WORD IMAGES

EDITED BY
GABRIELLA GUTIÉRREZ Y MUHS

FOREWORD BY
MARÍA HERRERA-SOBEK

WORD IMAGES

New Perspectives on Canícula *and Other Works by Norma Elia Cantú*

THE UNIVERSITY OF ARIZONA PRESS
TUCSON

The University of Arizona Press
www.uapress.arizona.edu

© 2017 by The Arizona Board of Regents
All rights reserved. Published 2017

Printed in the United States of America
22 21 20 19 18 17 6 5 4 3 2 1

ISBN-13: 978-0-8165-3409-8 (cloth)

Cover design by Leigh McDonald
Cover art by Veronica Eldredge

Library of Congress Cataloging-in-Publication Data
Names: Gutiérrez y Muhs, Gabriella, editor. | Herrera-Sobek, María, writer of foreword.
Title: Word images : new perspectives on Canícula and other works by Norma Elia Cantú / edited by Gabriella Gutiérrez y Muhs ; foreword by María Herrera-Sobek.
Description: Tucson : The University of Arizona Press, 2017. | Includes bibliographical references and index.
Identifiers: LCCN 2016039011 | ISBN 9780816534098 (pbk. : alk. paper)
Subjects: LCSH: Cantú, Norma E., 1947– Canícula. | Cantú, Norma E., 1947– —Criticism and interpretation.
Classification: LCC PS3553.A555 Z96 2017 | DDC 813/.54—dc23 LC record available at https://lccn.loc.gov/2016039011

♾ This paper meets the requirements of ANSI/NISO Z39.48-1992 (Permanence of Paper).

CONTENTS

FOREWORD

NORMA ELIA CANTÚ'S CULTURAL LANDSCAPES

Folklore and Aesthetic Activism

NORMA ELIA CANTÚ, creative writer, folklorist, literary critic, feminist, professor, public intellectual, and persona extraordinaire, has produced a significant body of work that adds greatly to the understanding and appreciation of Chicano/a literary and cultural production. Among her numerous contributions is the literary gem *Canícula: Snapshots of a Girlhood en la Frontera* (1995), categorized by the author herself as "a fictional autobioethnography." This collection of artistically constructed vignettes, some of them cleverly illustrated with personal photographs of self and family, are threaded, woven, or *hilvanados* (stitched) together to produce a brilliant, colorful tapestry of life experiences. Inscribed within the short narratives and family images are golden nuggets of perceptive political and cultural insights that can be savored over and over again as one reads and rereads each narrative. One reading of this work is not enough! In *Canícula*, Cantú offers us a kaleidoscope of experiences derived from her rich bilingual/bicultural heritage, which she inherited from her relatives, friends, and community. *La frontera*, the Texas/Mexico borderlands—more specifically, the Nuevo Laredo/Laredo area—provided a spectacular environment for learning about cultural traditions. The frontera borderline is a two-thousand-plus-mile stretch of land from Tijuana on the Pacific Coast to Brownsville on the Gulf of Mexico. It is mainly inhabited by members of two different ethnic groups, Anglo and Mexican, although of course a multiplicity of other populations also coexist in this area: African American, Asian American, plus numerous indigenous peoples. All of these inhabitants add to the cultural landscape in which Cantú grew up and thrived.

The short narratives that make up *Canícula* depict the life of a young girl from birth through the end of high school (1947–1965); it is brightly adorned with the cultural jewels garnered from a tradition rich in folklore. Ever the folklorist, Cantú mines this rich vein of *tradiciones* and produces a magnificent work of art that has been lauded nationally and internationally.

Having grown up in la frontera myself, in Rio Hondo, Texas, near Reynosa, Tamaulipas, Mexico, I can state that the borderlands capture us and implant themselves deeply in our hearts, never to disappear but, rather, flourishing and expanding with time. This memory of the borderlands is permeated with both pleasure and pain. Fond memories of friends, relatives, and a childhood lived in two nations—Mexico and the United States—bring pleasure. Crossing back and forth from north to south and from south to north was marvelous. Equally pleasurable was the experience of loving both cultures and both countries, of being bilingual, and of creating hybrid elements from each country, by, for example, playing with English- and Spanish-language structures and vocabularies.

The pain stems from the state of poverty in the borderlands. Middle-class people in the United States cannot possibly imagine that so much poverty exists in this amazingly affluent country, but it does. Pain explodes at the memories of poorly paid work and of toiling from sunup to sundown in the endless agricultural fields. The rows of cotton planted in the summertime, the tomatoes, jalapeño and serrano peppers, carrots, lettuces, cabbages, onions, cantaloupes, watermelons, and other edibles, all have to be harvested. These rows and rows of produce extend for miles and miles, and it is the Mexican and Mexican American worker who plants, nurtures, and harvests these crops. It is hard labor, especially in the hot Texas summer sun, as Cantú aptly describes in "Las Piscas" (3).* In addition, the acrid smell of racism, discrimination, classism, and gender oppression permeates the Texas landscape. The ethnic groups were strictly segregated during the pre–civil rights era of the 1960s: Mexican Americans and Anglo Americans seldom mixed; each had their own territories marked, if not by law, then by custom—it did not matter how, the division was there. Neither did it matter that the Mexican American communities were the majority and had

* Norma Elia Cantú, *Canícula: Snapshots of a Girlhood en la Frontera* (Albuquerque: University of New Mexico Press, 1995). All subsequent citations refer to this first edition.

been there for generations, before Anglo Americans arrived. It was Texas's own version of apartheid, and power solidly resided in the hands of Euro-Americans.

However, those bereft of political, social, and economic power construct cultural strategies that help them to survive, indeed, to spiritually flourish and thrive. That is the nature of the human condition: we are programmed to survive at any cost. One such strategy is to rely on cultural traditions that nourish the spirit, making a pueblo strong and resilient. Cantú's narrative, *Canícula*, encapsulates a brilliant artistic example of this strategy.

In this essay, I assert that Cantú's incorporation of folklore in her literary universe is linked to what I denominate as *aesthetic activism*. I define *aesthetic activism* as the use of the beautiful in the pursuit of social justice. That is to say, inscribed in what appear to be innocent vignettes of family life and experiences in la frontera is a series of encoded denunciations against a Texas/U.S. society that oppresses its citizens via discrimination, segregation, linguistic "terrorism" (Gloria Anzaldúa's term), domination, economic exploitation, and social, educational, and political disenfranchisement. Through numerous folklore genres, Cantú articulates a subtle form of social protest; it is almost imperceptible unless you undertake a systematic analysis of the folklore terms embedded in the text and identify their functions within it. The well-known folklore scholar Alan Dundes, in his article "What Is Folklore?," published in his edited volume *The Study of Folklore* (1965), defined the field by enumerating its genres and providing examples:

> Folklore includes myths, legends, folktales, jokes, proverbs, riddles, chants, charms, blessings, curses, oaths, insults, retorts, taunts, teases, toasts, tongue-twisters, and greetings and leave-taking formulas. . . . It also includes folk costumes, folk dance, folk drama (and mime), folk art, folk belief, . . . folk medicine, folk instrumental music, . . . folksongs (e.g., lullabies, ballads), folk speech (e.g., slang), folk similes, . . . folk metaphors, . . . and names (e.g., nicknames and place names). Folk poetry ranges from oral epics to autograph-book verse, epitaphs, latrinalia, . . . limericks, ball bouncing rhymes, jump-rope rhymes, finger and toe rhymes, dandling rhymes, . . . counting-out rhymes, . . . and nursery rhymes. The list of folklore forms also contains games; gestures; symbols; prayers; . . . practical jokes; folk etymologies; food recipes; quilt and embroidery designs; house, barn, and fence types; street vendor's cries; and even the traditional conventional sounds used to summon animals or to give them commands. There are such minor forms as mnemonic devices, . . . envelope sealers, . . . and the traditional comments made

after body emission. . . . There are such major forms as festival and special day (or holiday) customs (e.g., Christmas, Halloween, and birthday). (3)*

Cantú modestly states, in an interview undertaken by Gabriella Gutiérrez y Muhs and included in the current volume, "I jokingly call myself an undocumented folklorist, as I do not have a degree in folklore, nor have I ever taken courses or trained in the discipline. My work as a folklorist definitely complements my work as a scholar and as a creative writer." She goes on to state that "the research I do as a folklorist informs so much of my academic and creative work that I can claim the 'autobioethnographic' nature of my work." Indeed, she was learning folklore, as she informs us in the interview, even as a child picking medicinal plants with her grandmother. Cantú grew up accumulating cultural capital, but she was not made aware of the treasure she inherited from her relatives and her community until she enrolled at a university. It was only then that she learned the traditions she enjoyed and cherished from childhood were part and parcel of folkloric and anthropological studies.

The Chicana folklorist from Laredo, Texas, incorporates folklore traditions to structure what I call a vast cultural landscape. Her cultural landscape will be deployed to inscribe and lay out a cultural context in which her narratives are inlaid, not to serve as mere adornments, but to articulate her aesthetic activism, that is, her social protest. The title of the book itself, *Canícula*, is derived from a folk term used to describe the hot days of August and can be translated into English as "the dog days of summer." The word *canícula*'s etymological origin includes *canis*, or Latin for "dogs"; thus the reader should be prepared to find some sharp teeth, some strong bites, in the supposedly innocent vignettes.

Folklore is present in each of Cantú's narratives, including in folk speech found in the nicknames of the different characters, such as Tía Nicha, Pancho (Francisco), Memo (Guillermo), Panchita (Francisca), Pepa (Josefa), Espy (Esperanza), Tino (Valentín), Bueli (Abuelita), Nacho (Ignacio), Tía Chita (Jesuita), and Tía Toña (Antonia). Many of the vignettes are titled after the nickname of their protagonists; for example, an entry about Jesusa Vargas is titled "Tía Chita." She and her sister, Tía Toña, are viewed negatively by patriarchal society. The pejorative *solteronas*, a folk speech term similar to "old maids," is used to describe their single-woman status. These women are also negatively described with the

*Alan Dundes, "What is Folklore?," in *The Study of Folklore*, ed. Alan Dundes, 3 vols. (Englewood Cliffs, NJ: Prentice-Hall, 1965).

phrase *Se quedaron para vestir santos* (They have been left to dress the saints); that is to say, they are not married and therefore dedicate themselves to serving the church, to dressing and undressing the statues on the altars. These are mean and cruel depictions of middle-aged or elderly women who choose not to be married for whatever reason. The narrator, Azucena, mounts a spirited critique of these negative patriarchal folk constructions of unmarried women.

The narrative "Henrietta" (88–90) also offers a critique of class structures and the differences between rich and poor as exemplified even in a name. Henrietta, a Mexican American from the north, is called Henrietta—that is, she bears an English (denoting upper class) name, as opposed to the more quotidian Enriqueta (the Spanish translation) or, as the narrator exclaims, "even worse, Queta" (the nickname). Spanish in this case is devalued, and class differences within an ethnic group are exposed.

Folk speech is also related to racial taunts, such as Azucena's cousins calling her by the pejorative term *pocha*, meaning "Mexican American." Other negative taunts include *mojado/a*, meaning "wetback," which can be seen as racial stereotyping when it is used for a person who may not be undocumented or from Mexico.

Possibly the most outstanding deployment of a folk speech term as a denunciation of an oppressive political system is in the vignette titled "Políticos" (Politicians). The narrator protests against the corrupt Democratic and Republican political parties, whose leaders take the Mexican American voters for granted. The politicians included in the all-encompassing Spanish term *políticos* take money from the hardworking, economically deprived community and do not spend it on much-needed services for the towns and cities, such as paving the roads and streets in the barrios. They instead spend this money on more affluent areas, leaving the common people destitute and exposed to the dangers of floods and other catastrophic natural disasters.

Cantú depicts the strategies of survival used by Chicano communities, such as folk religious celebrations, which bring the pueblo together in solidarity and affirmation, aid the people in collectively resisting destructive outside forces, and give them opportunities to help one another. General religious celebrations are observed nationally and internationally, including the Christmas and Easter holidays, and are highlighted in the fictional narratives. However, to reiterate, even though the vignettes focus on religious rituals, they encapsulate political issues related to the oppressive economic status of Chicanos/as and/or gender issues associated with the systematic and overarching patriarchal oppression of the women featured in the stories.

Christmas celebrations are depicted as happy occasions filled with family- and friend-oriented activities. Nevertheless, the economic issue always exists in the lack of funds to purchase store-bought gifts. The presents the characters can afford consist of very humble handmade objects. The mothers cleverly sew clothes, while the children try their best to make do with inexpensive items, such as bags of fruit from their trees. The Cantú family also receives humble homemade presents or fruit from a gift-giving neighbor's garden. Nevertheless, Azucena will recall later that the peach preserves from her neighbor were the best she had and that as a child she looked forward to her after-school snack of peach preserve on her flour tortilla. Of particular interest is how Christmas is celebrated by incorporating both U.S. and Mexican rituals. For example, both Mexican and English-language Christmas carols are sung during the holidays. The Christmas "tree" in one of the periods of great economic lack consists of a branch from a tree in Azucena's family yard. However, the *nacimiento*, or Nativity scene, which is put away each year and brought out for Christmas, is described with pride, each object lovingly placed in the tableau. The different activities related to the nacimiento provide an opportunity for the community to get together in friendship and solidarity, affirmation and resistance. The traditional *acostas al Niño Jesús* (laying down of Baby Jesus in the manger) is performed on Christmas Eve. Posadas—the singing of Spanish-language carols from house to house, requesting a place to stay—are performed by friends, relatives, and neighbors each of the nine nights leading up to Christmas Day. The Tres Reyes Magos (Three Kings) are celebrated on January 6, and the *rosca de reyes*—a large, ring-shaped pastry with a ceramic Baby Jesus baked inside—is eaten at a party on this day. According to tradition, whoever finds the Baby Jesus in his or her piece of pastry is required to host the *levantar al Niño Jesús* festivities (the picking up of Baby Jesus) undertaken on February 2. In spite of their poverty, the people manage to survive and to reinforce their cultural identity together with their relatives, friends, and neighbors within the folk structure of these yearly rituals.

Folk food is always an important part of the religious celebrations. For Christmas, the candy-filled piñata is ever present, as are different kinds of teas and atoles (such as *champurrado*). So are the tamales, and the making of tamales—an intricate and labor-intensive process called *una tamalada*—can be an important event for bringing the people together. Members of the family, friends, and neighbors participate in this collective effort of making and cooking the tamales for Christmas Eve and Christmas Day.

As mentioned earlier, the Easter holidays are also part of the general religious celebrations (as opposed to the individual religious folk celebrations that I discuss below). Easter, like Christmas, is celebrated with friends and family. The customs related to how Chicanos celebrate Easter are detailed in various vignettes, and the same issues of economic deprivations are highlighted. For example, cascarones are constructed with empty eggshells that have been saved throughout the year. These eggshells are dyed, decorated, and then filled with confetti. On Easter Day the cascarones are smashed (gently) on the heads of friends and family members.

A more detailed account of a religious ritual is provided in the entries related to Halloween (October 31) and Día de los Muertos (Day of the Dead, November 1 and 2). Both are described, but the analysis and commentary about the Mexican Day of the Dead are more in-depth than those for the U.S. holiday of Halloween. The entry titled "Treeky-Treat," of course related to Halloween, contains a critique centered on how traditional customs are changing and not necessarily for the best. While the Day of the Dead is portrayed as a serious celebration of remembrance for those who have departed from earth, Halloween is presented as a more gruesome festivity. Cantú conveys this critique by describing the figure of Frankenstein, who appears at the cemetery in full costume, advertising a store. The people involved in the rituals of the Day of the Dead are solemn; they visit the cemetery to clean the tomb of a loved one and to place flowers on the resting place. Cantú also critiques the changing nature of the flowers. In the past the flowers were fresh or beautifully and artistically made with crepe paper, but in more recent times, the people use plastic flowers because, according to them, they last longer.

Religious folk celebrations that are personal—that is, related to an individual—are discussed throughout Cantú's vignettes. Baby baptisms are described in detail, especially the typical folk food consumed, and are at times associated with dysfunctional family dynamics. The first Holy Communion event, when a child receives the Holy Host for the first time, brings up both issues of poverty and questions of religious authenticity. The Catholic ritual takes place when the child is around seven years old, after he or she has prepared by learning the main principles of Catholic doctrine. In *Canícula*, scheduling errors cause the protagonist to celebrate her "first" Holy Communion twice. This leads her to question the "authenticity" of these rituals, which seem to be manipulated at will. The religious ritual of the wedding is likewise questioned in feminist terms, since after the wedding the hard life of a woman begins: the wife works hard from dawn to nighttime and has innumerable children. The vignette is aptly titled "Lola's Wedding," since Lola is the nickname for Dolores, which can be translated as "pain and suffering" (48).

The *quinceañera*, the religious celebration of a young girl's coming-of-age, transpires at her fifteenth birthday. She is presented as a "woman" to church and society. This celebration is somewhat related to the Anglo American debutante ball, although in the latter the young women are generally from upper-class society. In "Body Hair" (61) there is a reference to Azucena's quinceañera celebration, and the narrator has an opportunity to assert herself. The entry narrates how Azucena desires a pair of rhinestone-decorated flats, and her mother purchases a pair of the shoes for her. The father is incensed and forbids Azucena to wear them, stating that they are for *putas* (prostitutes). Azucena seldom wears them, abiding by her father's wishes, but for her quinceañera celebration she "defiantly" puts them on.

Funeral religious rites transpire when an individual dies; these are depicted in various vignettes, since death seems to be ever present for the poor. There are many religious folk customs related to dying: the wake, the funeral Mass, and the burial of a loved one at the campo santo, or cemetery. The stories contain several references to these particular rites, not only because the narrator's extended family experiences several deaths, but because a very important family member, Tino, Azucena's younger brother, is killed during the Vietnam War. This provides the narrator with an opportunity to critique the war, the killing of young, innocent soldiers, and to present the horrible trauma the family members suffer during this painful ordeal.

Closely tied to folk funeral rituals is the story of Lucita, a child barely twelve years old, who is killed by a stray bullet to the head from a man cleaning his gun. The mother never forgets and repeats this horrendous personal experience narrative whenever she can. The vignette also serves as a social protest against the use of guns.

A national secular festival, the parade, allows the narrator to comment on and critique how political figures, such as the president of the United States, are totally oblivious to the Chicano community. When President Dwight D. Eisenhower visits Laredo in the 1950s, he completely ignores the smiling brown faces of the people who are lined up in the street to welcome him, excitedly waving. This particular parade serves Azucena as an excellent platform from which to articulate her sense of outrage at insensitive, uncaring politicians' marginalization of and disrespect for the Chicano people.

Cultural oppression is evident in the "Declamación" (62) entry in relation to the folk practice of *ademanes*, or gestures. At her school, Azucena is to read an English-language poem. She begins to perform the poem in the style in which she has been taught to *declamar*, or declaim, Spanish poetry, using hand and arm gestures. The teacher immediately stops her and informs her that she is reciting the poem incorrectly. The culture clash between a Spanish poetry-reciting tradition and an English one is evident. Nevertheless, the student is crushed at being publically devalued.

The Escuelita (the endearment "Little School") is a site of Mexican American cultural affirmation, since this is where the Spanish language is taught to pre-kindergarten- and kindergarten-age children. In addition, Mexican culture is included in the songs and games the children play and sing, such as "Naranja Dulce" and "Doña Blanca." Other education subjects, such as arithmetic and writing, are also taught. These are all important methodological strategies in the learning process. Whereas in the Anglo American schools Spanish is forbidden and, indeed, the children are punished for speaking it by being fined, in Panchita's Escuelita the Spanish language and Spanish speakers are respected.

Cultural affirmation is also displayed in the "China Poblana One" entry, which features Azucena dressed up in Mexico's national costume. There is a certain incongruity here, for she is dressed up as a Mexican patriotic national to attend a George Washington's Birthday parade. Nothing could be more out of place, yet the child wears the colors of the Mexican flag—red, white, and green yarn—braided in her hair. The parents are certainly making a statement regarding cultural affirmation and not necessarily political nationalism. A second incongruous photograph, appearing in the entry "China Poblana Two," depicts Azucena's mother at the age of nineteen also dressed as a *china poblana*, in the Mexican national costume. The narrator highlights the strangeness of this photograph, saying her mother was not "even born in Mexico" (40). Here we have the story of the American citizen born in the United States but deported to Mexico with her parents during the 1930s Great Depression. Even today, this is a common occurrence, as American citizens of a young age are deported with their immigrant parents. The costumed mother offers the narrator an opportunity to articulate issues of deportation, loss of property, and pride, and she critiques the heartless American policies related to the deportation of families, which often result in family members being separated.

Possibly one of the book's most traumatic incidents is constructed through folk costume, in the entry "Cowboy Boots." Here the item of folk attire, a pair of cowboy boots, becomes an element related to the rape of a sixth-grade girl, Sanjuana, by an older man. Sanjuana's family is thrown into dire economic circumstances after the father's loss of work. The family is forced to send their young daughter to work at a grocery store owned by an Anglo named Tom. There, Tom rapes Sanjuana, who becomes pregnant and is forced to leave Laredo. Azucena, who is Sanjuana's good friend, becomes traumatized at the mere sight of cowboy boots.

Another case of rape is linked to yet another folk genre as depicted in the entry "Healing" (122–24). This time we encounter a *curandera*, or female folk healer, as one of the characters in the narrative. A young girl who has barely reached puberty, Manuelita, is raped and psychologically traumatized to the point of becoming unresponsive to the outside world. She is withdrawn and has a vacant look in her eyes. The girl and her mother journey to Matehuala, in San Luis Potosí, and then continue to a tiny mountain hamlet to see a curandera who is supposed to be a great healer. Azucena and her parents have also traveled the same route to seek help, since Mr. Cantú has arthritis in his hands and is desperately searching for a cure. When they arrive, Manuelita, the rape victim, has already been there two months, but the young girl has not responded to the curandera's ministrations. Azucena's father is not healed either.

Women in Cantú's vignettes are often portrayed as having knowledge of folk ailments and folk remedies. Women are also experts at folk arts and crafts, such as crocheting, embroidering, knitting, and quilting—useful skills that can sustain the family while the male head of the household is out of work or has migrated north in search of a job.

Norma Elia Cantú has constructed a splendid work of art through the incorporation of folklore genres in the construction of her aesthetic activism. These folklore genres are not employed merely as decorations but are the main elements in the depiction of a cultural landscape that anchors each narrative. Furthermore, each folklore element functions in a great number of instances as a platform from which the narrator can articulate her social protest or critique regarding issues of ethnic oppression and gender oppression in Anglo American and Mexican society. The folk items are so deftly and seamlessly integrated into the short narratives, the reader is barely aware of the brilliant manner in which these cultural artifacts are deployed.

María Herrera-Sobek
University of California, Santa Barbara

ACKNOWLEDGMENTS

After Juan Felipe Herrera:

For Aldo Ulisses Reséndiz Ramírez
For Marianne Mork and Veronica Eldredge
For Socorro Favela Rivera and Socorro Pellerino
For Eric C. Muhs, Enrico, and Eleuterio
For Mercedes and Pedro Martín and their entire family
For Martina Iñiguez and John Fraire, José, Alexia, and Erlinda Iñiguez
For Lucía Ochoa and Robert Nuñez, Andrea, and Cassandra
For Patrice Vecchione and Ken Weisner
For Mary Antoinette Smith and Christina Roberts
For Jeanette Rodriguez
For Connie Anthony
For Jodi O'Brien and Sabina Neem
For Fr. David Leigh and Jessica Ludescher Imanaka
For Sharon Suh, Catherine Punsalan, Donna Teevan, and Michael Jaycox
For Demetria Martínez and Helena María Viramontes
For Margarita Cota-Cárdenas
For Isaiah Crawford and Bob Dullea
For Guadalupe Vega, Graciela Vega, Shane, Cuahutemoc, and Kuriani
For Asunción and Serapia Vega
For Marú Márquez, Melyssa Jo Kelly, Vanessa Castañeda, and Jessica Gomez
For Lorna Dee Cervantes and John Martínez
For Kari Lerum and Shari Dworkin

For Shirley Flores Muñoz and Alex Flores
For Dan Goldberg
For Olga Díaz y Benjamín Cárdenas, Ana, and Camila
For Lain Hawkridge and Arlene Lee, for Sally Hawkridge and Tim Beken
For Steven Bender
For Carole Snee
For Patricia C. Lally
For Xánath Caraza and Raúl Sánchez
For Bob Flor and Jim and Catalina Cantú
For Raúl Sánchez
For Noemi Natividad, Rachael Brown, and Gabriela Boyle
For Nalini and Ganesh Iyer
For Annette and Frank Eldredge
For all my cousins, especially Ofelia Fabela, Remedios Mena, María Elena Reséndiz, Joel Frías, Conchita y Jesús Rivera, and all their children
For Adela, Manuel, and Lily Lechuga
For Yvonne Yarbro-Bejarano, Susana Gallardo, Rosalía Solórzano, and Rebeca Burciaga
For Winfield Hobbs and Patrick Perkins
For Paulette Kidder, Cynthia Moe-Lobeda, Katherine Dunbar, and Kathy Cook
For Nancy and James Vive
For Imme Bergmeier, Olga Colbert, Valentín Ferdinán, and Isabelle Gentili
For Forrest Gander and Kisha Xiomara Palmer
For Martha Shiah-Vega and José Ortiz for their work with youth and community
For my friends in México, Chile, France, and Spain, especially Rosa and Oscar Nuñez, and la familia Sosa-Delgado in Durango, and la famille Gentili in France
P/V

I am forever indebted to our copy editor from University of Arizona Press, Diana Rico, and to acquiring editor Kristen Buckles. I would also like to thank the dean of the College of Arts and Sciences at Seattle University, David Powers, and the associate dean, Kan Liang, for their support, as well as Rhonda Woods, Thorne Clayton-Falls, and especially Debbie Radbill.

WORD IMAGES

INTRODUCTION

NORMA CANTÚ'S *FRONTERA*

Exile, the Law, Space, Hybridity, and a Little Poetry

GABRIELLA GUTIÉRREZ Y MUHS

THIS READER BEGAN as a seed in my "Emerging Subjectivities in Chicana Literature" series at Stanford University, when I was a Chicana Fellow and graduate student in the late nineties. In the last almost fifty years since the first publications of Chicana/o literature by the Quinto Sol Press, Chicana/o literary scholars have concentrated on shedding light on the relationship between the subjects of Chicano literature and their sociohistorical context for mainstream America and the Chicano community. According to Ramón Saldívar, in his major contribution to subjectivity more than twenty-five years ago: "Rather than passively reproducing images of reality, the task of contemporary Chicano narrative is to defy, deform and thus transform reality by revealing the dialectical structures that form the base of human experience" (7). In the earlier decades, attention focused primarily on working-class characters who suffered racial and other kinds of social and political discrimination, an emphasis that overly simplified and dismissed the compelling differential experiences of Chicanos in the American landscape. Nonetheless, the quest for intentional and unintentional intersectional equity has truly been a ubiquitous nirvana that Chican@ writers have shared throughout time and is especially salient in the work of Latin@ writers, at large, today. Whether we follow Don Luis Leal's "Periodización" in stating that Chicano literature began in 1848 or consider that Chicano literature began in 1959 with *Pocho*, the first novel that intentionally talked about identity, ethnicity, and borders, we are still highlighting the importance of subjectivity and intersectionality in the United States. Intersectionality is exemplified in most literary oeuvres of today, and the protagonist of this project, Norma Elia Cantú, is a perfect example of someone who has sought intersectional analysis and influential exposure in every aspect of her life and work. She has altered the ways in which both business and literature are undertaken with a feminist-of-color agenda, as María Herrera-Sobek rightfully names her "an aesthetic activist," meaning that both aesthetics and inclusivity have been integral ingredients of her life's work. She unflinchingly yet gently urged inclusivity, particularly for young scholars and writers of color, whether as the president of Mujeres Activas en Letras y Cambio Social (MALCS), who established cultural practices like "passing the rebozo," or as the protagonist of her *cincuentañera*, defying and expanding tradition all at once. As a Chicana leader Norma Cantú has worked in Washington, DC, on national projects that affect Latinos and has represented Latinos in national and international government and community organizations, journals, and educational institutions. The expansion and inclusion of Chican@ cultural identity and its intersectional analysis have always been at the forefront of her projects. Her most recent endeavors have had to do with science and literature, as she writes a poem for each periodic table element.[1]

In *Transcendental Train Yard*, her 2015 collection of bilingual poems written in response to Marta Sánchez's serigraphs, Norma E. Cantú captures Mexican culture and reinscribes it into the Chicano/Latino consciousness along with artist Sánchez and critic Tomás Ybarra-Frausto, affirming the American railroad as a Mexican American historical and cultural icon. In his preface to the book, Ybarra-Frausto writes of the poems, "Their expressionistic dreamlike representations bring to consciousness reservoirs of feelings and primordial images from the Mexican collective unconscious" (vii). Folklorist Norma E. Cantú is prolific and transnationally infuses the importance of cultural and physical icons, like the train across borders, artistically—for example, by inserting the *trabalenguas* "*r* con *r* cigarro," which every Mexican child recognizes, into her poetry and magically making it a "legal image" in the U.S. popular memory during a time when U.S. nationalism is deadly. It is thus important that we honor her works by studying them at a deeper level, as there has never been a critical edited collection about her work. We are delving not only into her renowned novel *Canícula: Snapshots of a Girlhood en la Frontera* but also into her uncollected poems, analyzing these writings from various frameworks. Another volume analyzing her essays, as well as her editorial works and collaborations with critics, scholars, politicians, and artists—which infuse literature with art, politics, and science—would be necessary in order to fully shine a light through the spectrum of Norma Cantú's massive cultural significance. This book, although groundbreaking, does not suffice.

While recovery projects, such as María Ruíz de Burton's novel *The Squatter and the Don* (1885), broached issues of gender, sexuality, and poetry in works written by Chicanas, and writers of the 1970s did question the monopolization of Chicano identity by the male subject, it is really only in the past thirty years that a canonical body of Chicana literature representing a range of nonstereotypical Chicana subjectivities has been available at large. Chican@ writers are still addressing the differential experience deniers, who question the uniqueness and impact of the Chican@ experience.[2] The small boom (compared to what existed previously) in Chicana literature in the 1980s and 1990s afforded readers a new, more complex vision of Chicanas as multifaceted beings, producing representations that interweave gender and sexuality with racial and class identifications.[3] These more varied representations of Chicanas found formal expression in new hybrid genres in Chicana literature, which first emerged in the 1980s in texts such as *This Bridge Called My Back*, *Loving in the War Years*, and *Borderlands/La Frontera*.

Today Chicana writers and critics alike continue to be engaged in a communal project of fleshing out Chicana subjectivity in the fullness of its heterogeneity. I utilize *subject* as a verb, not as in "to subject," but as in "to subjectify" or "subjectifying." If subjectivity is "constantly being reconstituted in discourse each time we think of speak" (Weedon 1996, 33), the verb highlights the agency and power of Chicana writers such as Cantú to use novelistic discourse to intervene in the transformation of received subjectivities. Chicana scholars have worked diligently to further this project, anthologizing Chicana literature and writing literary criticism. I use the term *subjectifying entities* to describe this larger project (Gutiérrez y Muhs 2000).[4]

CANÍCULA: SNAPSHOTS OF A GIRLHOOD EN LA FRONTERA

This reader is not merely about Norma Elia Cantú's *Canícula: Snapshots of a Girlhood en la Frontera*, although the book was the catalyst that led many of us to Cantú's oeuvre. The visual aspect of photography—so important for people worldwide, and in particular for the Chicano community, when identity becomes portable—make *Canícula* an exceptional literary contribution. My migrant U.S. family makes an annual summer pilgrimage to Ciudad Juárez and Durango to take pictures for the *quinceañeras*, baptisms, and weddings that occurred during the previous year; by documenting these rites of passage in pictures, we inscribe our existence and ability to celebrate into a world view that denies victimization. And this element is central in *Canícula: Snapshots of a Girlhood en la Frontera*. Not only were our poor and working-class families proving that they had followed familial, cultural, and social traditions, but they were also able to prove, through a picture that became a document for them, that their lives were evolving in productive circumstances. Hence the importance of partnering some pictures, for a visual community, with literature, a strategy that made *Canícula* a sure read for a community hungry for visual literacy and visual representation. However, as stated previously, Cantú, like many Chican@ scholars of her time, feels the responsibility to contribute in diverse manners to the formation of a Chican@ canon, so she and her compatriots and literary siblings are also poets, short story writers, researchers, folklorists, cultural workers, and essay editors, among many other subjectivities. They assist her in carrying out this responsibility to expand subjectivity at all costs. I will describe in detail the contributing essays that form this collection at the end of this introduction, but I want to state that among the contributors to this reader we have scholars of the stature of María Herrera-Sobek (University of California, Santa Barbara), who has written a unique foreword to this collection. Ellen McCracken, in "Hybridity and the Space of the Border in the Writing of Norma Elia Cantú," lays a foundation for the way in which the borderlands that Cantú brings us to should be cultivated through our literary lens. María Socorro Tabuenca analyzes Cantú's poetic and creative voice in conjunction with her scholarly essays, something that has never been done, and law professor Steven W. Bender lays down the law for us in "Snapshots of Law and Life in the Midcentury Texas Borderlands," in which he cleverly provides the reader with "several 'snapshots' of the prevailing legal climate as it affected Norma Elia Cantú, her family, and more generally, the Latina/o community in Texas and northern Mexico . . . from her birth [in Mexico] in the late 1940s to her graduation from high school [in Texas] in 1965."

This collection is composed of a foreword; ten traditional literary essays; an introduction to the volume, "Norma Cantú's *Frontera*: Exile, the Law, Space, Hybridity, and a Little Poetry," and an essay introducing part 2, "Cantú's

Decolonial Imagination Through the Looking Glass," on teaching methodologies; and an interview with Cantú. The first part is made up of essays that individually describe one aspect of Cantú's oeuvre, as mentioned earlier. In part 2, I have placed the articles that will be instrumental in assisting teachers and professors to utilize *Canícula* in the classroom.

Norma Elia Cantú was appointed as the Norine R. and T. Frank Murchison Endowed Professor in Humanities at Trinity University in San Antonio, Texas, in 2016. She is professor emerita at the University of Texas at San Antonio and former professor of Latina/Latino studies and English at the University of Missouri–Kansas City. She published *Canícula: Snapshots of a Girlhood en la Frontera* in 1995 with the University of New Mexico Press. *Canícula* was so successful that the book became available in paperback in 1997, less than two years after its hardcover publication, and was issued in Spanish in the fall of 2000. *Canícula* is the second in a fictional trilogy of books. While the first volume of the trilogy does not exist, Cantú's description of the first "book" helps contextualize *Canícula* as a borderlands text. The first, *Papeles de mujer*, she describes as written entirely in Spanish and "consist[ing] of correspondence and documents that tell the story of a family in the geographical space between Monterrey, Mexico, and San Antonio, Texas, from 1880 to 1950" (Cantú 1995, xi). The second, *Canícula*, is a story told through family photographs, but the author clarifies that "what may appear to be autobiographical is not always so. On the other hand, many of the events are completely fictional, although they may be true in a historical context" (xi). *Cabañuelas*, the third book in the series, was finished by Cantú in 2016 and sent out for review.

Canícula is not a narrative with a beginning, a middle, and an end. It is a bildungsroman, or novel about coming of age, written in fragmented form. Eighty-five post–World War II vignettes, a prologue, an introduction, and twenty-three photographs make up this collection, which bears the subtitle *Snapshots of a Girlhood en la Frontera*. In the introduction, Cantú testifies to having written about these snapshots at random, without any particular order, as if she was pulling them out of a box. But in reality, the novel follows an internal progression based on age, from her earliest years through her time in high school. The period between high school and the narrator's present remains unvoiced, except for a tangential reference to her life in Madrid as a student. The text's time span is from the late 1940s to the mid-1960s, more specifically 1965, although it really ends in the 1990s through a series of memories and events that transport the protagonist back to her childhood. It is of paramount importance that the last third of the title of *Canícula* is also in Spanish; by calling it *en la Frontera* instead of *on the Border*, with a preposition and a noun the author is able to make the border a bilingual/bicultural space, which would not exist without Spanish. In order to underline that the author works and expresses the realities of both sides of the border (while emphasizing her American identity and highlighting the Spanish in the life of the various protagonists), I find it essential to include one essay originally written in Spanish, by María Esther Quintana Millamoto.

Canícula reconstructs a young girl's experience of a regional reality in a way that embraces universal themes through her memories. In fact, the book has already been translated into various languages other than Spanish (Cantú herself translated the Spanish version). Cantú's writing describes a border culture that is such not only because its members speak Spanish, are bilingual and bicultural, and are mostly located in Laredo and Nuevo Laredo, the United States and Mexico, but also because it encompasses a bicognitive reality. Sara Soledad García, utilizing Tino Villanueva's theories, has pointed out in her review of *Canícula* that Cantú writes about "the border from within the border," what Mary Louise Pratt calls "the contact zone" (607). Cantú represents the internal, moral, and linguistic borders that Chicanos cross every minute of their lives in different physical and psychological manners. *Canícula* reveals the binary notion of the border as many know it today to be: fragile and unreal. This is, of course, a direct result of her writing from the two Laredos, from the border region.

At first glance, *Canícula* seems much like Sandra Cisneros's influential *House on Mango Street*. The eye-opening research on the reception to Cisneros's text revealed many different responses from critics and affirmed the magnitudinal possibilities of impact of a book like *Canícula*.[5] Controversy over what genre the text belonged to undermined Cisneros's valuable contribution. Its fragmentation was ridiculed by some critics, who initially could not identify the work as a multilayered masterpiece. Some aspects of the responses to the book reinforced simplistic and formulaic ways of reading Chicana literature and created a false narrative of what Chicana literature encompasses, which explains in part why many critics were not open to reading Cantú's *Canícula* as a bildungsroman instead of a collection of vignettes. We also need to note that Norma Elia Cantú is following a vignette tradition that was initiated in Chicano literature in 1972 by the great Tomás Rivera, author of . . . *Y no se lo tragó la tierra/. . . And the Earth Did Not Devour Him*, and actually goes even further back, to the feminist Mexican authors Rosario Castellanos and Nellie Campobello. Their respective books *Balún Canán* and *Las manos de Mamá* are both novels written in the first part of the twentieth century, both written from the perspective of a young girl, and both composed almost in the bildungsroman tradition. Castellanos based the groundbreaking *Balún Canán* on her personal story of growing up in the southern state of Chiapas as the daughter of hacienda owners who left her to be raised by her Mexican indigenous nanny. She tells the story in the voice of a young girl; the child protagonist interprets the racist treatment of the upper class toward the indigenous campesinos. Campobello's *Las manos de Mamá* is an autobiographically based collection of vignettes from the perspective of a young girl who witnessed the violence in rural Mexico during the Mexican Revolution in the northern state of Durango.

In *Canícula*, Azucena, the protagonist, is fully realized as a character, which authorizes her version of the events narrated. In telling her life through descriptions of pictures, Azucena narrates a story not only about herself but also about every member of her immediate and her extended family. The novel's unique form, which the author refers to as fictional "autobioethnography," conveys a sense of empowerment and is constructed through photography, ethnography, and fictional autobiography.

This form produces a balanced treatment of subject positions that have remained instrumental or stereotyped in Chicano literature in the past. Cantú's text serves as a vehicle to "subjectify" identities that have remained eclipsed by other congruent realities: othermothers, *comadres*, *madrinas*, *niñas*, *madres*, *tías*, and *solteronas* (spinsters), as well as the shadowed grandmother and mother who have lost luster behind specific stereotypes. Cantú utilizes the photographs and the description of images to posit the existence of various Chicana/o subject positions and to engage the reader in a virtual reality validated and created through her agency and, since this book is also formulated with ethnographic data, that of her community.

Cantú begins her regional, very Chicana "autobioethnographic fiction" acknowledging the influence of Roland Barthes. Barthes appears in the prologue, which narrates the genesis of *Canícula* in the third person:

> In 1980 a car hits a man on a busy Paris street. Roland Barthes dies. The next morning, at the Café Colón in Madrid, a woman reads about the accident in El País over café con leche and churros. In Paris a few weeks later she buys *Nouvel Observateur* and reads it cover to cover; it's a special issue on Roland Barthes. His book *Camera Lucida: Reflection on Photography* is published. (1)

Without elucidating the connection—but by giving prominence to Barthes in the prologue to a book built around (remembered) photographs—Cantú invites the reader to construct one. In this way the author directs the reader to the relevance that autobiography, ethnography, and photography have in the telling of her story. It is important to reiterate here that the vignettes were inspired by photographs that were not present at the time of writing. The photographs, or imaginative descriptions of them, serve both as the locus for confession/disclosure in a controlled dialectical environment and as referents for nondisclosed realities.

Countering the historical nondisclosure of Chicana intimate writings, in the 1980s and 1990s Chicanas began writing their autobiographies. José David Saldívar has coined the term *border zone of conjectures* to explicate the phenomenon of the 1990s in particular, in which Chicana/o writers can and do become "narrative informants," to him and to other scholars specifically in anthropology (84). Cantú and other Chicana writers, such as Demetria Martínez, engage in this type of disclosure of the nondisclosed past as well, even as they continue to not disclose by showing, rather than telling, through narrative, photography, ethnography, and other forms of creativity. In *Canícula*, Cantú produces what I call "calloused nondisclosure" by painting her childhood, family, and community in primarily idyllic terms, passing over in silence issues such as sexuality, domestic friction, and violence in the literary construction of her life world. In the current volume, which began when I was writing my dissertation at Stanford in the 1990s, it is crucial for our understanding of Cantú's oeuvre that some of the authors, like Aurora Chang and Carlos Sibaja García, interpret her silences and theorize about them, as well as utilize them, in order to create classroom methodologies to teach about cultural identity, difference, diversity, and subjectivity to high school and college students. Regarding "calloused nondisclosure," I use the term *calloused* to reference the hardening effect of decades of hostile relations that produce nondisclosure inside and outside of Chicano communities. The nondisclosure Cantú evidences is also an art. For example, in the vignette "Políticos," what Cantú does not say is just as important as what is said. The reader might translate this word simply as "politicians," but Cantú writes the title of this vignette in Spanish, in which the term *político* means not only "politician" but someone who is arrogant, upper class, uppity, a crook, a weasel, and a person who pretends to be what he or she is not. She does not translate the term in the piece, as she does in others.

As in the above example, Cantú's writing allows diverse readerships to connect interactively with her literature in multiple and complicated manners, from different entry points. Here I am speaking not only about *Canícula*, her most famous work, but also about her poetry and essays. She presents readers the opportunity to enter a text from any number of levels, taking into consideration subjectivity, culture, language, class, gender, age, and sexuality. Cantú writes about the culture she grew up in, and those who share a similar cultural background will identify with the experiences, objects, and cultural practices she describes. While the text privileges the bicultural/bilingual reader, thanks to the vividness of her descriptions, readers from other cultural backgrounds are able to relate much of her writing to their own experiences and are motivated to learn more about Chicano culture. Journalist and folklorist Paddy Bowman states in a review of *Canícula* that Cantú speaks to Bowman's own working-class experience as a poor white child growing up in Appalachia:

> The book resonates with me for several reasons. The author and I were born in the same year; although I grew up Anglo in Appalachia, many historical events shaped our emerging selves. Her evocation of children's intense visceral senses returns me to my childhood self—seeing things from lower down, smelling and tasting my way through the day with my own beloved Anglo abuela, observing colors and people keenly, soaking up details but not always seeing the horizon. Colors flood every page of the book, vividly illuminating the black and white photos in readers' minds. (24)

Bowman's review resonates with what I call "Crayola dialectics," which inspire the reviewer to read more and understand the value of *Canícula* at a deeper level: "[*Canícula*] provides an elixir to heal, a way to know the bilingual, bicultural heart" (24).[6] Like crayons, color permeates *Canícula*. Although the pictures Cantú writes about, explains, and invents are all black and white, she describes them in color, alluding to the real color of her memories, in much the same way as the Crayola company presents myriad possibilities with their colors, 120 in the largest box in 2015, as well as a large array of other products of color. The inclusion of the public in naming some of the crayons in 1993 relates to Cantú's technique of drawing in different readerships through Crayola dialectics.[7]

The main vehicle of delivery in this narrative is the description, not of feelings, but of events that occur and are acknowledged and spoken in the voice of a little girl. Cantú vividly incorporates the senses of the reader and speaks about an entire cultural class practice and immigrant experience that are perhaps foreign to most other people. The technique of Crayola dialectics informs the representation of mothers and othermothers in *Canícula*, in whose shoes most readers can place themselves or who remind the reader of a relative within the long line of (other)mother subjectivities that make these women familiar. Her use of color and smell is part of her technique; she fills in the details of color, sound, self, and even specific names so as to include the reader in the protagonist's memories and to expand her memories into her reader's own aesthetic:

> I ride the rocking horse Buelito's built from discarded wood planks, painted the color of red coyotes—red as memories. My feet sandaled in brown huaraches from Nuevo Laredo with tiny green nopales and the tinier red pears, tunas, painted on the delicate leather. A white ribbon holds flimsy black curls away from my face; wisps of rebellious curls escape. Mami has made my sundress, blue like the sky, and embroidered tiny pink rosebuds on the handmade smocking—just like the ones she made when she worked as a seamstress at the dress factory. (6)

And again:

> Anamaría claims Pepa's not really my cousin, claims that Tía Trine and my uncle never married. But I don't care, she's still my favorite. She paints my nails with red, red polish; combs, braids, curls my hair. She was there to comfort me when Mami pierced my ears, strung red floss, then placed tiny gold loops through the needle wide holes. She treats me like a little sister. (11)

All readers can include themselves in this interactive book by comparing their grandmother, their third birthday picture, their first Communion picture, some church celebration in which they are dressed up, or their high school class with that of the book's protagonist, "in a continual process of mutual adaptation." Similarly, Cantú's Crayola dialectics technique manifests itself as the voice of the child with whom everybody can identify. More importantly, this metamorphosis relates to the broad spectrum of subjectivities she utilizes to tell her autobioethnography: comadres, madrinas, tías, grandmothers, solteronas, and child mothers, all of which are representative of the layered realities within the Chicana social structure and all of which are verbally photographed in *Canícula*. These subjectivities are the threads that weave the fabric of community in order to project a profile of the individual within her community, and they are what entice the public to want to know more about these agency-filled characters and try to identify with them.

Canícula equally presents theoretical ramifications of the concept of "othermothers," coined in African American feminist thought, in which women and even girls participate in the responsibilities of child-rearing within a mutually supporting network of social relationships.

EMERGENT DENOUEMENT

Cantú's texts are representations of community building as a cooperative project that women share in Chicano culture, in opposition to the individual focus on the nuclear family and the biological mother. Cantú shed light in the 1990s on these hidden or invisible subjectivities from a porous dialectical positioning. Mothers and grandmothers are reappraised vis-á-vis their historical appearance in Chicana/o literature. Comadres, godmothers, aunts, solteronas, child mothers, and Chicanos (men) are represented, at last, devoid of the veil that has enveloped and covered the subtleties of their quotidian realities. They are presented as active entities within the texts of the 1990s that contribute new facets of self within a broader Chicana/o spectrum. *Canícula* becomes the transcendent vehicle that illustrates and problematizes autobiography, ethnography, photography, intergenerational thematics, Chicana female subjectivities, family rituals, Chicana spirituality, and the border as a mental state.

The literary production of Cantú in the 1990s complements and innovatively contributes to the larger project of Chicanas/os "subjectifying" entities for Chicana/o and other readerships. Cantú represents new subjectivities that enlarge the spectrum of possibilities in canonical literature. Due to the visual and literary hybridity with which the author delves into the fields of subjectivity in relation to others, and by using autobiography, the exposure of the new spirituality of Chicanas, and the dialectics of the international, Cantú's work renews and enlarges the agenda of Chicana/o literature, placing Chicana subjectivities at the center of enormous margins.

In addition to (re)shaping tradition within *laredense* Chicano communities through her own personal endeavors, Cantú also records these traditions within her autobioethnographic fiction, which Chicanas and Chicanos will incorporate into their memories. She, the niña, madre, tía, solterona, madrina, and comadre, turns her subject positions into paintings that readers can closely observe through her literature and other activities. In this way, these subjectivities become an open book that must be read, analyzed, discussed, and rearticulated. In *Canícula*, regional nature, language, objects, and aesthetics reveal class and feminist issues that impinge, in turn, on the subjectivities of the characters in a circle of revelatory tendencies. While Cantú's work is regional, the framework of themes on which it is built can be appealing to a very wide public.

This volume is a collection of interpretations and methodological theories that combine to create, first, a reader to assist those who teach *Canícula* in their classrooms in theorizing Cantú's work and, second, a reader that allows *Canícula* and Cantú's other work to be utilized by lawyers, cultural workers and trainers, poets, and writers. Cantú's oeuvre is a revolutionary and evolutionary statement about the way in which autobioethnographic texts (which include testimonial work), even if marginal within their genre, can be employed to teach about and to interpret an entire world view of Chican@ life and culture in the United States in the last part of the twentieth century and the first part of the twenty-first. Critic María Esther Quintana Millamoto insists that her analysis of Cantú's work had to be written initially in Spanish, as a firm affirmation of the fact that there are several of us in the academy who navigate our daily lives, professionally and personally, in English and Spanish. In addition, it is of great importance to note that Norma Elia Cantú is one of very few authors who is able to write in English and Spanish; she in fact assisted in the translation of her book *Canícula* into Spanish, which, in my opinion, given the pictures she added to the Spanish version, makes for a different text.

In 2015 *Canícula* was reissued, a process explained in the additional introduction Norma Cantú provides the reader with in the new edition. Seventeen pictures are added to the initial twenty-three, two of the original pictures are replaced with two other pictures of the same event, and the cover of Tía Piedad's book is included, making this collection richer and more robust than the first edition. She also delves more deeply into community and masculinities by adding several vignettes that were not included initially, among them "Men Wearing Hats," "Neighborhood Boys," and "First Son."

In fact, each of the three publications of *Canícula*—the original 1995 edition, the Spanish-translation textbook *Canícula: Imagenes de una niñez fronteriza*, and the 2015 *Canícula* reissue—were made unique by the author. When she translated the book into Spanish as a textbook for the 2000 Houghton Mifflin edition, she left out at least one vignette, "Los Pulido"; changed the title of the vignette "Azalea" into "Susirio"; and showed a different photo of "Green Organza," one that appears neither in the 1995 edition nor in the 2015 English reissue. "La Cueva" (on page 95 of the 1995 edition) is also missing from the Spanish edition, yet it appears in the 2015 English edition.

The fictive belief that bilingualism is always literary as well as oral is another important discussion in our communities and in the academy. Many U.S. Latinos/Chicanos are not raised speaking Spanish in a country that highly devalues bilingualism (especially Spanish) because of its hierarchical view of language (see Amy Kaminsky's work on this). So we as contributors and editors honor Norma Elia Cantú's full bilingualism and her ability to often superbly translate meaning rather than direct language in *Canícula*. As writer Sherman Alexie recently stated about First Nation college students, "They are astronauts." I dare state the same about fully bilingual Chican@ authors. Language is our first intentional expression. Chicanos and Latinos are privileged because of their proximity to Mexico and Mexican culture. Nonetheless, the members of the baby boomer generation is the first to have the choice of recovering their Spanish language if, unlike Cantú, they did not grow up speaking their parents' language of origin. Renowned Chican@ authors have managed to recover their parents' language after having lost it in schools. Authors like Lorna Dee Cervantes, Ana Castillo, and even Sandra Cisneros managed a large generational project of recovery and survived growing up in a country that negated the possibility of them being bilingual and bicultural. They were made to choose the English-speaking subjectivity above the Spanish-speaking one, instead of being allowed to live intersectional lives.

ABOUT THE CONTRIBUTIONS: PART 1

Our book would not be complete without the participation of the prolific critic and renowned scholar of Chican@ literature from the University of California, Santa Barbara, María Herrera-Sobek, who gave us a foreword for our groundbreaking reader. We also begin this glorious book honoring Norma Elia Cantú with the renowned critic Ellen McCracken's magnificent contribution. In "Hybridity and the Space of the Border in the Writing of Norma Elia Cantú," McCracken examines the role of the vibrant borderspace in Cantú's writing in the context of the other border crossings she undertakes, such as genre hybridity, visual-verbal hybridity, and the intersection of competing critical, linguistic, and other cultural codes. According to McCracken, "While the geographic border described is the central space of tension and unity of her writing, she also frequently probes the postmodern intersections that replace the previously clear distinctions between genres, languages, and cultures. Cantú's representation of the border pivots centrally on the geographic space in which Mexico and the United States physically intersect, while at the same time probing several of the other tenuous cultural borders that postmodernity has brought into focus."

In "Community and Exile in Norma E. Cantú's *Canícula*," Jesús Rosales shows how *Canícula* can be read, first, as an important representative testimonial text that celebrates Mexican American culture, in which family forms an integral part of its essence; and, second and more intriguingly, as a personal manifesto that denounces the limitations experienced by the inhabitants of this border area. The community—including both Mexican Americans and Anglos—is responsible for perpetuating these restraints, which result in the protagonist's personal exile or escape from her particular regional homeland. The purpose of that departure is not to negate the culture that is left behind, but to come to embrace it, validate it, and integrate it into the ever-changing U.S. national ethos.

María Socorro Tabuenca builds up Norma Elia Cantú as a community pillar in "Norma E. Cantú: A *Fronteriza* and Chicana Creator and Critic." Her article focuses on reviewing some of Cantú's published and unpublished creative works, in addition to her scholarly works. In so doing, she conducts a survey of the importance of Cantú's work in Chicana/o and border studies, not only as a literary and folk critic but as a creative writer.

Innovative and prolific law professor Steven W. Bender brings us the legal presence in *Canícula*. In "Snapshots of Law and Life in the Midcentury Texas Borderlands," Bender supplies several "snapshots" of the prevailing legal climate as it affected Cantú, her family, and the Latina/o community writ large in Texas and northern Mexico, the geography of *Canícula*. Following the timeline of Cantú's childhood in the Texas borderlands, from her birth in Mexico in the late 1940s to her high school graduation in Texas in 1965, these legal snapshots address U.S. immigration policy, border crossings, public and private venues of segregation in the Southwest, and suppression of culture under Texas law. Overall, these legal snapshots aim to add richer context to Mexican life and *familia* in the borderlands that Cantú, her family, and her community navigated as a nonmainstream group of Americans, inscribing in this manner Chican@ historical and legal imprints into the literature of Cantú and her contemporaries.

Vanessa Fonseca examines the connection between the literary foremother and *nuevomexicana* Cleofas Jaramillo and the contemporary Chicana *tejana* writer Cantú. She draws parallels between Jaramillo and Cantú, as well as many other women whose works are considered precursors to Chicana literature. Utilizing the literary periodization of Chicana/Hispana/Mexicana women's writing offered by Tey Diana Rebolledo and Eliana S. Rivero in *Infinite Divisions: An Anthology of Chicana Literature* (1993), she traces the many literary strategies used by precursory writers from the contact period to the 1950s, all of whom established a rich tradition of writing that was highly influential to contemporary writers and that links them to Norma E. Cantú. In particular, Fonseca's work looks at the ways in which both Jaramillo and Cantú trace identity formation through the incorporation of multiple literary techniques that reflect the writers' own sense of geographic space and time periods.

Another author who addresses identity formation is María Esther Quintana Millamoto. Her critical piece, "La melancolía de una hija chicana: *Canícula: Imágenes de una niñez en la frontera*" was initially written in Spanish and has been translated by Aldo Ulisses Reséndiz Ramírez, Quintana Millamoto, and Adrian Ortega. She studies *Canícula: Snapshots of a Girlhood en la Frontera* as an ethnic coming-of-age novel, defined as "a novel by an ethnic woman about the identity formation of an ethnic woman, whether fictional or autobiographical in form, chronologically or retrospectively in plot" (Feng 1998, 15). One of the main attributes of these novels is the emphasis on the mother figure in the protagonist's psychosexual development. Mothers embody the native/hereditary cultures whose traditional and reduced view of women as caregivers is perceived by the heroines as a hindrance to achieving autonomy. But if, on one hand, ethnic mothers are the transmitters of patriarchal values, they also provide their daughters with a nurturing space that counters the oppression and discrimination of the hegemonic culture. Too, they pass invaluable knowledge (such as their native language) onto their daughters, which eventually becomes a cultural weapon they can use to fight against discrimination and to resist assimilation into the dominant culture.

Quintana Millamoto posits that *Canícula* foregrounds the protagonist's strong connection with her biological mother and her grandmother as crucial to her psychosexual development. Her article positions the sociopolitical context of these relationships as fundamental to Azucena's ambivalence: she wavers between rejecting her maternal role models for the sake of self-determination or keeping their teachings and risk giving up her independence. She argues that eventually Azucena achieves relational autonomy, recognizing her responsibilities to her family and community while separating from the domestic role embodied by her maternal figures. Also, the protagonist succeeds at integrating both the maternal native knowledge (her language, her sense of solidarity, her respect for her elders, among other things) and the more liberal views of women held by Anglo American culture. In this sense, the article proposes that although this novel takes up the traditional bildungsroman notion of autonomy and self-determination as important goals for Latina women, it does not mean that the protagonist is disposed to break her personal and communal relationships in order to achieve her individual goals.

ABOUT THE CONTRIBUTIONS: PART II

> *"A tool of colonial documentation and modern-day imperial and white supremacist voyeurism that often serves to reduce 'local,' 'native,' and 'ethnic' communities to nothing more than still subjects for Western/white curiosity and consumption, Cantú's use of family pictures and portraits turn the settler-colonial gaze on its head. No longer the outsider looking in but the insider looking out, Canícula makes no claim to be universal; instead, it clings to the image metaphors of the author's childhood set against the backdrop of the Laredo borderlands."*
>
> —ALDO ULISSES RESÉNDIZ RAMÍREZ

In "Cantú's Decolonial Imagination Through the Looking Glass," a timely introduction to the teaching part of this anthology, teacher and scholar Aldo Ulisses Reséndiz Ramírez unfolds before us a unique and extraordinary accordion that demonstrates Norma Elia Cantú's *Canícula* in fact has many bellows. He updates our vision through the criticism of Toni Morrison and David Barton and Mary Hamilton, guiding us through the folds of history, cultural memory, popular memory, identity, subjectivity, and many other layers that are available to us through the intersectional postmodern eye of scholars who unpack, so to speak, the many possibilities of utilizing the multisensory experience that is *Canícula* in the classroom.

Aurora Chang begins part 2 of this book with her contribution, "The Hidden Curriculum of *Canícula*: Critical Educational Lessons in Becoming a *Mujer*." She argues that in *Canícula*, Azucena illustrates the value and heaviness of the "hidden," and that it is within the seemingly quotidian and minute interactions of everyday life that Azucena learns the always consequential and often bittersweet lessons of becoming a mujer. Drawing from Chicana feminist epistemology, she adopts a combination of the concepts of hidden curriculum and community wealth to illustrate how Azucena uses her community cultural wealth to develop familial and resistance capital, ultimately utilizing the experiences of her *niñez* to inform her notions of and foster her fortitude in becoming a mujer. She concludes this striking methodological paper by discussing potential implications of using this type of work in classroom settings for the purposes of teaching and learning.

Another contribution that assists in reformulating *Canícula* for students is Carlos Sibaja García's "The Alternative Lives of Azucena in Norma Elia Cantú's *Canícula*." In his reading of *Canícula*, Sibaja García asserts that Cantú uses Azucena, the protagonist, to show us an understanding of both Mexican and American cultures and as a result creates her own enriched Tejana experience. At the same time, Azucena's story and her life are fragmented. Azucena learns early on to keep secrets, as Aurora Chang notes at the start of her chapter. Sibaja García further problematizes this notion by stating that the reader does not know what part of herself Azucena is showing at any given time. We see Azucena wondering what her life could be like, whether as a nun, a proper lady, or a mother, and her rejection of these "common" roles as almost inferior subjectivities. We do not know what Azucena grew into, but the possibility of Azucena being a lesbian exists in Cantú's text. We see that Azucena has negative associations with men and has an appreciation for older single women that differs from her view of the "traditional Mexican woman"—or is there one? Though her politics and lifestyle are never stated in *Canícula*, Sibaja García finds it clear that Azucena is a woman who does not conform to the traditional norms of gender. Several of her memories of childhood girlfriends reveal a strong attraction to them. The fact that Azucena does not openly state that she is a lesbian does not mean that we, as readers, cannot find hints indicating she does not prefer men.

In "A Discourse of Norma E. Cantú's *Canícula: Snapshots of a Girlhood en la Frontera* and the World of *Nepantla y Nepantlera*," Rose Rodríguez-Rabin states that *Canícula* is about growing up along the Rio Grande, specifically in Laredo, Texas. This chapter looks at the shifting position of the border culture and border people through the lens of the womanfolk. Rodríguez-Rabin juxtaposes what is perceived as autobiography and cultural theory with mainstream ideas of culture and folklore to disrupt traditional readings and scholarship.

Finally, in "*Canícula*: Self-Representation and the Glimpses of the Total Self," another article that teachers and professors may use to educate themselves about cultural pertinence for the purpose of teaching *Canícula*, Juan Velasco utilizes the term *automitografía* to address the open-ended quality of *mito* involved in Chicana autobiography and how that aspect connects not only with personal experience but with the voices that speak for culture and community.

Velasco examines Cantú's novel to see how mito reveals "the total significance of a certain event" and offers a vision of totality that emanates from experiences involving deep connections among the political, cultural, and personal. He analyzes how, in *Canícula*, the "significance" of certain events offers a vision of identity that connects in a unique way to the vision of healing wholeness embedded in Gloria Anzaldúa's notion of the total self: "Deconstruct, construct. She becomes a *nahual*, able to transform herself into a tree, a coyote, into another person. She learns to transform the small 'I' into the total self" (82–83). In fact, the recovery of those voices, the destroyed cultural practices, and communal voice as mitos become the signature of her automitografía.

NOTES

1. "WORD on KCUR 89.3: Norma Cantú reads 'Lithium,' 'Potassium,' and 'Sodium,'" SoundCloud.com, http://soundcloud.com/word-14/norma-cantu-reads-lithium-potassium-and-sodium?fb_action_ids=10204422222812720&fb_action_types=og.shares.
2. Here, I am referring to the unique experience of Chican@s in the American landscape, having survived colonialism, internal colonization, racism, and triumphed by creating a Chican@ homeland (Aztlán) and Chican@ identity that is still being theorized and formulated today.
3. When I interviewed writer/playwright Cherríe Moraga in 2000, she disagreed with me that there had been a "boom" in Chicana literature in the 1990s. She argued that there were a few more Chicanas published by mainstream publication houses, but that in comparison with African Americans, Asian Americans, and Native Americans, Chicanas were still published relatively infrequently (Cherríe Moraga, interview with the author, Palo Alto, CA, May 2000).
4. Just as Asian American theorist Traise Yamamoto utilized *mask* as a verb in *Masking Selves, Making Subjects* to stress the action and process of the entire project she was undertaking, I utilize *subject* as a verb. In this sense, Griselda

Pollock's definition of subjectivity as "social practices which constitute us as social individuals, subject of and for a social system" is also useful, particularly as she notes that "the relations of subjectivity and ideology have to be transformed at the points of their production," a transformation for which Chican@ literature and other cultural representations serve as significant sites for this transformation (164).

5. These discussions appear in Amy Sickels, "The Critical Reception of *The House on Mango Street*," in Herrera-Sobek (2010).
6. I utilize the word *Crayola* because of both the meaning of the word and the history of the company that produces Crayola crayons, Binney & Smith. Crayola "comes from 'craie,' the French word for chalk, and 'ola,' from 'oleaginous'" (Binney & Smith). The name was coined by Alice Binney in 1903. For fifty-five years the company produced eight Crayola crayon colors, selling millions of these individually packaged eight-color boxes. In 1958 Binney & Smith came up with the sixty-four-color assortment, packaged in a box with a built-in sharpener. This historical incident serves as a metaphor for me, the eight-color box referring to the limited and stereotyped range of images of Chicanos/as available to the general public, largely through cinema, and the sixty-four-color box referring to the more varied array of subjectivities now available through Chicano literature, especially literature by Chicanas.
7. The playfulness of the term *Crayola dialectics* is important to me because it connotes the possibility for change and agency both within the writing and from the outside. The participant observer who is the reader is also able to make changes to his or her personal interpretation. The noun *dialectics* in the term underscores this and adds to this moveable "situated knowledge," in which the public participates. The Marxian term *dialectical materialist* stresses the interactive properties of the open-ended relationship between author and reader.

WORKS CITED

Anzaldúa, Gloria. *Borderlands/La Frontera: The New Mestiza*. 2nd ed. San Francisco: Aunt Lute Books, 1999.

Anzaldúa, Gloria, and Cherríe Moraga, eds. *This Bridge Called My Back: Writings by Radical Women of Color*. 2nd ed. New York: Kitchen Table/Women of Color Press, 1983.

Barton, David, and Mary Hamilton. "Literacy Practices." In *Situated Literacies: Reading and Writing in Context*, edited by David Barton, Mary Hamilton, and Roz Ivanič, 7–15. London: Routledge, 2000.

Bowman, Paddy. "Book Reviews: *Canícula: Snapshots of a Girlhood en la Frontera.*" *Journal of the West* (July 1995): 23–24.

Binney & Smith. "History." Crayola.com. http://www.crayola.com/about-us/company/history.aspx.

Campobello, Nellie. *Las manos de Mamá*. Mexico City: Biblioteca Chihuahuense, 1937.

Castellanos, Rosario. *Balún Canán*. Mexico City: Fondo de Cultura Económica, 1957.

Cantú, Norma Elia. *Canícula: Snapshots of a Girlhood en la Frontera*. 1st ed. Albuquerque: University of New Mexico Press, 1995. Reprint, 2015. Page references refer to the 1995 edition.

———. *Canícula: Imagenes de una niñez fronteriza*. Boston: Houghton Mifflin, 2000.

———. *Transcendental Train Yard*. San Antonio, TX: Wings Press, 2015.

Herrera-Sobek, María, ed. *Critical Insights: "The House on Mango Street" by Sandra Cisneros*. Pasadena, CA, and Hackensack, NJ: Salem Press, 2010.

Feng, Pinchia. *The Female Bildungsroman by Toni Morrison and Maxine Hong Kingston: A Postmodern Reading*. Bern, Switzerland: Peter Lang Publishing, 1998.

Garcia, Sara Soledad. Review of *Canícula: Snapshots of a Girl en la Frontera* by Norma Cantú. *Ventana Abierta Revista Latina: Nuestra America* 1, no. 4 (1998). Spring Center for Chicano Studies, University of California, Santa Barbara.

Gutiérrez y Muhs, Gabriella. *Communal Feminisms: Chicanas, Chilenas, and Cultural Exile: Theorizing the Space of Exile, Class, and Identity*. Lanham, MD: Lexington Books, Rowman & Littlefield Publishing Group, 2007.

———. *Presumed Incompetent: The Intersections of Race and Class for Women in Academia*. Boulder: University Press of Colorado, 2012.

———. *Rebozos de Palabras: An Helena María Viramontes Critical Reader*. Tucson: University of Arizona Press, 2013.

——— [Gabriella Gutiérrez Favela Muhs]. "Subjectifying Entities/Emerging Subjectivities in Chicana Literature Through the Literary Production of Demetria Martínez and Norma Elia Cantú: Madres, comadres, madrinas, niñas madres, tías, abuelas y solteronas." PhD diss., Stanford University, 2000.

Kaminsky, Amy. *Reading the Body Politic: Feminist Criticism and Latin American Women Writers*. Minneapolis: University of Minnesota Press, 1992.

Leal, Luis. *Aztlán y México: Perfiles literarios e históricos*. Binghamton, NY: Editorial Bilingüe, 1985.

Moraga, Cherríe. *Loving in the War Years: Lo que nunca paso por sus labios*. Boston: South End Press, 1993.

Pratt, Mary Louise. "Arts of the Contact Zone." In *Ways of Reading*, 5th ed., edited by David Bartholomae and Anthony Petrosky, 603. Boston: Bedford/St. Martin's, 1999.

Pollock, Griselda. *Vision and Difference: Feminism, Femininity, and the Histories of Art*. New York: Routledge, 1988.

Rivera, Tomás. . . . *Y no se lo tragó la tierra/. . . And the Earth Did Not Devour Him*. Translated by Herminio Rios. Berkeley, CA: Quinto Sol, 1971.

Rebolledo, Tey Diana, and Eliana S. Rivero. *Infinite Divisions: An Anthology of Chicana Literature*. Tucson: University of Arizona Press, 1993.

Ruíz de Burton, María. *The Squatter and the Don*. Reprint. Houston: Arte Público Press, 1997. First published in 1885.

Saldívar, José David. *Border Matters: Remapping American Cultural Studies*. Berkeley: University of California Press, 1997.

Saldívar, Ramón. *Chicano Narrative: The Dialectics of Difference*. Madison: University of Wisconsin Press, 1990.

Weedon, Chris. *Feminist Practice and Poststructuralist Theory*, 2nd ed. Malden, MA: Wiley-Blackwell Publishing, 1996.

Yamamoto, Traise. *Masking Selves, Making Subjects: Japanese American Women, Identity, and the Body*. Berkeley: University of California Press, 1999.

PART I

CRITICAL ESSAYS

HYBRIDITY AND THE SPACE OF THE BORDER IN THE WRITING OF NORMA ELIA CANTÚ

ELLEN MCCRACKEN

WHEN NORMA E. CANTÚ'S *CANÍCULA* was published in 1995 and my article about her border writing appeared in 2001, a very different border between the United States and Mexico existed. Large numbers of Central American political refugees had come to the United States during the civil wars of the 1980s, and a number of Chicanos like Cantú supported the assistance that the Sanctuary Movement courageously offered them in spite of the Reagan administration's prohibition of such humanitarian aid. But Norma E. Cantú chose to focus her innovative 1995 book on the Laredo/Nuevo Laredo border space of her youth, the 1950s and 1960s, when most inhabitants of the area traced their family ties to Mexico. The rich cultural hybridity of the border in that period combined with Cantú's interest in the postmodern literary culture and theory developing in the 1980s to produce an innovative text about the border articulated through Cantú's hybrid optic joining the past and present.

Now in 2014, that hybrid border space of Laredo has been undeniably extended south beyond Mexico to Central America and north to the farthest reaches of the United States. The latest border "crisis" that has been building for several years involves tens of thousands of refugee women and children fleeing violence in Central America, who risk their lives to make a grueling, dangerous

Originally Published in *Studies in 20th & 21st Century Literature* 25, no. 1 (2001): 261–80.

journey because they need asylum in the United States. Laredo is only one of the key points along the border where these especially vulnerable Central American refugees find reprieve for a brief time on their journeys to other parts of the United States, where some have relatives or friends who can help them negotiate their attempts to save themselves from violence and death in their homelands. Our 2014 readings of Cantú's border writings must take this new reality into account.

What we might term "the teeming in-between space" that Cantú delineates—an extension of Gloria Anzaldúa's image of the *herida abierta* (open wound)—is even more so now as new groups of refugees pour into the city. Cantú's postmodern "autobioethnography" must now be read along with some of the stories emerging from the Central Americans who arrive in the Laredo border area. In one case, the coyotes helped a young woman and her child from Honduras get to the border, then sold them to traffickers in Nuevo Laredo, who demanded $17,000 ransom; her parents in Chelsea, Massachusetts, tried to borrow the money so that their daughter and grandchild could continue their journey north.[1] The story this woman tells to interviewers in Massachusetts is a new kind of hybrid "autobioethnography" that spans the space from Honduras to Laredo to Massachusetts—a teeming herida abierta.

Can Cantú's striking word and image portrait of Tino in *Canícula*, her young brother who pretends to point a gun at the camera on Easter 1952, be unconnected to the plight of the children coming to Laredo from Central America in 2014? As Cantú poignantly comments on the prolepsis of this visual image—a foretelling of Tino's arrival home in a flag-draped casket from Vietnam—is it not also a foretelling of the death that the contemporary U.S. government foists upon those refugees it deports to their dangerous countries or callously admonishes to stay home in the first place?

Indeed, the family immigration history that Cantú recounts in *Canícula* links her strongly to today's Central American refugees, who are trying to make a life for themselves in the United States and facing the threat of deportation. Her grandparents and their two young daughters were deported to Nuevo Laredo in 1935, losing their truck and all their belongings to corrupt customs officials. A poignant example of the open wound of the border is one daughter's memory of seeing another little girl wearing a pretty dress she had sewn herself. The family would return "home" in 1948, when Cantú was one. Today's Central American deportees may not have that opportunity.

Cantú delineates the rich popular religiosity of her youth on the border, such as the *mandas* (vows) the family makes in the Santo Niño de Atocha church in Nuevo Laredo, the pilgrimage to the shrine of the Virgen de San Juan, and her grandmother's candles to the image of this Virgin by her bedside. In 2014 an important element of Latino popular religiosity in Laredo involves a strong interfaith effort to assist Central American refugees when they arrive in this teeming border space. Many grassroots volunteers along with key church hierarchy have joined efforts to restore a modicum of human dignity to the travelers. The Holding Institute, a clearinghouse for donations, helps 100 to 150 arriving immigrants per day. Catholic Social Services, Bethany House, and the First United Methodist Church provide key support and members of the hierarchy, such as Bishops James Tamayo and Jim Dorff, who made public presentations on July 2, 2014, in Laredo to ask for aid for the refugees. Mandas and prayers no doubt continue, but this crucial community response to the plight of the women and unaccompanied children now augments traditional popular religious practices.

In 2014, as we revisit Norma E. Cantú's classic writings on the border, the "open wound" has expanded geographically north and south, but more and more people are joining efforts to humanely alleviate the refugee crisis in border spaces such as Laredo. Cantú's narratives become new texts in today's context, helping to locate the arriving migrants as part of the long trajectory of diaspora, originally centered in Mexico and now expanded much further south and north. As we add these new aspects of the teeming in-between space to our reading of her work, the example of the humanitarian relief that the border volunteers strive to provide offers a model for a positive outcome to this narrative.

HYBRIDITY AND THE SPACE OF THE BORDER IN THE WRITING OF NORMA ELIA CANTÚ

Studies of postmodernity in the late twentieth century have emphasized the erosion of the comfortable dividing lines by which we neatly separate and categorize reality. The concomitant indeterminacy is disquieting for some but celebrated by others as the site of renewal and a refreshing hybridity unfettered by fixed binary categories. The erosion of epistemological borders does not entail their dissolution; the act of crossing borders relies upon and sometimes indirectly validates the very presence of the border that is to be transcended.

In the case of geographical borders—that separating the United States from Mexico, for example—porosity and firm separation are in constant interplay. The official efforts of governments to establish unassailable borders coexist with the constant flow of people and ideas across the divisional barriers. And like the epistemological borders that postmodernism both denies and indirectly affirms, the geographical interstices between countries are the site of both openness and stricture for those who recreate them in literary texts.

One such border narrativist is Norma E. Cantú, who writes from the space between Mexico and the United States comprised of land in northern Nuevo León and South Texas, centrally punctuated by the two dots on the map that represent the cities of Nuevo Laredo and Laredo. This geographical locale is both a unit and a bisected space in which the official separation of national borders is continually undermined and eroded on the cultural, economic, and social levels. On many levels it functions as a postnationalist space in which the traditional definitions of national identity are reevaluated. At the same time, however, residues of distinct nationalism continue, echoing the deep historical memory of the conflict between unity and separation that marks the area. Cantú recounts the popular story still circulating in Laredo that when the U.S. border was drawn to separate the two Laredos, some Mexicanos disinterred their dead to rebury them on the Mexican side.[2]

Cantú captures the unity of this officially divided territory in the illustrated map at the beginning of *Canícula*, her 1995 hybrid memoir (fig. 1). Along an area of the Río Grande/Río Bravo that runs nearly north/south, the cities of Laredo and Nuevo Laredo oppose each other as east and west, strikingly displaying the deep incursion of the United States southward into Mexico and the parallel geographical presence of Mexico into the land area now occupied by the United States. For Cantú, the unified area depicted by the map emblematically represents the complicated unitary space of her family's history and evolving identity on both sides of the border. It functions as one visual point of entry into her life narrative—a visual signifier that is both accurate and inaccurate representationally. Employing Gloria Anzaldúa's motif of the border as an open wound, Cantú suggests that the ostensibly smooth and unified appearance of the two geographical divisions on the map is in fact teeming with contradictions and the unsettling narratives to come.

FIGURE 1. Map, *Canícula: Snapshots of a Girlhood en la Frontera*, by Norma Elia Cantú, page x.

This essay examines the role of this vibrant border space in Cantú's writing in the context of the other border crossings she undertakes, such as genre hybridity, visual verbal hybridity, and the intersection of competing critical, linguistic, and other cultural codes. While the geographic border described above is the central space of tension and unity of her writing, she frequently probes as well the postmodern intersections that replace the previously clear distinctions between genres, languages, and cultures. Cantú's representation of the border pivots centrally on the geographic space in which Mexico and the United States physically intersect, while at the same time probing several of the other tenuous cultural borders that postmodernity has brought into focus.

Working both as a creative writer and a professor of literature, Cantú frequently transcends the divisions between genres and academic fields. Her varied writing evidences a creative conjoining of cultural criticism and literary creativity that erodes standard categorical borders marking genre divisions. Merging cultural studies and ethnography, she charts new paths of scholarly endeavor. Already in 1982, in her PhD dissertation written at the University of Nebraska, she broadened the boundaries of traditional English literary study by examining the tradition of the *pastorela*, focusing on an example of this Christmas shepherds' play that has been performed for many years in Laredo. Arguing that emphasis either on a literary analysis or on the folk quality of the play would be flawed, she combines disciplines to understand the complex nature of the text as a literary and oral artifact and as folk ritual. Perceiving herself to be following in the footsteps of folklorists such as Jovita González, Cleofas Jaramillo, and Aurora Lucero-White Lea as well as going beyond their work, Cantú spent a year in Spain sponsored by a Fulbright-Hays research grant to study the Spanish origins and developments of the Christmas shepherds' play for her interdisciplinary study.[3]

More recently, Cantú has written on the popular tradition of the Matachines, the dancers in Indian costumes who venerate the Holy Cross in Laredo during religious festivals on May 3, December 12, and December 24. Again she returned to the Spanish roots of the tradition by researching in Spain in 1985. She terms the Fiesta de la Santa Cruz "a site of not necessarily syncretic expression but of postmodern development of a centuries old tradition in a geographical site that is at the interstice of two major cultural worlds—the U.S. and Mexico—yet firmly rooted in . . . the private world; that is, the world of a community in contact with and affected by U.S. hegemonic forces and yet true to its values and worldview" ("Soldiers," 11–12). That is, not only does her study transcend disciplinary boundaries, but it analyzes the geographical and temporal hybridity evidenced in the ancient tradition of the Matachines dance performed to this day in Laredo.

In another study, Cantú examines the *quinceañera* celebration, the rite of passage ceremony for fifteen-year-old girls, viewing the tradition as a communal and individual performance with religious and social elements. As in the other studies, Cantú breaks down borders further by integrating her own experiences of these cultural rituals in her scholarly analysis. Here, she ethnographically presents her own quinceañera Mass years earlier with both insiders and outsiders in mind: "The aisle seemed interminable, my knees were shaking, and I was trying not to hobble, for that day I wore high heels for the first time. After Mass, we went home to hot chocolate and *repostería*, a kind of pastry that is traditional for the Christmas season, which in Mexican tradition extends until February 2, the Feast of Candlemas, or *el día de la Candelaria*" ("Quinceañera," 7). She is both author and subject in these ethnographic studies, one of the local informants whose experience openly shapes the scholarly narrative she herself writes.

As Cantú worked on the study of the Matachines in 1993, she found that even more of her own personal stories surfaced as she wrote, and she decided to focus immediately on writing them. Later, after giving them an order and a narrative frame based on the motif of photographs randomly selected from a storage box, Cantú published her first major work of creative writing, *Canícula* (1995), which joins the tendencies of her scholarly and poetic writing in an experimental, partially fictional, ethnographic account of her own life and family traditions. Transcending traditional generic classifications, this collage of eighty-five vignettes and twenty-three interspersed photos is a hybrid of the visual and verbal, fiction and autobiography, the novel and the short story, and ethnography and creative writing. Cantú settles on the neologism "fictional autobioethnography" to classify the book, a creative new genre that merges this both fictional and veridical account of the self and community.

Inspired by Rita Mae Brown's *Six of One* and Maxine Hong Kingston's *Woman Warrior: Memoirs of a Girlhood Among Ghosts*, Cantú attempts to write an experimental narrative about her life on the Texas-Mexico border. She tells her own story from the late 1940s to the mid-1960s in the "land in between"—the single geographic unit we now know as the border area around the cities of Laredo and Nuevo Laredo, depicted in the hand-drawn map that opens the book. Inextricably connected to the lives of her family and community, this self-narration recounts the daily life, work, traditions, fiestas, and history of her family, friends, and the larger Mexicano population of the borderlands. Using the real names of those who have died and fictional names for the still living (the names of eight flowers stand in for the eight girls in her family), Cantú describes the everyday and the extraordinary—from the repaying of mandas at the Santo Niño de Atocha church in Nuevo Laredo to the tragic death of her brother Tino in Vietnam in 1968. The disturbing memories of repatriation, the poll tax, and picking crops under the hot summer sun join the pleasant remembrances of performing *declamaciones* (recitations) on special occasions, watching Hopalong Cassidy on television, memorable outings, and fiestas.

Celebrating the epistemological questioning common in postmodernist experimentation in the late twentieth century, *Canícula* intentionally blurs the border between fact and fiction from the beginning. Undermining the common readerly expectation of "truth" in autobiography, the text lies openly from its first sentence, as Cantú situates the book as the second part of a nonexistent trilogy she pretends to have written. In a disquieting paradoxical statement, she notes: "In *Canícula* the story is told through the photographs, and so what may appear to be autobiographical is not always so" (xi). The authorial "I" here asks readers to question the presumed truth value of both photographs and first-person accounts; just as photographs may be incorrectly interpreted as truthful representations of one's past life, so too, must readers be wary of that other representational strategy in the book, verbal autobiography, which readers might falsely trust as completely truthful.

The book challenges readers to discern what Roland Barthes (1977) has termed "the photographic paradox" at work in the photos Cantú carefully integrates into the text. Despite the ostensible documentary level of photographs, Barthes notes, numerous hardly visible techniques add the highly subjective code of connotation to the denotative level. To emphasize this, Cantú sometimes deliberately mismatches photographs and narratives (pages 75, 117), reverses a photograph (page 4), omits photos (page 26), retouches photographs (pages 21, 22), or lies about a photograph (pages 14, 130). She reverses the family photograph on page 4, for example, to emphasize her sense of standing apart from and outside of the family unit at that time (fig. 2);[4] she forges her fictional name (one of the eight flowers that represent the eight daughters), "Azucena Cantú," in the retouched immigration and citizenship documents pictured on pages 21 and 22 both to call into question facile markers of identity and to deconstruct the veridical aura of documents and photographs (figs. 3 and 4). And the avowed photographic impetus of the book turns out also to be a lie, since Cantú first wrote the stories and then later decided upon the motif of photographs randomly selected from a box as the frame to hold the stories together.

Cantu's border crossing between the visual and verbal in this hybrid text engages in both terms of the dichotomy that Linda Rugg poses for photographs that "enter the autobiographical act": one, "the rescue of autobiographical referentiality through the presentation of the author's body in the world," and two,

FIGURE 2. Family photograph, *Canícula: Snapshots of a Girlhood en la Frontera*, by Norma Elia Cantú, page 4.

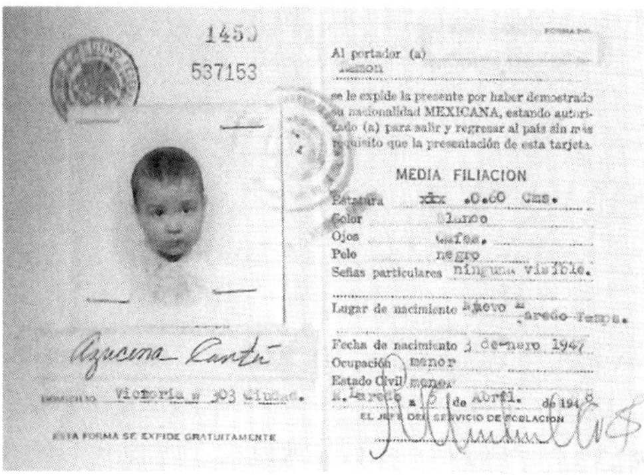

537153

Al portador (a)

se le expide la presente por haber demostrado su nacionalidad MEXICANA, estando autorizado (a) para salir y regresar al país sin más requisito que la presentación de esta tarjeta.

MEDIA FILIACION

Estatura .0.60 Cms.

Color

Ojos

Pelo negro

Señas particulares ninguna visible.

Lugar de nacimiento

Fecha de nacimiento

Ocupación menor

Estado Civil

de Abril. de 194

EL JEFE DEL SERVICIO DE POBLACION

Azucena Cantú

Victoria # 303 Ciudad.

ESTA FORMA SE EXPIDE GRATUITAMENTE

FIGURE 3. Photo of U.S. immigration papers, *Canícula: Snapshots of a Girlhood en la Frontera*, by Norma Elia Cantú, page 21.

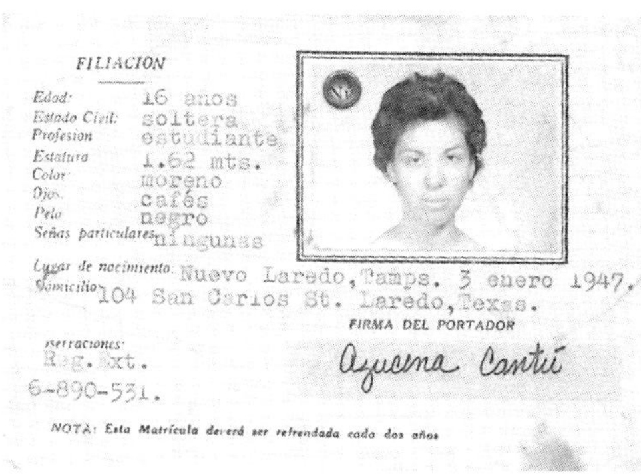

FILIACION

Edad: 16 anos

Estado Civil: soltera

Profesion estudiante

Estatura 1.62 mts.

Color moreno

Ojos cafés

Pelo negro

Señas particulares ningunas

Lugar de nacimiento Nuevo Laredo, Tamps. 3 enero 1947.

Domicilio 104 San Carlos St. Laredo, Texas.

FIRMA DEL PORTADOR

Azucena Cantú

6-890-531.

NOTA: Esta Matrícula deverá ser refrendada cada dos años

FIGURE 4. Photo of immigration document, *Canícula: Snapshots of a Girlhood en la Frontera*, by Norma Elia Cantú, page 22.

FIGURE 5. Family photo, *Canícula: Snapshots of a Girlhood en la Frontera*, by Norma Elia Cantú, page 14.

the undermining of "the integrity of referentiality through multiple or posed presentations" (1). The inclusion of photos and the playful deceptions Cantú engages in with them ask readers to understand the self as multiple and unitary at the same time, as both fixed and changing, and as unfinalized. Although on an initial level the visual and verbal appear to complement each other, allowing the two "semiotic Others" (Mitchell, 156–57) to remedy one another's insufficiencies, Cantú's playful postmodernist deceptions work to dislodge the epistemological certainty of both the verbal and visual levels. Conflicting verbal phrases confuse the anchorage of the photo on page 14, for example (fig. 5). Although a handwritten inscription on the photo itself delimits it as "Easter 1952," the text below suggests that the occasion of the photograph is Tino's ninth birthday party, in which he wields a toy gun, proleptically imaging his own death in Vietnam ten years later. Beyond the postmodern questioning of epistemological certainty, Cantú suggests that this repeated image from the past not only eerily foretells her brother's death but warns us to question children's ostensibly innocent play with war toys.

Together, text and image in *Canícula* ask us both to trust and distrust traditional signifiers of identity. The identification documents in figures 3 and 4 have been "falsified" to correspond to the fictionalized identity of the narrator of this autobioethnography. Readers float between trustworthy and untrustworthy visual and verbal signs in these images—ostensibly truthful photographs and documentary notations such as the birthplace, date of birth, and seals. Yet the

FIGURE 6. High school photo, *Canícula: Snapshots of a Girlhood en la Frontera*, by Norma Elia Cantú, page 130.

surname "Cantú," which has only appeared paratextually on the book's cover, title page, and in the acknowledgments, now appears beneath each photo with the fictional first name "Azucena." What we assume to be Cantú's own handwriting lends a spurious documentary reliability to each document, although the possibility of a one-year-old child signing her name to the first document disrupts that certainty. The matching signatures tease us to uncover the adult Cantú's "forgery" of her own documents in the hybrid visual/verbal border crossing of this book.

In the text below the final photo on page 130 (fig. 6), Cantú lies to readers that she is the girl whose "pink headband holds back a sixties flip" and who wears a white sweater. The girl with the flip and headband has no sweater, while the figure resembling Cantú in the photo does. Cantú indicates with these deliberately contradictory visual and verbal signifiers that identity is unfinalized and unstable; readers must continually question assumed truths and abandon the security of epistemological certainty. The hybrid narrative that promises to describe the self ethnographically in fact foregrounds its own unreliability and its status as a simulacrum.

Barthes (whose 1980 death and posthumous book *Camera Lucida* Cantú refers to in the prologue) distinguishes between the levels of studium and punctum in photographs. In many photos only the level of studium is present, a general arena of interest that attracts us to the image, the photographer's intention present in the photo, his or her means of drawing us to look at an object in a certain way. The punctum, in contrast, is an element—usually a small detail—of some photographs that "pricks" a given viewer in a particular way and produces an altogether different experience of the photograph; "it is this element which rises from the scene, shoots out of it like an arrow, and pierces me" (Barthes 1981, 26). In many photographs, only the studium functions, depending upon a particular viewer's experience of the photograph.

Cantú's verbal narrative strives to communicate both the studium and the punctum of the photos she includes in the book. Her words guide us to "read" the general representational characteristics of the photo either present on the page or imagined. We are to understand the overarching cultural meaning of the posed first Holy Communion photo of the young Cantú on page 56 (fig. 7), kneeling, wearing a veil and white dress, and holding a candle and missal. The studium of this photo, Cantú implies, is the standard image of the perfectly outfitted young girl, dressed like a bride, participating for the first time in the standard Catholic ritual of Communion. The accompanying narrative introduces an element of the photo's punctum that Cantú wishes to communicate to readers: the missal she holds in the photo has "a picture of a blonde child receiving communion from a long-haired, red-robed Jesus on the cover." The photo before us stands in contrast to the stereotypical image of ideal childhood innocence the young Cantú and thousands of other children of color were expected to pray with in their childhood.

The punctum operates on a more literal level in figure 5, discussed above, in which the play gun that the young Tino shoots toward the viewers creates the experience of an emotional and physical wound. Like the piercing arrow shooting out of the photograph of which Barthes spoke metaphorically, the gun in this image foretells a literal death, which Cantú narrates in the accompanying text. The border between text and photo in this section is literally the "wound" that Gloria Anzaldúa describes in one of the epigraphs of *Canícula*. And as Barthes elaborates further on in *Camera Lucida*, the real punctum of photographs is that they foretell our own death. Almost as if he were speaking of the photograph Cantú shows us here, Barthes notes:

> The photograph is handsome, as is the boy: that is the *studium*. But the *punctum* is: *he is going to die*. I read at the same time: *This will be* and *this has been*; I observe with horror an anterior future of which death is the stake. By giving me

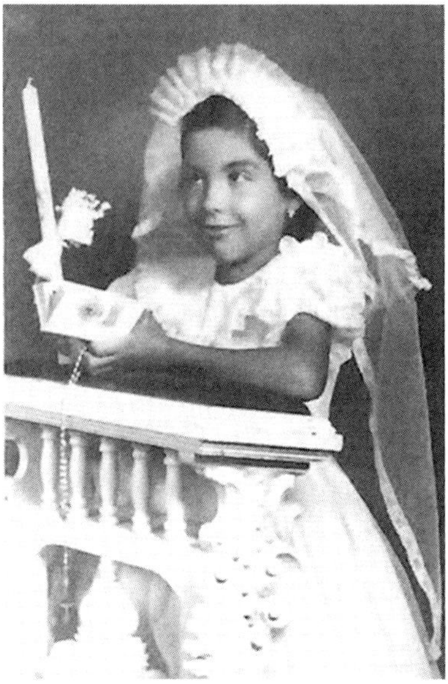

FIGURE 7. First Communion photo, *Canícula: Snapshots of a Girlhood en la Frontera*, by Norma Elia Cantú, page 56.

> the absolute past of the pose (aorist), the photograph tells me death in the future. What *pricks* me is the discovery of this equivalence. (96)

In fact, Barthes notes further on, the common punctum of all photographs is "the imperious sign of my future death" (92). Cantú's autobioethnography, indebted to Barthes's theory and his own death, is a hybrid photo-text that represents life while foretelling death.

Cantú's insistence on the continuum between fiction and reality that is so often celebrated by postmodernist writers is one of several levels of hybridity in the book involving linguistic, cultural, generic, disciplinary, and geographic border crossing. In an unpublished essay, "How I Wrote *Canícula*: Musings on Writing, Reading, and Life," Cantú summarizes her own intriguing hybrid identity as a literary critic, an ethnographer, and a creative writer with respect to the book: "All in all, the critic had to write *Canícula*, and the novelist had to be the soul for the mind. . . . How can someone who does all these things: write literary criticism, folklore, ethnography and fiction—separate these into neat little boxes labeled and set aside?" (7).

In earlier creative writing, Cantú merged disciplinary concerns more subtly by developing an ethnographic overlay in fiction. Because a cousin on her father's side of the family had settled in Omaha, Nebraska, years earlier, Cantú's father allowed her to leave home to attend graduate school there, assured that his relatives would watch over her. Based on that experience, she wrote "Nebraska Family: A Triptych," which implicitly patterns itself on the visual model of a three-paneled painting. It recounts three tales of life in Nebraska, focusing on a daughter who is just turning fifteen, her mother, and her grandmother. Cantú views the three women as versions of a single story and through the triptych form presents three key feasts—Thanksgiving, a quinceañera, and a wedding, which represent, respectively, a secular U.S. celebration, a tradition that emphasizes Mexican roots, and an official Catholic Church ceremony marking the union of an Anglo and a Mexican. Through this narrative, Cantú notes, she came to know her "other" family.[5]

Cantú crosses temporal and historical borders in several poems that are structured by revisionist readings of historical women and goddesses. In "Trojan Horse," the authorial voice imagines herself as the active rescuer of others and as one who changes the world and "bears the power of triumphant entry." Beyond beauty and betrayal, she is neither the figure of Helen of Sparta nor Malinche, but the bearer of a gift that may or may not last forever. She invites the reader to "take my skeletal hand, / look into the eyes of night, / Come into the blinding light / Storm the fortress, / rescue those who need rescuing / offer the proper offerings" (44–45). Joining the perspective of contemporary feminism and the recuperation by Chicana feminists of the figure of Malinche to a reconceptualization of women from previous centuries, Cantú merges distinct temporal periods into a hybrid artifact of difference and unity. The poem's social message works as a counter model to traditional images of both ideal and negative femininity, suggesting that women's power is connected to helping those in need with the gift of oneself.

In the 1994 poem "Action, Thought, Spirit," Cantú engages in what Néstor García Canclini terms "multi-temporal heterogeneity" as she merges temporally and culturally distinct images in a unitary, hybrid utterance. She argues that Santa Teresa is to be celebrated not only for her mysticism but for her action; contemporary women, whether working with "test-tubes or computers," should imitate Teresa's commitment to action or the warrior goddess Coyolxauhqui, who led the attack against Coatlicue in Aztec mythology. Cantú focuses on the practical side of Teresa, who perhaps "was a woman just trying to get things done" as she traveled throughout Spain to various sacred sites. St. John of the Cross, Cantú suggests, could have learned a lesson from Teresa, as should young women today. Cantú again crosses geographical, cultural, and temporal borders in the 1997 poem "Diosas," written entirely in Spanish, as she creates a modified litany to goddesses such as Tonantzin, Coatlicue, Gaia, and the Virgin Mary; instead of the usual repeated supplications of the litany, Cantú's poem chants affirmative statements about an alternate hybrid pantheon of female goddesses who suffer with women today, crying for their daughters who suffer on earth.

Much of Cantú's writing engages in the linguistic hybridity of bilingualism common to border writing. She carries this linguistic experimentation further in the 1998 short story "El luto," dividing the narrative into a Spanish and an English section to represent the separate worlds of a mother and daughter. Whereas Spanish and English intersect with each other in *Canícula* and many of Cantú's other texts, here she reestablishes a firm separation between the two codes to reflect the border tension between the worlds of the mother and the daughter. Offering an updated version of the biblical narrative about Ruth, "El luto" suggests that the contemporary Ruth will engage in filial piety while at the same time breaking with traditional expectations for women in Mexican culture. Unwilling to follow the prescribed mourning rituals after the death of her father, who had deserted her and her mother, plunging both into greater poverty, Ruth nonetheless continues to live at home and care for her mother, while her sisters pursue exciting careers elsewhere. As wide a gap exists between mother and daughter culturally in the story as between the Spanish and English sections of the story, but Ruth's sensible rejection of public mourning for the father who was not a father suggests that she successfully negotiates the tradition of the biblical Ruth's goodness and her own contemporary needs of identity and autonomy.

Cantú's 1999 story published on the Internet, "Farewell in Madrid," carries the motif of linguistic hybridity further by showing how distinct cultural signifiers merge with one another. The story deploys the central motif of equivalencies—linguistic, actantial, and generational—to work through a woman's pain as loved ones pass in and out of her life. The technique of the crossword puzzle, whereby one set of signifiers is substituted for an equivalent set, frames the story: the title, "Farewell in Madrid," is the query seeking the substitute signifier "adios," while the ending word, "father," is the substitute signifier not only for the crossword query but for the larger question that the story as a whole subtly poses. The narrative about the imminent departure of the protagonist's son for college is superimposed on the memory of her own painful separation from a lover in Spain a generation earlier; the revelation of an equivalent for the lover's identity at the end is the answer to the story itself as a metaphorical crossword puzzle. Cantú deliberately includes ambiguity so that the reader must move, sometimes confusingly, back and forth between equivalent linguistic, actantial, and generational signifiers, highlighting the homologous structure and the overlay of the two key moments in the protagonist's life. Just as the six-letter word "father" substitutes by fitting exactly in the crossword puzzle space, so does the story itself substitute for the mother's telling her son about her private memories of her time with his father.

Cantú's innovative scholarly and creative writing—two parts of a continuum—provides seminal information about Chicano/a identity, the border, hybridity, and postmodernity. Her writing is centrally concerned with the tensions of borders that are eroding yet firmly in place, that serve as the site of both exuberant, experimental transcendence and the concrete pain of the herida abierta. As an important postmodernist writer of the border experience, Cantú probes temporal, cultural, and genre hybridity, the dynamic intersections of the visual and verbal, and the teeming in-between space of the geographical border between the United States and Mexico from which her creative writing and cultural criticism arise.

NOTES

1. Richard Knox, "Even in Mass., Hundreds of Central American Refugees Seek Care," WBUR Radio, Boston, http://www.wbur.org/commonhealth/2014/08/22/central-american-refugees-chelsea.
2. Norma E. Cantú, lecture, University of California, Santa Barbara, November 4, 1998.
3. See the introduction to Cantú's book manuscript, "Soldiers of the Cross: Los Matachines de la Santa Cruz," 4.
4. Cantú, lecture.
5. Norma E. Cantú, interview with Ellen McCracken, Santa Barbara, CA, February 17, 1999.

WORKS CITED

Barthes, Roland. *Camera Lucida: Reflections on Photography*. Translated by Richard Howard. New York: Hill and Wang, 1981.

———. *Image—Music—Text*. Edited and translated by Stephen Heath. New York: Hill and Wang, 1977.

Cantú, Norma Elia. "Action, Thought, Spirit." *Prairie Schooner* 68 (Winter 1994): 163–64.

———. *Canícula: Snapshots of a Girlhood en la Frontera*. Albuquerque: University of New Mexico Press, 1995.

———. "Diosas." *Blue Mesa Review* 9 (1997): 71.

———. "Farewell in Madrid." *Proyecto Sherezade*. Edited by Enrique Fernández, June 1999. https://home.cc.umanitoba.ca/~fernand4/adiosing.html.

———. "How I Wrote *Canícula*: Musings on Writing, Reading, and Life." Unpublished essay.

———. "El luto." *Ventana Abierta* 1 (Spring 1998): 46–51.

———. "Nebraska Family: A Triptych." *Nebraska Humanist* (Spring 1995), n.p.

———. *The Offering and the Offerers: A Generic Illocation of a Laredo Pastorela in the Tradition of Shepherds' Plays*. PhD diss., University of Nebraska—Lincoln, 1982.

———. "Quinceañera." Unpublished manuscript.

———. "The Semiotics of Land and Place: Matachines Dancing in Laredo, Texas." In *Dancing Across Borders: Danzas y Bailes Mexicanos*, edited by Olga Nájera Ramirez, Norma Elia Cantú, and Brenda M. Romero, 97–115. Urbana: University of Illinois Press, 2009.

———. "Trojan Horse." In *Floricanto Sí: A Collection of U.S. Latina Poetry*, edited by Bryce Milligan, Mary Guerrero Milligan, and Angela de Hoyos, 44–47. New York: Penguin, 1998.

García Canclini, Néstor. "Memory and Innovation in the Theory of Art." *South Atlantic Quarterly* 92, no. 3 (1993): 423–43.

Mitchell, W. J. T. *Picture Theory: Essays on Verbal and Visual Representation*. Chicago: University of Chicago Press, 1994.

Rugg, Linda Haverty. *Picturing Ourselves: Photography and Autobiography*. Chicago: University of Chicago Press, 1997.

COMMUNITY AND EXILE IN NORMA E. CANTÚ'S *CANÍCULA*

JESÚS ROSALES

Hace tiempo yo me fui para olvidarte
Te dejé sin saber que me querías
Y hoy que vuelvoa implorar por tu cariño
Vestida de blanco te encuentro hincada en el altar.
—"VESTIDA DE BLANCO," AS SUNG BY CARLOS GUZMÁN

THE EPIGRAPH ABOVE is taken from the opening lines of "Vestida de blanco," a song that launched the singing career of Carlos Guzmán, a South Texas performer who is mentioned in the section titled "Declamación" in Norma E. Cantú's *Canícula*.[1] Guzmán began his singing career in the 1960s and presently continues to enjoy artistic success, performing with Las Leyendas de Texas, a group of Tejano singers that also includes Freddie Martínez Sr., Sunny Ozuna, Agustín Ramírez, Carlos Miranda, and Joe Bravo, all significant names—a dream team—to fans of Tejano music.

To those who are unfamiliar with these names and the significance that Las Leyendas have on Tejano culture, it is difficult to convey the profound sense of pride that Tejanos have for their *patria chica*. One can say that the themes of their songs are no different than the everyday life *sufrimientos* that consist of broken hearts and platonic love, of nostalgic yearnings for *tiempo perdido* or *lo que pudo ser*, remembrances of things past, as well as the beauty of life and family unity, topics that are common in any culture. However, there is something different about Tejanos. One can witness it at any Chicano/a dance at some university outside of Texas, for when a Selena or Flaco Jiménez song is played, *lo juro por ésta*, one voice will erupt from somewhere on the dance floor with a thunderous "¡Qué viva Corpus Christi!" Like wildfire, additional praises will rapidly engulf the room: "¡Qué viva San Antonio!" "¡Austin!" "¡Robstown!" "¡Cristal!" "¡Aliiiiiiice!" One can also observe this outpouring of pride by viewing any YouTube performance of a Tejano artist—for example, witness Little Joe's emotional introduction, "Orale, Santa Raza. Here's my brown soul," before performing his signature song, "Las nubes," to a packed auditorium in a concert in Victoria, Texas, on December 11, 2010.[2] The passion expressed in these two examples is so intense and sincere that, *la neta*, for one fleeting moment, one wishes to have been born Tejano.

Lo juro, once again—*ya es un doble juramento*—that there is something culturally unique about Chicanos in Texas. It is encapsulated in the phrase *puro tejano*, a state of mind that unfortunately *nos enajena* but at the same time makes us Chicanos/as proud—proud of who we are or what we can become.[3] "Puro tejano" is an appropriation of a way of being so uniquely special that the phrase incarnates *carnalismo*, a term that unquestionably embodies a passionate Mexican American cultural understanding.

In Norma E. Cantú's *Canícula*, one senses this "puro tejano" sentiment permeating the descriptive canvas on which she paints her portrait of a Mexican American woman growing up in the border area of Laredo, Texas, United States, and Nuevo Laredo, Tamaulipas, Mexico.[4] Her story, not clearly identified as an autobiography, is narrated as a series of short episodes and includes photographs to authenticate the story line.

This essay attempts to reflect on how the Mexican American community of South Texas nurtures sentiments of cultural pride and belonging toward Cantú's *Canícula*, a book that embodies a celebration of Mexican American culture and in which family holds an integral part of the culture's essence. However, *Canícula* is also a personal manifesto that denounces the limitations experienced by the inhabitants of the Laredo–Nuevo Laredo border area and puts the responsibility for perpetuating these restraints on the shoulders of the community (which includes Anglos); the result is a personal exile, or *un escape*, from that particular regional community. The purpose of the departure is not to negate the culture that is left behind, but to embrace it, *llevarla en el bolsillo*, validate it, *como un pasaporte*, and urgently integrate it into the always-changing U.S. national ethos.

COMMUNITY AND FAMILY: CON TODO Y HOMBRES

In an interview with Gabriella Gutiérrez y Muhs, when asked if she identifies *Canícula* as an autoethnography, a work of fiction, a novel, a vignette, or a testimony, Cantú offers the following explanation of her work:

> I on purpose chose to call it a creative auto-bio-ethnography. . . . The reason I chose that, first[, is] creative, because not all of it is autobiographical, some of it is fictionalized, but also it blurs that line between what is fiction and what is life. And I like that. I like to say that life is a fiction, but that fiction is life. And then the autobiographical part of it is obviously the photographs, the fact that I use documents from my own personal life, [to] give it that verisimilitude. On the other hand it is ethnography. I should maybe say on the third hand, it's also an ethnography. It is ethnography of a community as seen from [the point of view of] a little girl, from some participant observer if you will, of the community, cultural lines.[5]

It is clear that with this definition of *Canícula*, Cantú is presenting her text under what Stuart Hall identifies—in relation to a reader's response theory and his interpretation of encoding/decoding—as a dominant-hegemonic position in reference to the reading of the text.[6] In other words, the author will dictate a subjective and dominant point of view of the story, allowing the reader to understand its meaning exactly the way it was intended to be interpreted by the author. As a result, for a Chicano/a reader who shares similar cultural characteristics with the author, it is easy to sympathize with the protagonist's Mexican American coming-of-age experience in *Canícula*. For this reason, in my reading of Cantú's story, the sender (Cantú) and the receiver (me) share indistinguishable cultural Chicano/a biases. *Por ejemplo*, we both proudly embrace our Mexican background, including the fluent use of Spanish and the inherited subtleties of our culture, ranging from the similar *antojitos* that we eat and the childhood games that we played to the admiration for Mexican popular culture icons that contribute so much to our imagination. When Cantú includes the iconic name of Pedro Infante as part of her reality, song lyrics like "Amorcito corazón, yo tengo tentación de un beso" and movie scenes from *Nosotros los pobres* easily come to mind, triggering a romanticized yearning to be intensely more *mexicano* than we Chicanos/as can actually be(come).

The narrative sketches in *Canícula* oscillate between experiences lived in Laredo, Texas, and those lived in Nuevo Laredo, Tamaulipas; between identifying the border through the Rio Grande or el río Bravo; and between the cultural characteristics presented by popular culture from the United States and from Mexico. And though *Canícula* is written in English, the Spanish presence is ubiquitous, lurking like a pesky shadow that depicts itself at times in a tangible way (through the use of specific Spanish words) and at other times only by way of the cultural Mexican essence of the lived ambience in a Mexican-influenced South Texas.

The world that Cantú presents in *Canícula* is one that, in general, determines positive cultural elements of Chicano/a and Mexican culture from both sides of the border. One of the most important ones is the relationship that Nena (Azucena), the protagonist of the story, has with her family and members of her community. Her parents and grandparents provide her not only with a welcoming home environment that nourishes her cultural life but also with a historical stability that allows her to enjoy a cultural Mexican American tradition dating back centuries in the South Texas and Northern Mexico areas.

Within these spaces Mexican culture nourishes Nena's senses and imagination. Many Mexican cultural subtleties exist throughout the book, including the candy that the protagonist eats (*el pirulí*, *las colaciones*); the words associated with community life (like asking for *el pilón* at the local *tiendita*, smashing *cascarones*, acting *chipil*, using *engrudo* as both glue and food); the elements of Mexican pop culture that she admires (including movie star Dolores del Río, singer Alberto Vázquez, the soap opera *Gutierritos*, and songs like "Amor eterno" and "Angelito"); and words related to religion (*los Aleluya* to refer to Protestants; *el Santo Niño de Atocha* to symbolize Catholics' obsession with religious images'; Matachines dancers, who are associated with many religious feasts; and *el romero y la ruda*, healing herbs used by *curanderos* to cure common maladies).

Mexican culture will continue to nourish the teenage Nena as she secures a Mexican identity, along with the more mature elements represented by her reading of the section "Cartas que se extraviaron" (Lost Letters) of a *Confidencias* magazine, "una revista para mujeres que leo a escondidas durante las siestas" (12) ("a women's magazine I'll read secretly during siesta time" [8]).[7] From these letters she creates stories of what her future might bring:

> Me imaginaré que las cartas de amor son para mí, o que las escribí apoderándome de los cuentos trágicos. Juego a ser una gran artista de cine—María Félix,

> Miroslava, Silvia Pinal—con una toalla como traje, Dahlia y yo bailábamos como lo hacen las actrices en las películas. (12)

> I'll . . . pretend the love letters are for me, or that I wrote them, making the tragic stories mine. I pretend I'm a leading star—María Félix, Miroslava, Silvia Pinal. (9)[8]

Mexican female film icons from la Época de Oro del Cine Mexicano (the Golden Age of Mexican Cinema) are the protagonist's nonfamily role models, the ones who open up a world of possibilities, for they are presented as strong women who have the power to negotiate, challenge, and even overturn women's roles within the commanding Mexican patriarchal system.

The community of women in *Canícula*, made up of both movie stars (like the names mentioned above) and family and friends (*abuelitas, tías, amigas*), offer a profound cultural support in the *crecimiento*, or upbringing, of the young protagonist of the story. However, the role that men play is equally important. Most of the men in *Canícula* are presented in a positive way, including Nena's grandparents and friends of the barrio. Three, however, merit special consideration: Nena's father, her brother Tino, and tío Mase.

As expected, Nena's father, lovingly referred to as Papi, holds a dear place in her heart. He is present directly or indirectly throughout the text and generally portrayed with utmost respect. Papi is described as a man who is concerned for the welfare of his family, unwilling to compromise his family life for work (he shows this by quitting his construction job so as not to be constantly away from the family). Among many other positive human characteristics, he is also financially responsible (he does not want credit accounts); he cares for the family's harmony and mental health (by taking them to restaurants and *días de campo*, or picnics, and regularly participating in family functions like birthday parties and social events); he shows concern for his children's future (by buying an encyclopedia to encourage their education); he takes traditions seriously (he buries the *ombligo* of Nena when she is born); and he is a dreamer (he is not afraid to dream what he wanted to be or do in life) as well as a realist (he believes in God when his son is healed and loses his faith when his son is killed in the war).

In the short *estampa*, or narrative, titled "El caballo de Papi" ("Papi's Horse"), Nena describes a photograph of her father sitting on top of his beloved horse, Rocinante, as a young man in Mexico, followed by a short narration of a trip that she took with him as an older man to his home town of Allende, Coahuila. Describing the photo, Nena presents her father as a proud man whose wholesome smile seems to indicate that he is sitting on top of the world as he enjoys the beauty of his Mexican rancho, "donde el campo se extiende hasta el cielo" (27) ("where a field extends into the sky" [15]). For some reason, so many Mexicanos who leave their homeland to find economic opportunities in the United States yearn to someday return to *descansar en paz* or retire in this earthly paradise. Unfortunately, the reality of leaving their beloved country and the dream of someday returning to it result in a never-ending dramatic sojourn that tragically lingers in their minds until they finally realize *que ya están viejitos*, that they are growing old, and that the dream of returning home is slowly fading away. According to Nena, this is exactly what happened to Papi's desire to return to his homeland:

> Hasta hace poco hablaba de volver a México, de establecerse en un pueblo pequeño: Vallecillo, Sabinas, Anáhuac.—Un ranchito para volver a sembrar—, decía. Pero ya no menciona estos planes, resignado a vivir con su incapacidad artrítica, a su vida de jubilado en Laredo. (27)

> He used to talk of going back to Mexico, of settling in a small town, Vallecillo, Sabinas, Anáhuac. "A ranchito, to plant again," he'd say. He doesn't mention these plans anymore, resigned to arthritic disability, to retirement in Laredo. (15–16)

The quote highlighted above serves as a useful metaphor, for it encapsulates the lifetime saga of many Mexicanos, who, like Papi, leave their country at a young age on a journey of no return, sadly coming to the realization that their wishful *cuando regresemos* never will exist. Ironically, this also encapsulates the future saga of Mexican Americans, who, like several characters in *Canícula*, including the protagonist, will eventually leave their own geographic space to encounter a similar fate.

Like Nena's father, Tino plays an important part in Nena's life and in a way, because of his untimely death in the Vietnam War, serves as a sentimental bridge that connects all three. In the short narrative "Tino," Nena includes a snapshot of herself and three other children playing in the yard of a house. Tino stands slightly apart from the group, his hand extended, as if pointing a gun at the camera. Nena specifies that Tino always enjoyed playing a fictional soldier, something that became a reality ten years later, when he enlisted in the army. The narration that started at a family gathering to celebrate Nena's birthday party ends by describing another family gathering, the mourning of Tino's death.

Tino's death was a tragedy that affected the entire family. Nena, however, was affected by the loss in a more intimate and peculiar way than the others, for it appears to haunt her throughout her life as a result of the sense of culpability her father placed upon her. In the narrative "Hábito de monja" ("Nun's Habit"), Nena talks about how, when she was a young girl, the Roman Catholic Church encouraged kids to follow a religious path and enroll in a seminary (for boys) or a convent (for girls) to prepare for the priesthood or nunhood. This religious path did not interest Nena at all, but she writes that this option could have been something her brother Tino might have considered, for he was recruited to enter the seminary by the local priests. Unfortunately, his family did not encourage (nor discourage) him to follow this career path.

In hindsight Nena believes that, after Tino's death, her father felt a huge sense of guilt for causing his son to ignore the opportunity to enter the seminary. His feeling of guilt was so great that Nena surmises he needed to share it with others to mitigate the pain:

> Tal vez por eso me culpó a mí, la mayor, porque no le hablé, yo que hablo inglés, que soy la mayor. Pude haberlo convencido de que no fuera de voluntario, que esperara terminar high school por lo menos. Tal vez entonces hubiera sido otra cosa. (208)

> Must be why he blamed me. I, the oldest, the one who spoke English, why I didn't talk to my brother? He usually listened to me. I could've told him not to enlist, to wait till he finished high school at least. Maybe then something else would've happened. (117)

Two things stand out in this statement. One is the parental responsibility that was placed upon her. Being the oldest of the children and fluent in English, Nena was given responsibilities meant for parents or grown-ups. Her father, seeing her as the "speaker" of the house (in a way, a father-figure prototype), made her feel guilty for not convincing Tino to finish high school, a decision that led to his death in Vietnam at age seventeen. This tragedy mentally hurt Nena, not because she was not able to convince Tino to enter the seminary or finish high school, but because their father instigated the guilt that so profoundly affected her life.

Besides Papi and Tino, tío Mase is a vital male figure in Nena's life. First, tío Mase is deeply connected to the protagonist's immediate family and serves as an added source of nostalgic remembrances of her childhood. Tío Mase (Maximiliano, Max) is Nena's mother's cousin and the Holy Communion godparent of her brother Tino. He served in the Korean War, returned to South Texas, took advantage of his GI Bill, and became a family man. His wife, Lucía, who was his high school sweetheart, and their eight children (seven females and one male) spend countless days at Nena's home, sharing memorable moments with her family. In the section titled "Mase," Nena describes this closeness with her uncle's family:

> Mientras Mami, tía Lucía y Bueli platicaban, tío Mase y Papi veían la lucha libre en la tele; nosotros jugábamos a la *touch*, la *roña* o a los *retratos*. Jugábamos *bebeleche* cuando podiamos dibujar el diagrama en la tierra. Al obscurecer pasabamos a los juegos de el *bote* o a las *escondidas*. (87)

> While Mami, Tía Lucia, and Bueli visited and Mase and Papi watched wrestling on TV, we played "a la touch," or "la roña," or "retratos." We played "bebeleche" where we could draw the hopscotch diagram on the ground and "a las escondidas." (50)

The image that Nena offers is one that many of her readers can relate to. It nurtures memories of watching *luchadores* like Santo and Blue Demon grapple with *las momias de* Guanajuato and playing games *al aire libre* like *los encantados* and *la lotería*.[9] But another reason why tío Mase is significant in Nena's life is the indirect influence that he has on her formation as a creative writer. Tío Mase owns a printing business, and his *taller*, or workshop, captivates the young girl's mind. By witnessing the transformation of words onto paper, Nena is able to physically see words that existed only in her mind. As she points out: "Me encantaba esculcar en su taller al fondo del solar, el olor a tinta, a papel, olor a palabras recién impresas, negras como la suerte en el blanco, color de cascarón, de los anuncios de bodas" (87–88). ("I loved to snoop in the little shop behind the house: the smell of ink, of paper, of freshly printed words, black as fate on the eggshell white of wedding announcements" [50]).

Nena describes in meticulous detail the day that she accompanied her parents to print her *quinceañera* invitation and the image of her uncle that became ingrained in her memory: "el sudor le corre por la frente y los brazos, viste camiseta blanca y pantalón café. El cinturón de piel se obscurecía con el sudor" (88) ("sweat runs down his forehead, down his bare arms, he wore an undershirt and brown pants, the leather belt darkened by the sweat" [51]). These unfading images undoubtedly inspired the protagonist's love for the printed word and in describing them she credits tío Mase for opening a world to her that she never knew existed.

To balance the positive representations of the males in Nena's family, Cantú does offer her share of male *abusadores*, characters who are usually linked, not to the family, but to friends, or *conocidos*. But overall, Nena's experience with men is tantamount to the nurturing cultural experience that she lived in South Texas. Papi, Tino, and tío Mase offer a link that connects her life as a child with the woman and writer that she will become in her later life. Sadly, that educated woman will be able to return to her past only through printed memories of a world that, like her father's *campo mexicano*, is lost forever.

COMMUNITY AND EXILE: UN ESCAPE

In *The Decolonial Imaginary: Writing Chicanas into History*, Emma Pérez intends to provide the Chicana with a specific historical space, one that has previously been negated by mainstream male-oriented historical representations. In an effort to reinterpret or rewrite this history, Pérez aims to remove the "'his' out of the 'story'" (xiv).[10] She begins her reconstruction by digging through historical archives in order to unearth the previously ignored or forgotten history of women. Pérez affirms that "archeology seeks to uncover discursive practices by unmasking them" (xvi). As an archaeologist of Chicana history, she aspires to do exactly that. Pérez argues that "differential consciousness" (a concept credited to Chela Sandoval) is useful to her in recreating the history of the Chicana. According to Sandoval, Pérez explains, the "differential consciousness" allows the mobility or shifting of identities among differential powers as needed. For example, it becomes easy to change or alternate ideological concepts (liberal, socialist, feminist, et cetera) according to the specific circumstance for which the particular concept seems most appropriate. With the use of this concept Pérez introduces a third space, feminist in nature, which she calls "the decolonial imaginary": "Like differential consciousness, the decolonial imaginary in Chicana/o history is a theoretical tool for uncovering the hidden voices of Chicanas that have been relegated to silences, to passivity, to that third space where agency is enacted through third space feminism" (xvi). Pérez uses archaeology figuratively to excavate words and their innate meanings and to analyze those who have created Chicano historiography. She argues that traditional historiography produces a fictitious past and that, as a result, authors have regrettably negated the cultural differences of the "other." In this respect, Pérez tries to create an imagined history that will form a consciousness reflecting the reality of present Chicana history.

If we read *Canícula* with these concepts in mind, we can see it is more than a celebration of a South Texas Mexican American border culture: it is an act of defiance and *rebeldía* against that same culture, which means so much to the author. In other words, besides accentuating her rich cultural world and family unity and pride, Cantú also recognizes the limitations of a stagnant community that requires social change and challenges its people to grow outside of that restricted space.

In the opening pages of *Canícula*, Cantú includes a physical map of the region she writes about (fig. 1). It is a square depiction that encloses a specific space marked by lines and black dots that denote rivers and towns. We can identify this area, using a romanticized Tejano spirit, as a self-declared República del Río Grande or, using an outsider's critical approach, as *la tierra abandonada*, a historically neglected region in desperate need of a meaningful social integration with the surrounding states.

This *tierra abandonada*, like many other Chicano urban barrios in the United States, is one where ambiguity and uncertainty abound, as do hope and *ganas* to excel. All the good and the bad that encompass a Chicano reality can be found here. It is a microcosm that represents any marginal community that struggles with everyday challenges. There is a wealth of talent in its streets and *pueblitos*, but it is seldom exploited and celebrated. It is a tierra that, in the worst of times, reminds us of Juan Rulfo's Comala, a land lost in the shadows of dust and solitude.[11]

To describe this sense of abandonment, allow me to share a trip that I made from Corpus Christi, Texas—where I lived for fifteen years—to Laredo. As one leaves Corpus and travels on Highway 44 to Laredo, one senses *la grandeza tejana*, a land *plana* covered by a blanket of endless blue sky, without a mountain in sight. If one decides to adhere to the speed limit of the road and take time to meditate over the wonder of the scenery, some Chevy truck or GM SUV will sooner or later zoom by you, for the driver wants to beat you to a seamless unknown destination. The journey will come to a halting stop once you reach Robstown. Some drivers will merge onto Highway 77 and travel to Kingsville; others, like me, will follow the signs leading through the town to reconnect us to Highway 44 (which was somehow interrupted by Highway 77). Forty minutes later, accompanied by the still blue, cloudless sky and endless flat land, one has swiftly passed by the small towns of Banquete and Agua Dulce and crossed into the heart of Alice. It is here that one is tempted to stop at a local taqueria (El Jalisiense on Main Street) and order several bacon-and-egg breakfast tacos (flour tortilla, "*mixteados*") and a cup of coffee, *con crema por favor*.

By the time one reaches San Diego, Texas, there are two *bolitas* of foil inside the brown paper bag that minutes before contained the breakfast tacos. I take a sip of my coffee while I pass through the Duval County Courthouse, recalling the ambitious *Plan de San Diego* and the plight of Gregorio Cortez.[12] Just before reaching the town limits I spot numerous abandoned structures; other are occupied, but these stand as broken-hearted businesses clinging to life through the spirit of their faded *rótulos* announcing Panadería La Esmeralda or Lucy's Café. Some houses are caving in to nonexistence; surprisingly, others are surviving, for I see a *viejito* stepping out from one of them. A rickety screen door remains half open behind him as he approaches the road, waiting for my car to pass so he can cross the street to *saludar* another viejito—no doubt a ritual practiced for ages.

The viejito's house reminds me of impressionist *cuadro* that challenges its spectator to decipher its ambiguity. The body of the structure is *chueco*: it is tilted toward one side, as if mimicking the tree that stands in the front yard, deformed by the power of the wind. The structure next to his is an abandoned home with one large hole in the roof, as if a large rock had fallen on top of it, *descalabrándolo*.

At the outskirts of San Diego the last business that one sees is a *llantera*, a tire shop, where a couple of local mechanics sit patiently waiting for a car to leave the road so they can pull a rusty nail from a flat tire that has punctured it. There is no urgency in their faces, and it might seem that this area is lifeless. But life does exist. I witness it in the numerous flowers growing in tin coffee cans on many of the *solares* and the *pan de campo* that is sold from an open-doored minivan parked in an empty, unpaved parking lot. Life is moving, but not at the same pace as for those who live outside of these *comarcas*.

Freer is the last town to pass before reaching Laredo. Here one checks the gas gauge, for there will not be any gas service for the next sixty miles. I fill the gas tank, check the tire pressure, and refill my coffee cup at the local store. Before I proceed I take a picture of the giant rattlesnake, the local legendary landmark in a lonely and imperfect spot that challenges the immensity of the sky.

It is here in Freer where I separate from Highway 44 and take Highway 59 left/south onto a two-lane road to Laredo. Those who turn right/north will eventually reach George West, Beeville, "crossroads" Victoria, eventually Houston. I turn left, and in an hour or so I reach the outskirts of Laredo. As I approach the city, to my right I glimpse the Casa Blanca Lake and the standing buildings of the city's new university, Texas A&M International. Slowly, structures start to appear in the scenery on both sides of the road: more llanteras, a shop with colorful clay pots lined up, a cemetery with faded artificial flowers decorating its graves. It is at these particular spots that I realize Cantú's border city and cultural domain have been reached.

To travel through these South Texas roads (including Highway 77 to Brownsville, Highway 83 to Crystal City or Eagle Pass, and 281 to Falfurrias, Edinburg, and McAllen, among many others) and compare the landscape to the highways and less harsh topography north of San Antonio, to the green slopes of the hill country that embraces Boerne, Kerrville, Fredericksburg, and New Braunfels, or to the mighty cities of Austin, Houston, and Dallas is to comprehend the disparity that exists between South Texas and the rest of the state. Cantú's region is rich with culture but still poor in opportunities for the Mexican Americans who make up more than 90 percent of the South Texas population.

When we delve into the history of the state of Texas and understand the cultural conflicts that have existed among the Anglo American, Mexican, and Mexican American people since the early decades of the nineteenth century, we can understand Cantú's yearning for family and cultural survival. But equally important is Cantú's desire to document this story (not his-story) and yearn for a life outside of it. Not to abandon it, but to grow because of it.

It is under this critical perspective, the negotiating code, or the mixture of accepting and rejecting elements that make up the text, that the reader *mete su cuchara y engancha* his or her critical perspective of *Canícula*. It is under this scrutiny that we see the limitations that emerge from living in this part of the country—limitations caused by the history of the area (the Texas Republic that relives the "Remember the Alamo!" mentality, the illogical Mexican-American War, the notorious King Ranch, the hated Texas Rangers . . .), which left South Texas in a state of economical, political, and educational poverty that continues to this day.

In *Canícula* we see hints of the hardships suffered by Mexican Americans. The map included in the beginning of the book charters the battleground. Within the limits of this space is described a community of working-class people who struggle with economic uncertainty. Many people from this part of the country toil as migrant farm workers, migrating part of the year to other states to pick crops and saving their money to survive on when they return to Texas and face unemployment. Nena's father, for example, was forced to look for work as far north as Gary, Indiana, and in Texas he worked at different jobs throughout his life. Seeing no hope in the future, many males are forced to enlist in the army as a way to move out of their beloved, but at the same time *maldita, vecindad.*

Canícula, then, becomes a *denuncia*, a social protest against the dominant culture's exploitation and neglect of the Mexican American community of South Texas. The minimal representation of Anglo characters in Nena's story says it all. By not including Anglos in her coming-of-age memories she conveys the segregation—at all levels—that existed between the Anglo and Mexican American communities. And yet, the Anglo community that is in Nena's world in reality is undeniably visible, for it has manipulated her world throughout the history of Mexican Americans for close to two hundred years.

But Cantú's criticism is not centered solely on Anglo American domination. It also denounces the negative elements of her culture's patriarchal system that are ingrained in the daily life and whose stubborn existence suffocates women's personal progress.

Cantú's *Canícula*, metaphorically packaged in a shoebox full of pictures and short written anecdotes of her life, permits the author to protest the limitations of her culture, in particular those associated with women. Her intent is, as Pérez points out at the beginning of this section, to take the his-story (both Anglo and Mexican American) out of the overall story and her regional space. By doing this Cantú not only denounces the lack of the Mexican American presence in the national picture, but also denounces the machismo so prevalent in the Mexican American psyche.

Cantú's shoebox story structure is a symbolic literary mechanism she uses to remove herself from that past as well as to become a self-proclaimed exile (un escape) from it. Each snapshot and short narrative piece, or estampa, in the story becomes a legitimate *sello*, or stamp, that authorizes those memories to confer an eternal rest.

Canícula is a contestation that denounces dismal social conditions that exist in Cantú's community. Her cultural paradise becomes a *barrio abandonado* that is clinging to its culture as a way of enduring the remembrance of living under the shadow of a conquest.

Like Highway 59 in Freer, where one chooses to continue to the left to Laredo or to the right to Houston, *Canicula* is a reading that bifurcates, a testimony of both love and criticism for Mexican and Mexican American culture. It is appropriate that Cantú's testimony ends with a recollection of her high school years, both when she graduated in 1965 and later, at her 1990 reunion:

> Algunos de nosotros jamás nos alejamos y otros jamás volvemos. Algunos regresamos una y otra vez. Algunos amamos y otros odiamos. Algunos amamos y odiamos a la vez ésta, nuestra frontera. Algunos recordamos, otros nos olvidamos. (238)

> And some of us never leave, and some of us never come back. Some of us keep coming back. Some of us love, and some of us hate, some of us both love and hate our borderlands. Some of us remember, some of us forget. (131–32)

Cantú embodies these oppositional feelings for her *frontera*, as expressed in the quote above. The love for her culture will always bring her home to participate in life celebrations (birthdays, quinceañeras, weddings, *lutos*) that will continue to take place in Laredo and Nuevo Laredo; on the other hand, her return will be defined only as a temporary visitation, for she is coaxed to live outside of that nurturing space and participate unreservedly in the shaping of the increasingly multicultural reality of mainstream society.

CLOSING REMARKS: VESTIDA DE BLANCO, HINCADA EN EL ALTAR

So we go back to the epigraph of the beginning of the essay: "Hace tiempo yo me fui para olvidarte" (I left a long time ago to forget about you) / "Te dejé sin saber que me querías" (I left you without knowing that you loved me) / "Y hoy que vuelvo a implorar por tu cariño" (And now that I return to implore for your love), / "Vestida de blanco te encuentro hincada ante el altar" (I find you dressed in white kneeling before the altar).[13] Carlos Guzmán's song embodies dramatic representations of love, exile, redemption, and loss. It dramatizes an exhausted story line in which the protagonist leaves home in search of the fictitious promised land, only to realize, by means of trial and error, that this mythical place never really existed. In a desperate quest for redemption, the exiled traveler returns to the initial point of departure to recuperate what was left behind. But yesterday doesn't exist anymore. It becomes evident that one can only pretend to retrieve the past that was left behind through the fallacy of a fragile memory. *Canícula* does not intend to surrender to the audacity of that possibility.

NOTES

1. Carlos Guzmán was born in a small community in South Texas. His real name is Margarito Guzmán. He is extremely popular in the Tejano music scene. He has performed with major Mexican singers and also appeared in several Mexican soap operas.
2. I recommend the following YouTube video to get the feel of Little Joe's performance of "Las nubes," a monumental song in Tejano and Chicano music: http://www.youtube.com/watch?v=J-YIBj8cuao.
3. An issue of the journal *Puentes: Revista México-chicana de literatura, cultura y arte* was dedicated to Tejanos. Leading writers and critics from Texas (Rolando Hinojosa, Norma E. Cantú, Rosaura Sánchez, Juan Rodríguez, María Herrera-Sobek, José Ángel Gutiérrez, and Arnoldo De León, among others) reflect on what it is to be "tejano." "Puro tejano," *Puentes: Revista México-chicana de literatura, cultura y arte*, no. 6 (Fall 2008).
4. Norma E. Cantú, *Canícula: Snapshots of a Girlhood en la Frontera* (Albuquerque: University of New Mexico Press, 1995). The book was translated into Spanish as *Canícula: Imágenes de una niña fronteriza* by the University of New Mexico Press (Boston, New York: Houghton Mifflin, 2001).
5. Gabriella Gutiérrez y Muhs, *Communal Feminism: Chicanas, Chileans, and Cultural Exile; Theorizing the Space of Exile, Class, and Identity* (Lanham, MD: Lexington Books, 2007), 20.
6. Stuart Hall, "Encoding/Decoding," chap. 10 in *Culture, Media, Language*, ed. Stuart Hall, Dorothy Hobson, Andrew Lowe, and Paul Willis (London: Hutchinson, 1980).
7. The quotes used in this essay are taken from the Spanish translation of *Canícula*. They are included to provide an opportunity for an English reading public to read and appreciate the Spanish version.
8. The Spanish translation of *Canícula* is slighty different from the original English version of the text. In this particular quote the English sentence ends with "Silvia Pinal"; the Spanish one goes on and includes Dahlia in the description of the scene. All the English quotes in this essay are taken from

Canícula: Snapshots of a Girlhood en la Frontera (Albuquerque: University of New Mexico Press, 1995).

9. Santo and Blue Demon were two of the most celebrated and iconic Mexican wrestlers of the twentieth century. Both were movie stars, appearing as action heroes in films such as *Santo y Blue Demon en el mundo de los muertos*, *Santo y Blue Demon en la Atlántida*, and *Santo contra las momias de Guanajuato*.
10. Emma Pérez, *The Decolonial Imaginary: Writing Chicanas into History* (Bloomington: Indiana University Press, 1999).
11. Comala is Juan Rulfo's fictional town in his celebrated short novel, *Pedro Páramo*.
12. The *Plan de San Diego* was a document written in Mexico by supporters of Venustiano Carranza in 1915, during the Mexican Revolution. The *Plan* called for Mexico to recapture the southwestern U.S. states of Texas, New Mexico, Arizona, and California. Gregorio Cortez was a Mexican American social bandit who became a folk hero to Mexicans and Mexican Americans in South Texas in the first decades of the twentieth century.
13. The translation to Guzmán's song is mine.

NORMA E. CANTÚ

*From Chicana/*Fronteriza *Writer and Critic to Public Intellectual*

MARÍA SOCORRO TABUENCA

But I didn't convince Mrs. Watkins
that my destiny lay in math. . . .
She trusted my love of words
didn't see my love of numbers.
And thus my path was set . . .
—NORMA E. CANTÚ

IN 1993 I CAME ACROSS the work of Norma Elia Cantú. At that time she had only published several poems and short stories, and her academic work concentrated mainly on Chicana/o literature, literacy, and folklore.[1] More than twenty years have passed since that literary and personal encounter, and I am certain that Mrs. Watkins's trust in her writing has been essential to her vision and path, her trail and dream. Norma E. Cantú's creative work is not limited to its foremost piece, *Canícula: Snapshots of a Girlhood en la Frontera* (1995). She has also published short stories, poems, and *testimonios* and has produced other, as yet unpublished creative work, such as "Cabañuelas: A Love Story" (a novel under review), "Papeles de mujer" (a novel written in Spanish), "Champú, or Hair Matters" (a novel), and "Meditación fronteriza: Poems of Life, Love, and Work" (poetry collection).[2] Her scholarly publications include a variety of topics; she has focused primarily on such subjects as border literature "*de este lado*," traditional border dance, Chicana traditions, the works of Gloria

Anzaldúa, teaching English to Chicanas/os, food, Chicana/Latina women in math and sciences, and Chicana feminist theory. She has also worked on professional reports about traditional arts and folklore for the Smithsonian's National Museum of American History, the Southern Arts Federation in Atlanta, the Idaho Commission on the Arts, and the Tennessee Arts Commission.

Most studies of Cantú's work comment on her autobioethnography, *Canícula*, and a good number of them focus on the border richness of the text. A dynamic and heterogeneous border space exists inside *Canícula*, where one can find a mix of overlapping elements and codes, such as autobiography and ethnography, the visual, the oral, and the written, and the linguistic, the cultural, and the territorial. In fact, to date, Norma Cantú's other creative and critical work also shows these multiple inter- and transdisciplinary characteristics, a result of her academic training, her personal experience, and the fact that she is a multifaceted individual with many talents and abilities, capable of maneuvering with gentleness and agility across the borders of creative writing, academia, and social practice, as well as those of geographical space. By "social practice," I refer to Cantú's classroom involvement with and mentorship of her many students and her role as editor and co-editor of books. Her commitment to spread Chicana/o cultural production, particularly from the U.S.-Mexico border and especially from Texas, is always present. In this regard, she has devoted time to editing such volumes as *Paths to Discovery: Chicanas in Mathematics, Science, and Engineering* (2008) and *Moctezuma's Table: Rolando Briseño's Mexicano and Chicano Tablescapes* (2012) and to jointly editing other important and varied volumes, such as *Entre Malinche y Guadalupe: Tejanas in Literature and Art* (2016), *El Mundo Zurdo: Selected Works from the Meetings of the Society for the Study of Gloria Anzaldúa, 2007 and 2009* (2009), *Inside the Latin@ Experience: A Latin@ Studies Reader* (2010), *Dancing Across Borders: Danzas y Bailes Mexicanos* (2009), *Telling to Live: Latina Feminist Testimonios* (2001), and *Chicana Traditions: Continuity and Change* (2002). However, Norma E. Cantú has not only worked for the Chicana/Latina border community within the academic world and in renowned organizations like the American Folklore Society, the Federation of State Humanities Councils, and the National Endowment for the Arts, she has also actively participated in the community in general, offering workshops, readings, and other kinds of volunteer work to immigrant communities.[3]

From this overview of her published work and her extracurricular activities we can perceive a tireless advocacy to bring marginalized, obliterated, or neglected people and topics into the academic and public arena.[4] Such constant advocacy places her among those she has called "organic intellectuals" (Cantú, "Whose Story," 2) and moves her away from "American [and other Chicana/o] intellectuals [who] appear to have entered a period of non-engagement, cherishing their autonomy over engagement and retreating into the ivory tower" (Patrick Saveau, quoted in Cushman, 328).[5] I don't know if Cantú will agree with my statement, because in her lecture, "Whose Story Is It Anyway? Autobiography on the Border," she mentioned that many Chicana/o scholars are reluctant to call themselves intellectuals, perhaps "because of its elitist associative semantic weight" and also because, for her and others, "the term connotes class as well" (2). This connotation is based on the fact that growing up in the barrio she was never in contact with intellectuals; her English teacher believed that the head of the smeltery where her father worked was an intellectual. However, if we trace Cantú's academic, creative, and political work and take into account Edward Said and Ellen Cushman's concepts of the public intellectual, she is unquestionably the perfect fit.[6] For Said, the public intellectual is

> an individual endowed with a faculty for representing, embodying, articulating a message, a view, an attitude, philosophy or opinion to, as well as for, a public, in public. And this role has an edge to it, and cannot be played without a sense of being someone whose place it is to raise embarrassing questions, to confront orthodoxy and dogma (rather than to produce them), to be someone who cannot easily be co-opted by governments or corporations, and whose *raison d'être* is to represent all those people and issues who are routinely forgotten or swept under the rug. (3)

And as Ellen Cushman writes:

> The kind of public intellectuals I have in mind combine their research, teaching, and service efforts in order to address social issues important to community members in under-served neighborhoods. . . . When public intellectuals not only reach outside the university, but actually interact with the public beyond its walls, they overcome the ivory tower isolation that marks so much current intellectual work. They create knowledge with those whom the knowledge serves. Dovetailing the traditionally separate duties of research, teaching, and service, public intellectuals can use the privilege of their positions to forward the goals of both students and local community members. In doing so, they extend access to the university to a wider community. Public intellectuals challenge the value system of academe

> by starting with the assumption that all language use and ways of knowing are valuable and worthy of respect. Academics can serve this role in two ways: service learning and activist research. (329–30)

And precisely, Cantú achieves this communion between her writings and her social practice, between her texts and her political views.

This essay focuses on the study of some of Norma E. Cantú's critical and creative works and identifies how the work of the public intellectual, in accord with Ellen Cushman and Edward Said's definitions, is illustrated therein and the importance of her place of enunciation in her texts.

I believe that her path toward becoming a feminist public intellectual can be clearly analyzed in her testimonios "Getting There Cuando No Hay Camino" and in "A escondidas: A Chicana Feminist Teacher Who Writes/A Chicana Feminist Teacher Who Teaches." In "Getting There," she describes how she was able to graduate first from high school, then from college, and finally from a doctorate program. For each academic level, she narrates school and family experiences, as well as experiences of her community. In "A escondidas," she goes into details about what she calls "the various selves that I am" (123). This is an essay divided into ten short sections, in each of which her "self being" analyzes how she became a Chicana, professor, feminist, and writer, as well as citing her literary influences and enumerating the women who had impact on her life, like her grandmother, mother, aunts, great-aunts, girlfriends, neighbors, and close friends. Her college-life self seems to be the one tracing her path. Cantú recalls:

> My graduate work was arduous because I had not been exposed to much of what other students had and because being the only Chicana/o in the department I felt a tremendous responsibility, I had to work much more than the other students. Yet I always felt I was barely prepared. I also worked with the community, visited the prisons, did translations, had a Spanish-language radio program, wrote poetry and managed to keep a high grade point average. There were so many incidents in which I confronted racism that it would take a book to tell all of them; suffice to say that I made myself strong and thick-skinned—*hice concha*—to survive. I was still the same person, but I had grown; I had matured and developed survival skills that served me well. ("Getting There," 66)

From her phrase "I had not been exposed to much of what other students had" we can infer that perhaps the other students had received better educations because of their social class and ethnicity. This implies that the rest of her classmates (who were not Chicanas/os) either attended private schools outside Laredo—or outside the U.S.-Mexico border area—and/or that public and private education in other places was better than the education given to the Chicana/o community from Laredo and from other places in the United States. However, what was seen by her as a disadvantage actually helped her to acquire and create more knowledge and take a well-defined political view toward her community. In this regard, we notice a continuous resistance: instead of withdrawing from college because she felt "barely prepared," her presumed cultural weakness strengthened her not only to resist the numerous signs of racism she encountered but also to overcome adversity by working for the Chicana/o and Latina/o communities (as a radio broadcaster in Spanish, translator, prison volunteer). The use of the Spanish phrase *hacer concha*, which means "to survive without becoming someone else," implies she reappropriated her own "*sitio y lengua*" (Pérez, 161–62). That is, by choosing this particular phrase and making the decision that she will no longer listen to racist criticisms, she exercises her agency because she has decided to embrace her sitio y lengua. In so doing, not only does she claim the language, the mother tongue, and the discourse for herself, but she also takes over the historic space, the geographic site, and the philosophical space both for her and for the Chicana/o community.[7] Such space includes the U.S.-Mexico border and the rest of the American and global geography where Chicana/o people are located.

In her testimony, Cantú acknowledges that finishing her PhD in 1982 was unusual, since it wasn't very common for a Chicana to graduate then, not even from high school. With no role model to follow, she was about to make the path herself. Instead of retreating to the ivory tower once she completed her doctoral work (as many do), she returned to Laredo and decided to "create knowledge with those whom the knowledge serves" (Cushman, 328) and to "represent all those people and issues who are routinely forgotten or swept under the rug" (Said, 3), perhaps because she herself had come from "under the rug."[8] In fact, "A escondidas" narrates the episode in which she discovers and defines herself as a Chicana, when a Midwest school manager introduces her as "Spanish" in an attempt not to insult her by calling her "Mexican." Having been asked the question "How would you like me to call you?" she writes: "I don't hesitate a minute. 'Chicana' I answer. Prior to that, I would've said Mexican American but that one incident was like watershed after all the discrimination and the racism I had quietly experienced and often excused. I would define myself and 'Chicana' was exactly the term that would define me" (124). This moment of definition as a Chicana calls my attention, because it confirms the specific instance of her identity construction, in addition to the fact that she no longer needed to hacer concha, to ignore or excuse the racism of which she has been a target. This new identity—the real one, the political, the one found under the skin and not on top of it (concha)—is the one that she will continue to use until today. Furthermore, with this newfound Chicana identity, she overthrows and resists the Anglo American hegemony. She declares, "I call myself a Chicana for many reasons: my ethnic heritage, my ideological position, and my identity. But the most important one is that I know who I am, what I feel I am: *soy Chicana*" (124), a statement through which Said's definition of the public intellectual seems to resonate: "an individual endowed with a faculty for representing, embodying, articulating a message, a view, an attitude, philosophy or opinion to, as well as for, a public, in public" (3). Once again she will recover her sitio y lengua as an enunciation space of her own and of her people.

Before continuing my discussion of Cantú´s creative work, I want to turn my attention to her critical and editorial work, since I believe that it is linked to what Cushman calls "activist research," and in this sense she not only extends "access to the university to a wider community" (329), but she also brings the wider community to the university. This objective is clearly evident in her choice of doctoral dissertation topic: the *pastorela*, its traditional representation in Laredo, Texas, and relevant community issues and traditions.[9] In her analysis of pastorelas, Cantú goes beyond the traditional English literary research and incorporates an overlooked topic by combining folklore and literary studies for a deeper analysis of the genre. She is able to understand the text's complexity through the inclusion of oral and literary elements, such as the Christian religious ritual. Thus, besides following the path of Cleofas Jaramillo, Jovita González, and other folklorists, she starts interweaving the dialogue between her/the community (in this case, Laredo) and U.S. academia (which was mostly white during those years). "Chicana Life-Cycle Rituals," another of Cantú's critical works, is a study of the *quinceañera* and *cincuentañera* celebrations. She argues that in Chicana/o communities, both events work as cultural identity markers that separate these communities from the American mainstream. Both embody a strong symbolic content, and even though they take place in spaces that are oppressive for women, like churches and ballrooms, such social spaces are transformed into a generic space by these rituals. While the quinceañera represents the sexual awakening, the ticket for young girls into womanhood and social acceptance, the cincuentañera represents the "change of life," the beginning of menopause, but mainly it celebrates the person's achievements.[10] Through a detailed analysis of objects and rituals (dress, rosary, church, godmother, godfather, dance, and so forth), Cantú succeeds in showing us both traditions as

> the social glue that marks the celebrant and the community engaged in a celebration ethnically as Mexican or Latina [in which] the honoree is a woman. *Cincuentañeras* and *quinceañeras* affirm cultural tradition and then celebrate the individual's history within the context of the group. Both help the individual undergoing the transition to cope, to achieve the transition but not alone, incorporating symbols that have cultural meaning on personal and community levels. (32)

The study of these traditions is important because it demonstrates how Chicana/o communities resignify the celebrations at the same time as they contest and resist the dominant culture. And in these ethnographic studies Cantú acts as "both author and subject . . . , as one of the local informants whose experience [not only allows her to] openly shape the scholarly narrative she herself writes" (McCracken, 5) but also to "*interact* with the public beyond [the university] walls" (Cushman, 330).

Her ethnographic work about the Matachines de la Santa Cruz, begun in the late 1980s, and a Spanish version, published in 1992, was entitled "Los Matachines de la Santa Cruz de Laredo, Texas: Un acto de resistencia cultural." This work, which was later turned into a more elaborated article, "The Semiotics of Land and Place: Matachines Dancing in Laredo, Texas," and into a book, *Soldiers of the Cross: Los Matachines de la Santa Cruz* (forthcoming), is another study that establishes the aforementioned interaction outside the university's walls. Captivated by this dance since she was a little girl, she obtains the tools provided by the academy and starts interviewing, recording, and faithfully translating the dance of the Matachines. As a way to preserve traditions and cultural identity, she recovers, in writing, a ritual that has been taking place in Laredo since the beginning of the twentieth century. This is a ritual dance done by indigenous and mestizo groups in Mexico and the southwestern United States. According to Cantú, one main feature of the dance is that despite social variations caused by the change of space and the dancers' profession (many are migrants), the festivity tradition has stayed stable because of "the [individual's] religious faith, . . . the faith in the community and the strong social contract between them" ("Los Matachines," 234). For instance, the Matachines group studied by Cantu was established in a neighborhood called La Ladrillera. Matachines come together in such places: their families have lived there for more than eighty years, and new groups of Mexican and Central American immigrants reside there as well. Yet, even with all these different people and cultures, the group keeps its integrity; The community unification combined with the religious faith nourish an important cultural identity in this Laredo neighborhood; the phenomenon also represents the community's survival and resistance in the United States, specifically in South Texas. In the interactions between Cantú and her informant families, Cantú carries out what Cushman calls "activist research," defined this way: "the activist ethnographic research insures that, at every level of the ethnographic enterprise—from data collection through interpretation to write-up—the researchers and participants engaged in openly negotiated, reciprocal, mutually beneficial relations" (332). In this regard, I consider Cantú as a "post-occidental intellectual able to think at the intersection of the colonial languages of scholarship and the myriad languages sub-alternated and banned from cultures of scholarship through five hundred years of colonialism" (Walter Mignolo, quoted in Cushman, 328). Thus, in the traditions of the pastorela, the quinceañera, the cincuentañera, and the Matachines she recovers sitio y lengua, which, through their rituals, have been used by communities as a resistance space.

"Meditación fronteriza: Poems of Love, Life, and Work," an unpublished poetry book, comprises five sections: "Songs of the Borderlands," "Reading the Body," "In the Country of Art," "Going Home," and "Meditación fronteriza." Some of the poems included in the book have already been published in other places.[11] Each poem corresponds to the section with an analogous thematic. Some are written entirely in Spanish, with an English translation; others are bilingual; and a few are in English only. The first section focuses on the Mexico-U.S. border through elements such as the river, the crossing, the flora, the fauna, historic reminiscences, and personal or external situations (that become personal), like the undocumented crossing and its dangers. The second section is centered on the body, from different perspectives: a migraine, the purple color of a birthmark and of the marks left by violence, perceptions of a variety of body shapes and weights. It also includes reflections on the mental effort implied when a person thinks in a different way than the traditional majority. And, finally, it investigates combining different goddesses from various mythologies to form one single mystic body. The third section is more heterogeneous, covering traditional festivities like the December holidays, Easter, and bullfighting, or *la fiesta brava*, and it includes poems honoring others, either for pure admiration or to pay tribute. In this section, we can find the poem "Of Math, Words, and Mrs. Watkins," from which my epigraph is taken. The fourth section has a nostalgic air; it basically talks about farewells, welcomes, encounters, and disagreements. The fifth and last section includes two poems only: "Hablando de la vida y la muerte" and the long poem or poetic prose from which the book's title comes.

The book opens with "Canto a la tierra," a bilingual poem with a nostalgic tone for the border that was, is, and will be. The author performs a recovery of the ancient peoples who inhabited the place: "los Carrizo / los Comecrudo, los Coahuiltecos / . . . Esta tierra de mis antepasados" (5), a community that is gone but that she reclaims through her "dreams, desires, nostalgias," and writing. The geographical space is inherently linked to the personal and to the collective by her expression "my dead ones / my first bloods" (6). This poem plays with images and language in Spanish, but when she gives the English version, it includes a stanza that refers to the ancient tribes' traditions and is not incorporated in the Spanish text. She shows a sync in the past-present time by indicating how the new cycle of life and the born-die-bury tradition are now and how they were centuries ago. This movement allows her to create a permanent presence in this geography and to regain the space. By symbolically burying the ancient and current dead, she sets her roots in this world and takes back the Spanish, the English, and the Spanglish languages; in other words, she reconquers her/their/our sitio y lengua, as she does in other works. This act of recovery is present throughout the book in different ways. For instance, "She Was a Bobolo Grandmother" tells the story of a Bobolo woman who commits suicide as a protest against the conquest violence because a *conquistador* kills her baby grandson. What is interesting in this poem is that besides Cantú showing the Bobolo woman's resistance, she also exposes her in a different, broader context of the Nuevo Santander border, comparing her sacrifice with that of a Vietnamese monk and inserting this anonymous woman within a wider geography and community. In the last strophe we can see this at work:

> So, she set herself afire
> calmly sitting at the very spot that would become
> the center of the town's plaza of the town of Nuevo Santander,
> the flames burning all her pain and hate
> no marker honors her death

and no one knows her name
but the historian chronicled her death,
and thereby she lives. (9)

Not only does the woman sacrifice herself by setting herself on fire, which connotes purification, but she also does it in the middle of what would become the town's heart in the conquered land. She commits a violent act against herself to protest against violence and to avoid being witness to violent actions that will continue until the present. Moreover, what is even more noteworthy and paradoxical about her death is that, even though there is no name plate or monument in Nuevo Santander to acknowledge what had happened there, nor is her name even known, knowledge of the event has persisted throughout time because her story was recorded in writing by the chronicler/conqueror's hand. In other words, by recounting this episode Cantú does the opposite of condemning the Bobolo woman dispossessed of her land and her lineage to anonymity and silence: she is granting her—and all Bobolo people and, by extension, all conquered and dispossessed people—a place in history, in her story.

Her poetry is not an exception to the approach Cantú has preferred in most of her academic and other creative work. In her poetry, her voice is present and continues to tell her story along with other stories of people less fortunate than herself, such as the undocumented people who have risked drowning in the middle of the river while trying to cross or those who risk suffocating while locked in train wagons or in trailer containers. Her own crossing into the United States and from there to Spain meant leaving not only the space but the cultural and social baggage behind. However, her abandonment discourse moves beyond the personal because she intertwines it with other stories related to many stories. The stories include accounts of those who have crossed the river, through that river that "instiga llanto y gemidos profundos" (10), through that river whose plants have been "testigos del dolor y el amor" (11), as expressed by Cantú in "Hablando soñando." She comments:

¡Lo que hemos tenido que dejar para llegar aquí!
Muñecas de trapo, mi colección de LPs de los 60s, los CD de los 90s, el barrio de mi niñez, las cartas, sí tus cartas de amor, depresión aguda como la noche, la solidez de la casa paterna, ilusiones de paz, de alegría, Che Guevara, el Marxismo, mis ideas de justicia, la iglesia de mi niñez con sus flores de mayo, todo lo que cargaba a cuestas desde la guerra que aún no termina. (10)

This means that the poetic voice places itself in the same space where individual and collective borders cross, and by connecting her own experience with that of those who have migrated voluntarily or involuntarily, she makes her own story the story of the migrant community. The last line turns suggestive, since it could evoke not only a specific war—although it mentions Marxism and Che Guevara—but also a longer war, one that has been evolving since the beginning of humankind. In the U.S.-Mexico border region, the line suggests a war between both countries for the conquest of Texas and then of a larger territory. In general—since she talks about Spain, Che, and Marxism—it could be, as I stated, a continuation of a great war that includes all wars and that haven't ended because our time/space has not ended yet.

Poems like "The Killing Paths," "Border Bullets," and "Song of the Borderlands" contain the same types of references to the undocumented crossing that we have observed in the works discussed earlier, and they present the river as an augury of death. The very fact that river is crossed implies the certainty of not making it, which creates a dialogue with the river that has to be crossed to get to Mictlan, the underworld of the Aztecs, or the River Styx, which the ferryman Charon helps souls to cross to get to the world of the dead in Greek mythology. What draws attention in Cantú's case is that the river is precisely the thing that prevents the crossing, and many times causes death, while in the Aztec and Greek mythologies, the river is just a place of transition between life and death, not the actual place of death. Another constant in these poems is the trip that might end in an unknown place or in death, as in "Border Bullets." Another repeated motif is found in "The Killing Path," whose trip of "they" becomes ours and also leads to death:

> They travel the path faithfully
> generous and onerous
> regretting the choice but seeing no option except death
> slow and sure
>
> They travel the path
> they travel the path
> they travel
> we travel the path
> we travel the path
> we travel. (18)

Here we can see again the necessity of being one with the others; her trip becomes ours, therefore her death is ours. In "Song of the Borderlands," a section described as "a poem for choral reading for six voices (three male and three female)" (19), once more the author makes allusion to the river crossing, to the dead left in it or in other spaces. Above all, however, this is a song to the recovery of geographical space and to the Chicana/o people. Therein she talks about two conquests, the Spanish and the Anglo American, and how Spaniards and Anglos imposed a language above the Other, a culture above the Other. She does it in such way that she does not evade her social responsibility. In order to keep the collective memory alive, she voices tragedy and injustice.

Preserving the collective memory, in the section "Reading the Body" Cantú presents "Decolonizing the Mind," in which she not only rearticulates the Chicana/o identity but ignores any link to a particular space or nation-state, including all nationalistic symbols such as flags, parades, and fallen soldiers.[12] This section also includes two poems that mostly examine women's issues. In "Body/My Body" (37) the lyric voice stops to examine how the narrator was a target of bullying for being skinny, but she also comments on the fact that being overweight may also trigger such behavior. In the end, she resolves the conflict by claiming both—being overweight and skinny—and by transforming her body into every woman's body. The piece also critiques the ideology of how "women's beauty" should be. By incorporating all types of bodies in one, Cantú resists cultural norms and returns to women one of their most precious possessions: their own bodies. In the poem "Diosas," Cantú takes over a mixed body by naming goddesses of diverse mythologies (Tonantzin, Toci, Coatlicue, Ixchel, Gaia, Lilith, La Virgen María) and "creates a modified litany [in which] instead of the usual repeated supplications of the litany, Cantú's poem chants affirmative statements about an alternate hybrid pantheon of female goddesses who suffer with women today, crying for their daughters who suffer on earth (McCracken, 17). However, inasmuch as I agree with McCracken, I also believe that Cantú is proposing something even more radical: the formation of an alternative mystic body. In this sense, the voice of the female spiritual community overthrows the Catholic Church's great religious-master discourse, which holds up Christ as the head of the mystic body. Cantú proposes a fused female body that links different religious and spiritual beliefs, and through a litany structure she breaks from the Catholic tradition to create this new mystic female body, apart from patriarchy and colonization. She also places spirituality above religion, community above individualism.

Another recurrent element in some of her poems—and in her autobiographical and academic essays as well—is the inclusion not only of U.S. cultural conventions but also of both cultural traditions that gave birth to Chicana/os, the Mexican and the Spanish. This is something unusual in Chicana/o writing. Generally when Chicana/os write about Spain it is through the painful experience of the conquest of the indigenous. However, Cantú includes both topics, and while acknowledging the violence of the conquest, she also recognizes the rich tradition of Spain and its importance in her Chicana identity formation. Cantú embraces all four cultures—indigenous, Spanish, Mexican, and U.S.—to recover her ancestors' "*sitios y lenguas.*"

Two poems comprise the last section of the book, in which Cantú enters into a dialectical communication with an audience that goes beyond the U.S.-Mexico border, anticipating that her argument will be received. She speaks for those who have been dispossessed of their personal belongings, their culture, and their own lives, and just as she has done elsewhere throughout the book, she intertwines these voices with hers, resulting in the inclusion of a "we" referring to individuals as well as to a global community. I focus on this last characteristic to point out how this vision of a global community is constructed in the poem "Hablando de la vida y la muerte." Each stanza begins with a group of marginalized, deprived, vulnerable, or murdered people and ends with a solidary community, although some people in the community are not aware of others' problems:

Cuando hablo de los que yacen muertos
en el río al amanecer
o de los que pierden
        brazos
                piernas
y hasta la vida
por el afán de irse al norte
hablo de todos nosotros
aún los que jamás han pisado mi frontera

Cuando hablo de los desaparecidos
los que perseguidos por pensar,
        por hablar,
                por escribir,
                        por ser,

los que con el miedo a cuestas huyen,
o no,
hablo de todos nosotros
aún todos los que jamás han tenido idea de lo que es militar por un ideal

Cuando hablo de los miles de muertos en las guerras
los heridos,
los exterminados en hornos o en fosas
My Lai, Auschwitz, Hiroshima
hablo de todos nosotros aun los que con historia y con conciencia
niegan su historia y su conciencia

Cuando hablo de Tlatelolco
Tenochtitlán
Wounded Knee
Rwanda
Acteal
Juárez

Hablo de nosotros, de todos nosotras
Y hablo de ayer y hablo de ahora. (93–94)

Here, she employs the same strategy of concentrating many different bodies in one. In this poem we see Cantú's strong determination to create a collective awareness regarding the many massacres and genocides around the world and to consider a global community that includes everyone, because we, too, could be one of those massacred bodies. She also aims to create an endless and cyclic poem, because she knows that the topic has no end; violence did not end in the past (*en el ayer*), and unfortunately it cannot end in the present (*ahora*), as in various territories in the world the bloodshed still continues. There are at present many places globally where people are "swept under the rug" (to use Said's expression). However, Cantú knows that by naming these people, she and we can bring them out from "under the rug" and can create one healed body out of many, many wounded bodies. Her poem acquires a universal value not only because she embodies every war in one war and every body in one body but also because she inspires a sense of immediacy and urgency to take action. Right at this moment I could add to her list Ayotzinapa, Syria, Kosovo, Ukraine,

Palestine, Iraq, Somalia, Ciudad Juárez, Michoacán, and Laredo, among other places that have been subjected to violence, especially from the state. With this poem, Cantú reflects what is suggested by Walden Bello: "Truths only become true through action . . . one must accept that there is an inevitable and permanent tension between theory and practice, between thought and action, between truth and power, and thinking that this tension can be eliminated is one of the worst illusions a public intellectual can fall into."[13] This means that when Cantú reevaluates and reassesses, in a favorable light, marginalized communities that are harassed or destroyed by the state, solidary communities arise. Within this process, the writer holds an important responsibility, because the role of the writer as public intellectual is to point out the truth(s) even if it is (they are) not convenient from the political point of view. In this sense, I believe that through the brief journey of Norma Cantu's texts presented here, we have confirmed her ability to take what is private into the public arena and combine theory with social practice. Thanks to her activist research and her committed creative writing, she has unburied stories of the nameless to give them a place in history, in her story. Thus, we have observed Norma E. Cantú's capacity to transform the personal and individual into a solidary community, and above all, we have been and will be able to keep reflecting on her work as a critic, writer, and public intellectual.

NOTES

1. In 1993, when I was reviewing border authors for my PhD dissertation, I ran into her work. Of the writers from the U.S. side of the border, she was, for me, the most *fronteriza* because she had—and still has—the true experience of crossing the U.S.-Mexico border back and forth, with family on both sides. That same year I had the pleasure of meeting Professor Cantú at an *encuentro* in Mexico City, and for the last twenty-plus years we have shared many discussions about borders, borderlands, and the similarities and differences between various communities along the U.S.-Mexico border, among other topics. She has always been very generous with her time and comments on my work.
2. Some of the writings included in this essay, including the epigraph, belong to "Meditación fronteriza: Poems of Life, Love and Work," an unpublished poetry manuscript by Norma E. Cantú. The manuscript is now under revision. It was sent to me by Professor Cantú so that I could include her unpublished

work in this article. My deepest gratitude to Dr. Cantú. I will be quoting from "Meditación fronteriza" throughout.

3. Other places where she has done work include the Mexican American Cultural Center, Esperanza Peace and Justice Center, Martinez Street Women's Center, Society for Advancement of Chicanos/Hispanics and Native Americans in Science, and various elementary and high schools in Texas, California, and Colorado.
4. I want to clarify that the titles I mentioned are the titles of the books in which she is credited as author, editor, or co-editor. I do not refer here to the innumerable academic articles and creative works that have appeared throughout the years in anthologies, newspapers, magazines, and other collective volumes, nor to her blog about the Camino de Santiago.
5. In her paper "Whose Story Is It Anyway? Autobiography on the Border" she studies the personal narratives of Chicana/o border writers Beatriz George, Norma Benavides, Albert Salazar, and José Sánchez, taking into account Antonio Gramsci's ideas of the "organic intellectual" to underscore how these writers, "although coming from varied 'functions in the world of economic production,' felt the impulse to *write* and thus assume one of the most visible markers of the 'intellectual'" (130).
6. We can even consider her social mobility from the barrio to the university and beyond.
7. As explained by Pérez, *sitio y lengua* rejects the colonial ideology because it is rooted in a capitalist patriarchy, and therefore it also rejects its products, which include sexism, racism, homophobia, and others. Third World women—Chicanas—seize a space of empowerment apart from white men, white women, and men of color to create their own sitio y lengua as an alternative to patriarchy.
8. Cantú mentions that in those days it was very rare for Chicanos in general to graduate from the university. Consequently, Chicanos who had doctorate degrees were highly unusual. Even more unusual were Chicanos/as who participated or went back to the community even when they were involved before or during their university years with the *movimiento*. The short story by Rosaura Sánchez "Entró y se sentó" is a very good example of this. The story can be found in *He Walked In and Sat Down, and Other Stories* by Rosaura Sánchez, trans. Beatrice Pita (Albuquerque: University of New Mexico Press, 2000).
9. According to Angélica Galicia, *pastorelas* "are plays that recreate the biblical passage where the shepherds follow the Star of Bethlehem to find the Christ

Child. In order to reach the birth place of the Redeemer, they have to experience a series of changes in fortune and confront the Devil, who will do everything possible to prevent them from completing their mission. It is at that moment that the Archangel Michael intervenes to defend the shepherds on their journey." Angie Galicia, "Las Pastorelas: A Centuries Old Christmas Tradition," *Inside Mexico*, November 30, 2015, http://www.inside-mexico.com/pastorelas.htm.

10. It will be interesting for future reference to analyze this celebration regarding its traditional meanings or what it still means in some societies: the death of sexual desire and/or the death of maternity.
11. Poems include: "Diosas," *Blue Mesa Review* (1977): 71, and "The Body/My Body," "Border Bullets," and "Meditación fronteriza," *Chicana/Latina Studies* 6, no. 1 (Fall 2006): 90–92.
12. The significance of this is increased by the fact that her brother was killed in Vietnam.
13. Walden Bello, "Challenges and Dilemmas of the Public Intellectual," Walden Bello.org, http://www.waldenbello.org//?s=Public+Intellectual.

WORKS CITED

Cantú, Norma E. "A escondidas: A Chicana Feminist Teacher Who Writes/A Chicana Feminist Writer Who Teaches." In The Latina Feminist Group (Luz del Alba Acevedo, Norma Alarcón, Cecilia Alvarez, et al.), *Telling to Live: Latina Feminist Testimonios*, 123–31. Durham, NC, and London: Duke University Press, 2001.

———. "Cabañuelas: A Love Story." Unpublished novel.

———. "Champú, or Hair Matters." Unpublished novel.

———. "Chicana Life-Cycle Rituals." In *Chicana Traditions: Continuity and Change*, edited by Norma Cantú and Olga Nájera-Ramírez, 15–34. Urbana and Chicago: University of Illinois Press, 2002.

———. "Getting There Cuando No Hay Camino." In The Latina Feminist Group (Luz del Alba Acevedo, Norma Alarcón, Cecilia Alvarez, et al.), *Telling to Live: Latina Feminist Testimonios*, 60–68. Durham, NC, and London: Duke University Press, 2001.

———. "Living La Vida Santa: My Chicana Spirituality and Activist Scholarship." In *Fleshing the Spirit: Spirituality and Activism in Chicana, Latina, and*

Indigenous Women's Lives, edited by Elisa Facio and Irene Lara, 202–17. Tucson: University of Arizona Press, 2014.

———. "Los Matachines de la Santa Cruz de Laredo, Texas: Un acto de resistencia cultural." In *Entre la magia y la historia: Tradiciones, mitos y leyendas de la frontera*, edited by José Manuel Valenzuela Arce, 131–47. Madrid: Plaza y Valdés Editores, 1992.

———. "Meditación fronteriza: Poems of Life, Love, and Work." Unpublished bilingual poetry collection.

———. *Moctezuma's Table: Rolando Briseño's Mexicano and Chicano Tablescapes*. Rio Grande/Rio Bravo Series. College Station: Texas A&M University Press, 2012.

———. "Papeles de mujer." Unpublished novel.

———. *Paths to Discovery: Chicanas in Mathematics, Science, and Engineering*. Los Angeles: UCLA Chicano Studies Research Center, 2008.

———. "The Semiotics of Land and Place: Matachines Dancing in Laredo, Texas." In *Dancing Across Borders: Danzas y bailes mexicanos*, edited by Olga Nájera-Ramírez, Norma Elia Cantú, and Brenda M. Romero, 97–115. Urbana and Chicago: University of Illinois Press, 2009.

———. "Whose Story Is It Anyway? Autobiography on the Border." Paper presented at the National Association for Chicana and Chicano Studies Annual Conference, Tucson, AZ, April 1, 2001. http://scholarworks.sjsu.edu/naccs/2001/Proceedings/12.

Cantú, Norma E., and María E. Fránquiz, eds. *Inside the Latin@ Experience: A Latin@ Studies Reader*. New York: Palgrave Macmillan, 2010.

Cantú, Norma E., Christina L. Gutiérrez, Norma Alarcón, and Rita E. Urquijo-Ruiz, eds. *El Mundo Zurdo: Selected Works from the Meetings of the Society for the Study of Gloria Anzaldúa, 2007 and 2009*. San Francisco: Aunt Lute Press, 2009.

Cantú, Norma E., and Olga Nájera-Ramírez, eds. *Chicana Traditions: Continuity and Change*. Urbana and Chicago: University of Illinois Press, 2002.

Cushman, Ellen. "The Public Intellectual, Service Learning, and Activist Research." *College English* 61, no. 3 (January 1999): 328–36. http://www.jstor.org/stable/379072.

Hernández-Ávila, Inés, and Norma Elia Cantú, eds. *Entre Malinche y Guadalupe: Tejanas in Literature and Art*. Austin: University of Texas Press, 2016.

McCracken, Ellen. "Hybridity and the Space of the Border in the Writing of Norma Elia Cantú." *Studies in 20th Century Literature* 25, no. 1, article 13 (January 1, 2001): 1–20. http//dx.doi.org/10.4148/2334-4415.1502.

Nájera-Ramírez, Olga, Norma E. Cantú, and Brenda M. Romero, eds. *Dancing Across Borders: Danzas y bailes mexicanos*. Urbana and Chicago: University of Illinois Press, 2009.

Pérez, Emma, "Sexuality and Discourse: Notes from a Chicana Survivor." *Chicana Lesbians: The Girls Our Mothers Warned Us About*, edited by Carla Trujillo, 159–84. Berkeley, CA: Third Woman Press, 1991.

Said, Edward. *Reflections on Exile and other Essays*. Cambridge, MA: Harvard University Press, 2003.

———. "The Reith Lectures: Representations of the Intellectual." *The Independent*, June 23, 1993. http://www.independent.co.uk/life-style/the-reith-lectures-representations-of-the-intellectual-1493404.html.

SNAPSHOTS OF LAW AND LIFE IN THE MIDCENTURY TEXAS BORDERLANDS

STEVEN W. BENDER

INTRODUCTION

SERVING AS HER FICTIONAL autobioethnography, *Canícula: Snapshots of a Girlhood en la Frontera* skirts the timeline of Norma Elia Cantú's childhood in the Texas borderlands, from her birth in the late 1940s to her graduation from high school in 1965. This essay supplies several "snapshots" of the prevailing legal climate at that time as it affected Cantú, her family, and more generally the Latina/o community in Texas and northern Mexico. Born in Nuevo Laredo, the Mexican sister city to Laredo, Texas, Cantú grew up in Laredo and attended Texas schools there, but her life, as was true for many Mexican Americans, was one marked by repeated border crossings both physical and psychological.[1] Addressing U.S. immigration policy, border crossings, segregation in the Southwest, and suppression of Mexican culture under Texas law, the legal snapshots supplied below aim to enrich the context of Mexican life and *familia* in the borderlands that Cantú navigated.

LOS INMIGRANTES

Born in Mexico to a U.S.-born mother, Cantú was deemed a Mexican national,[2] but she could readily navigate immigration laws and surmount borders existing at the time.[3] Throughout the book's events, Cantú and her family, both immediate and extended, routinely crossed the border between the United States and Mexico—sometimes for just a few hours, for a doctor visit or church service in Mexico, and other times for a lengthier stay. More fundamentally, during her early childhood in 1948, Cantú crossed borders to make Laredo, Texas, her home and went on to enjoy a distinguished academic career in the United States.

In contrast to its discriminatory aim to restrict immigration from southern and eastern Europe, the Immigration Act of 1924 (which governed Mexican immigration until 1965) facially treated Mexicans more favorably than Europeans, Asians, and Africans by means of the Western hemisphere exemption that imposed no numerical limits on Mexican immigration to the United States. Urged by Southwestern agricultural and industrial interests, this exemption shielded Mexicans from artificial immigration limits applicable to entrants from other parts of the world, yet Mexicans were never allowed unrestricted access into the United States, particularly in periods when their labor entry was unneeded and unwanted. Operating to control Mexican entry like a faucet, various administrative restrictions (most notably the denial of entry of those deemed potential public charges, given their apparent lack of wealth) were eased to allow virtually unlimited entry during times of labor demand and stiffened to deny entry to Mexicans in times of economic distress. Sometimes even the unrestricted allowance of Mexican immigration wasn't enough to meet U.S. demand for low-wage workers, as evidenced by the recruitment tool known as the Bracero Program, initiated by the Mexican and U.S. governments in 1942 to serve the wartime demand for agricultural and other labor at a time when Japanese workers were interned and many other U.S. workers were diverted to the military. Despite its many abuses of Mexican workers, the Bracero Program survived until late 1964, when Congress finally responded to those abuses and let it lapse rather than add labor protections. Overall, the program brought some 4.8 million Mexican laborers across the border.[4] Given the state's particularly bad record of abusing and terrorizing Mexican immigrant workers, the Mexican government blacklisted Texas from the program during the years 1943 to 1947.[5] Disregarding the prohibition, Texas growers simply beckoned Mexican immigrants to cross the border as undocumented workers rather than as bracero laborers, a practice in which the U.S. Border Patrol acquiesced to allow Mexican undocumented workers to enter the United States on foot into the waiting trucks of Texan farmers.[6] These entries coincided with the absence of any meaningful border security infrastructure, which came a few decades later.

The bracero labor recruitment program allowed as much temporary guest labor entry as U.S. employers needed, and the Western hemisphere exemption permitted potentially unlimited long-term migrant entry. Despite the presence of administrative means to shut this immigration faucet as needed, when labor demand waned sufficiently, U.S. federal, state, and local officials joined forces to sweep up Mexican residents already within the United States and deport them to Mexico. As Cantú documents in *Canícula*, one of the two most pronounced campaigns of deportation sweeps occurred during the Great Depression, before her birth, when some of Cantú's family, including her Texas-born grandfather and mother, were forced to leave Texas for Mexico, losing all their belongings in the process.[7] In the deportation frenzy that accompanied the Depression, many of the deported were U.S. citizens targeted solely for their Mexican appearance under the prevailing belief that Mexicans, no matter their immigration or citizenship status, were undeserving of government welfare during the crisis. Vigilantes aided this government deportation effort, chasing off Mexican residents, and signs in Texas warned Mexicans to leave town.[8]

Returning to the United States in the late 1940s, Cantú's mother crossed as a U.S. citizen at a time when the ongoing cycle of Mexican laborer invitation and exile tilted toward allowing Mexican entry. Although not mentioned in the book, Cantú survived the next onslaught of mass deportation to sweep the borderlands and the Southwest—the derogatorily named Operation Wetback campaign. Active between 1954 and 1959 and resulting in the deportation of some 3.7 million Latina/os, most of them Mexican, and some of them U.S. citizens denied an opportunity to defend their deportation, the military-like operation used planes and ground teams to round up its targets. After the economic turmoil subsided, and along with it the imperative of deporting Mexicans, the borderlands quieted as its residents awaited a substantial change in immigration policy in 1965, which would rewrite the face of undocumented immigration in the U.S. imagination and prevails to this day.

NO MEXICANS OR DOGS ALLOWED

Cantú grew up at a time when Mexicans were overtly regarded as second-class citizens in the terrain that Mexico once governed.[9] Akin to the emblematic segregation of blacks and whites in the United States was the oppression of Mexicans in Texas and much of the Southwest, where Mexicans, African Americans, and dogs were lumped together in their exclusion from white spaces. Enforced both by local laws and private discrimination, segregation dominated the Texas landscape until the civil rights era (which brought such reforms as the federal Civil Rights Act of 1964, outlawing discrimination in places of public accommodation) halted the reign of de jure discrimination against Mexicans and other marginalized groups. Though perhaps it was not as prevalent in the Mexican-dominated borderlands, nevertheless some 117 Texas towns practiced segregation against Mexican residents, most through local laws.[10] Segregation, though generally undiscussed in the text of *Canícula*, governed all aspects of Texas life. Mexicans were excluded from public parks and swimming pools (except for "Mexican Day," before the pool was cleaned). Businesses pervasively excluded Mexicans from restaurants, barbershops, and dance halls and segregated them to movie theater balconies and even away from whites-only cemeteries. Signs reading "No Dogs, Negroes, or Mexicans" littered the Texas landscape. Restrictive housing covenants excluded Mexicans (and blacks) from whites-only residential developments in cities such as San Antonio. Officials kept Mexicans from sitting on juries, until the U.S. Supreme Court ruled the practice unconstitutional in a case originating in Jackson County, Texas, a few hours from Laredo, where officials claimed Mexicans were seen as white and therefore could not complain about convictions by all-Anglo juries, though the racialized sign in the courthouse basement bathroom reading Colored Men and Hombres Aqui suggested otherwise.[11]

SEPARATE AND UNEQUAL: TEXAS SCHOOL SEGREGATION

Consistent with the widespread separation of Tejanos from Anglo Texans, schools in the Southwest practiced overt segregation in the first half of the twentieth century. Attempting to justify its "Mexican schools," Texans generally relied either on stereotypical conceptions of the "dirty Mexican" or on the supposed impossibility of educating Mexicans whose native language was Spanish in the same classroom as English-speaking students. These justifications effectively swept all Mexican children into inferior schools separate from Anglos. Surviving into the 1970s was the practice of segregating students with Spanish surnames into separate classrooms simply on the assumption, untested, that they did not speak English well enough.[12] Also relied upon to separate the Mexican students were perceptions of their uncleanliness. A University of Texas report in 1923 called for separate schools for impoverished Mexicans in order to protect Anglo kids from their filth:

> Many of the [Mexican] children are too ill-clad to attend school with other [Anglo] children. The American children and those of the Mexican children who are clean and high-minded do not like to go to school with the dirty "greaser" type of Mexican child. It is not right that they should have to do so. There is but one choice in the matter of educating these unfortunate children and that is to put the "dirty" ones into separate schools til they learn how to "clean up" and become eligible to better society.[13]

Some school officials were even more overtly racist in justifying separate schools for Mexican American children—in 1929 officials in Nueces County (with its county seat of Corpus Christi) bluntly explained segregating Mexican American children because "they are an inferior race, that is all."[14] Augmenting the separation of Mexican American children from Anglos in Texas (and the rest of the Southwest) was the expectation, sometimes rigidly enforced, that Mexican children would simply not remain in public school beyond the sixth grade, at which point they had reached their designated station in Texas life.[15] In addition to being separate, the Mexican schools were decidedly unequal, often consisting of ramshackle buildings with less land for recreation and inferior bathroom facilities in comparison to Anglo schools.[16]

In advance of the Supreme Court's 1954 decision in *Brown v. Board of Education* invalidating segregation of black and white students in Topeka, Kansas, elementary schools because it constituted inherently unequal treatment, Mexican Americans were challenging their own discrimination in Texas schools.[17] A 1930 Texas court ruling invalidated the practice of segregating Mexican American children without regard to their English language ability but allowed separate schools for non-English-speaking students.[18] Yet the discriminatory practices continued. A subsequent lawsuit in the late 1940s resulted in a 1948 consent decree, with the state of Texas declaring that school districts must discontinue segregation that was based solely on Latina/o heritage, but allowing segregation of Mexican first-graders if the district could demonstrate a linguistic or pedagogical justification.[19] Because the state failed to establish a mechanism for compliance, local school officials ignored the desegregation order.[20]

By the time Norma E. Cantú began her education in Texas, culminating in a doctorate at the University of Nebraska–Lincoln, Texas schools ostensibly were barred from segregating students on the basis of Mexican heritage. But the vestiges of segregation remained throughout Cantú's education and beyond.[21] Perhaps most important, even integrated schools in poor school districts suffered from facilities and resources that were inadequate for effectively educating their often Latina/o students. In 1973 the Supreme Court gave the green light to long-standing district inequalities by rejecting a constitutional challenge to the Texas system of school finance relying on property taxes, which conferred revenue advantages on wealthier districts.[22] As the poorest U.S. city in 1960 and still the fourth poorest city by 1990, Laredo faced, as it still does, the challenge of educating its decidedly Mexican American–dominated student body and somehow breaking the ongoing cycle of poverty.[23]

NAVIGATING THE ENGLISH-ONLY CLASSROOM

As legal scholar Juan Perea revealed, segregated schools in Texas and the rest of the Southwest were intended to teach Mexican American children their inferiority and need for subservience to Anglos.[24] One strategy for teaching subservience and inferiority was to degrade and destroy the Spanish language—the native tongue and household language of most Mexican Americans in 1900s Texas. As Mexican immigrants came to Texas in large numbers in the 1900s, adding to the U.S.-born Mexicans already there for generations, Texas schools enforced an imperative of educational instruction in English as part of a broader campaign to subordinate and suppress the Mexican culture. Enacted in 1918 and surviving until Congress passed the Bilingual Education Act in 1968, Texas law for decades imposed criminal penalties for teaching children in languages other than English—except, of course, in a foreign language class taught to older students, such as French, where bilingualism, at least in languages other than Spanish, was valued.[25] Texas school officials carried the law's anti-Spanish policy to further extremes by notoriously punishing children who spoke Spanish to each other anywhere on the school grounds, even in school districts whose students were nearly exclusively of Mexican origin: "As late as the 1950s [Texas] children who spoke Spanish in school were made to kneel on upturned bottle caps, forced to hold bricks in outstretched hands in the schoolyard, or told to put their nose in a chalk circle drawn on a blackboard."[26] As Norma E. Cantú writes in *Canícula*, her Mexican American friend and classmate who understood but couldn't actually speak Spanish fell outside the anti-Spanish rules—"she never had to pay a fine or write lines as punishment for using [Spanish]."[27] Demonstrating the reality of tough punishment for speaking Spanish at school, a legal scholar later wrote of his brother being forced by his Texas elementary schoolteacher to write "I will not speak Spanish on school grounds" five hundred times.[28]

Although the schoolyard punishments are less overt in Texas today, the imperative of speaking and teaching English to schoolchildren is no less ingrained in Texas law and culture. An Amarillo, Texas, judge illustrated the prevailing cultural sentiment in 1995 when he ordered a Latina mother in a child custody case to stop speaking Spanish to her five-year-old daughter or lose custody of her: "You're abusing that child and you're relegating her to the position of a housemaid. Now get this straight. You start speaking English to this child because if she doesn't do good [*sic*] in school, then I can remove her because it's not in her best interest to be ignorant. The child will hear only English."[29] Whether in school or in the home, apparently, Spanish is subordinated and devalued, despite being the currency of communication in the Laredo borderlands.

1965: GRADUATION AND A NEW IMMIGRATION REGIME

Concluding *Canícula* with the occasion of her high school graduation as part of the class of '65, Cantú went on to teach in or near the borderlands throughout much of her academic career. The year 1965 is monumental, not for her ascendancy toward teaching, but for the legal recasting of the Mexican migrant population in the United States as the face of unwanted and undocumented immigration, to be kept out by armoring the U.S.-Mexico border with an infrastructure that aims to exclude Mexico and Mexicans both physically and symbolically.

In the decades before 1965, Mexicans had the flexibility to enter the United States as guest workers or as immigrants seeking a permanent residence. As discussed above, the Bracero Program provided a ready means of connecting Mexican guest workers to U.S. employers, and the absence of any limits on annual Mexican migration meant that Mexican migrants desiring to live long-term in the United States could both enter the country and aspire to eventual U.S. citizenship. But developments in immigration law and policy coinciding with Cantú's graduation in 1965 rewrote the landscape for Mexican migrants and contributed to the vilification of Mexicans in the United States. Abuses in the Bracero Program led Congress to let that guest labor program lapse in December 1964. Shortly thereafter, in 1965, Congress enacted the Immigration and Nationality Act, which dismantled the Western hemisphere exemption and imposed a 120,000-person hemispheric cap on migration. As the next step in undoing the good neighbor relationship between Mexico and the United States in immigration allowances, in 1976 Congress subjected Mexico (and other Western hemisphere countries) to the same per-county annual limits as the rest of the world, limiting permanent visas to just 20,000 entrants annually, along with the possibility of family reunification with immediate relatives and work commuter and other limited visa programs. Going from the prior rules allowing virtually unlimited entry in times of labor demand to the current rules of stingy Mexican entry helped transform the vilified face of undocumented migration to a Mexican one. As one commentator summarized the dramatic tightening in permissible legal entry for Mexicans, "Mexico went from enjoying access to 450,000 annual [Bracero Program] guest worker visas and an unlimited number of residence visas to having no guest worker visas at all and just 20,000 visas for permanent residence."[30] Because U.S. employers kept calling for cheap labor, particularly desiring vulnerable undocumented laborers who would hesitate to unionize or object to wage and other labor violations, Mexican migration continued in large numbers, but mostly as undocumented migration. Soon, the appearance of an uncontrolled southern border led to laws (such as the Illegal Immigration Reform and Immigrant Responsibility Act of 1996 and the Secure Fence Act of 2006, championed by both Republicans and Democrats) and appropriations for installing border infrastructure that caused thousands of migrant deaths. The image of the undocumented, lawless Mexican migrant coincided with the border buildup in ways that scarred the borderlands and our relations with Mexico and its workers, who have long supplied vital U.S. labor needs. The final snapshot below examines borderlands migration against the backdrop of the unceasing U.S. demand for cheap Mexican labor, and also for illicit drugs, while the Mexicans who supply these needs continue to be vilified.

NUEVO LAREDO: THEN AND NOW

> *"Night arrives; boys from Amarillo and Texas A&M pile out of vehicles, urinate on the bumper, emit war whoops, and stagger off toward Papagallo's [brothel in Nuevo Laredo]. . . . All along the border, Mexican women are receiving American men and their dollars in their bed."*
>
> —ALAN WEISMAN, *LA FRONTERA: THE UNITED STATES BORDER WITH MEXICO*[31]

Born in Nuevo Laredo, but raised and schooled across the border in Laredo, Cantú had a childhood that embodies the connectedness of border sister cities and borderlands culture. The outcome of the Mexican-American War in 1848 first separated these two Spanish/Mexican settlements on either side of the Rio Grande.[32] Given its location and heritage, Laredo's residents have tended to be those of Mexican background—by 2010, almost every Laredo resident was Mexican (91.6 percent). Well depicted in *Canícula*, the cultural odyssey of these border sister city residents has always been one of border crossings. Cantú writes of regular trips across the river to Nuevo Laredo for groceries, to attend church on Sunday, to see doctors, and to visit sick relatives. As she grows older, her classmates also cross into Nuevo Laredo, presumably to drink away from their parents' watchful eyes. Life in borderlands Texas is one beyond borders. Cantú poetically describes the border as a revolving door for borderlands residents of all ages:

> We've been shopping at the Mercado Maclovio Herrera in Nuevo Laredo; we carry bags [Mami] calls redes full of meat, sugar, tomatoes, groceries. . . . Sometimes she sends Tino and me [across the border] to run these errands. We make the rounds at the mercado, go to the butcher's and buy red juicy meat and have it ground by Raúl who winks as he puts in a pilón; we go to Rangel's for cookies—galletas marías and morenas—and sugar, piloncillo, and dark aguacates [avocados] which he carefully cuts in half, satisfying U.S. Department of Agriculture requirements he extracts the pit so we can legally cross them to the United States and closes them again, like fine carved wood boxes. We carefully count out the money, figuring out the exchange pesos to dollars. . . . We walk, cross the bridge, resting every half block or so, resting our arms, sore from carrying the heavy redes. We take the bus home.[33]

As I have written elsewhere, in the U.S.-Mexico borderlands and beyond, the reality despite the recent infusion of border infrastructure has been and continues to be that whatever is needed or desired by one country will be supplied by the other.[34] During Prohibition, U.S. residents crossed into Mexican border towns such as Nuevo Laredo to quench their thirst for alcohol, as underage U.S. youth continue to do in light of Mexico's lower drinking age and the fact that the age limit is not always enforced. Vice goes beyond alcohol, as Nuevo Laredo boasts one of the border's largest red-light districts, offering legal prostitutes to Texans young and old. And not just Texans and other U.S. residents enter the Mexican borderlands; historically, if goods are unavailable in Mexico or subject to tighter regulation or to significant trade duties, then they have been smuggled south into Mexico. In 1978 alone, for example, smugglers brought an estimated $2.8 million in televisions from Laredo into Mexico.[35] Today, the most often smuggled commodities headed south are guns and cash to fuel the Mexican drug cartels, which are rewriting the story of the borderlands into one of murder and mayhem. Since the inception of the Mexican drug war in the last decade, tens of thousands have perished in the bloody borderlands to ensure the survival of the trade serving the insatiable demand of U.S. residents for illicit drugs. Some of the dead are innocent victims, including children. Nuevo Laredo often is in the cross hairs of the Mexican cartel turf battles. In 2012, for example, on a particularly bloody Friday, authorities discovered nine bodies hanging from a Nuevo Laredo overpass and, a few hours later, fourteen human heads inside coolers left outside city hall—their headless bodies were found stuffed inside plastic bags in an abandoned minivan near the international bridge to Laredo. Drug violence has tended to stay south of the border, sparing U.S. border cities such as El Paso but interrupting the normal border crossings of U.S. residents whose lives once spilled across the border. No doubt a borderlands coming-of-age, if occurring today rather than during Cantú's youth in the 1950s and 1960s, would be a much different journey against the backdrop of the ongoing drug war and the border buildup intended to keep Mexicans and drugs from crossing into el Norte.

Coinciding with Cantú's high school graduation and the restrictive Immigration and Nationality Act discussed above, 1965 saw the advent of the Border Industrialization Program, effectively replacing the Bracero Program. Rather than bringing Mexican workers into the United States, it was intended they would come to Mexican borderlands factories (known as "maquiladoras") to assemble goods destined for the United States and taxed only on the value added—primarily the cheap Mexican labor assembling raw materials supplied from the United States and returned as automobiles, televisions and other electronics, and appliances. Maquiladoras eventually sprouted along the Mexican borderlands, as in Nuevo Laredo, which hosts dozens of these tax-favored factories. But the demand for cheap migrant labor was unquenched within the United States, which drew millions of Mexicans in subsequent years, many of them as undocumented immigrants and many of them vulnerable women and children—some fleeing the dismal opportunities and oppressive working conditions in borderlands maquiladoras, which favor young women as their employees.[36]

As with most other Mexican immigrants, Cantú's lifework has advanced the United States and augmented our diverse cultural heritage. Overall, the Mexican migrant experience helps reinforce the reality that the human spirit has no borders, whether in academia or in the borderlands. Perhaps our immigration laws will someday acknowledge and celebrate the power of the human spirit and its unquenchable instinct for survival and economic opportunity, rather than construct costly, largely ineffective, often deadly symbols of cultural separation in a *frontera* landscape of cultural connectedness.

NOTES

1. See generally Gloria Anzaldúa, *Borderlands/La Frontera: The New Mestiza* (San Francisco: Aunt Lute Books, 1987).
2. "We sit for hours waiting at the consulado on Farragut Street until our number is called and the cheery clerk talks to Mamagrande, takes the papers to a mysterious back room to have the cónsul sign, and finally returns. The papers flourishingly signed and decorated with an official stamp—I am declared a Mexican national. I can travel back to Mexico without my parents." Norma Elia Cantú, *Canícula: Snapshots of a Girlhood en la Frontera* (Albuquerque: University of New Mexico Press, 1995), 21.
3. In order to qualify for U.S. citizenship at birth, without regard to immigration laws, someone born in the 1940s needed to have both parents be U.S. citizens or to have been born in the United States. See "Citizenship Through Parents," U.S. Citizenship and Immigration Services, http://www.uscis.gov/us-citizenship/citizenship-through-parents.
4. Steven W. Bender, *Run for the Border: Vice and Virtue in U.S.-Mexico Border Crossings* (New York: New York University Press, 2012), 123.
5. Carlos Kevin Blanton, "The Citizenship Sacrifice: Mexican Americans, the Saunders-Leonard Report, and the Politics of Immigration, 1951–1952," *Western Historical Quarterly* 40 (2009): 299, 305.
6. Bender, *Run for the Border*, 124. See also Oscar J. Martínez, *Border Boom Town: Ciudad Juárez Since 1848* (Austin: University of Texas Press, 1978), 112, suggesting the Border Patrol played an even more active role by arresting undocumented crossers and "paroling" them to Texas growers.
7. Cantú, *Canícula*, 5.
8. Bender, *Run for the Border*, 122.
9. See generally Steven W. Bender, *How the West Was Juan: Reimagining the U.S.-Mexico Border* (San Diego: San Diego State University Press, forthcoming 2017).

10. Juan Francisco Perea, "Mi profundo azul: Why Latinos Have a Right to Sing the Blues," in *"Colored Men" and "Hombres Aquí": Hernandez v. Texas and the Emergence of Mexican-American Lawyering*, ed. Michael A. Olivas (Houston: Arte Público Press, 2006), 91, 93.
11. In *Hernandez v. Texas*, 347 U.S. 475 (1954), it was found that persons of Mexican descent constituted a separate class distinct from whites for antidiscrimination purposes.
12. Statement of Norma V. Cantú, a Texas law professor, in Marcus Guerra, ed., "*Hernandez v. Texas*: A 50th Anniversary Celebration," *Texas Hispanic Journal of Law and Policy* 11 (2005): 11, 16.
13. David Montejano, *Anglos and Mexicans in the Making of Texas, 1836–1986* (Austin: University of Texas Press, 1987), 228, discusses how the perceptions of the dirty Mexican were anchored to racialized perceptions of subordinate Mexicans and the realities of poverty and thus the possibility of actually being elevated to "better society" was elusive.
14. Jorge C. Rangel and Carlos M. Alcala, "Project Report: De Jure Segregation of Chicanos in Texas Schools," *Harvard Civil Rights–Civil Liberties Law Review* 7 (1972): 307.
15. Leticia Magda Garza-Falcón, *Gente decente: A Borderlands Response to the Rhetoric of Dominance* (Austin: University of Texas Press, 1998), 173, discusses resistance to this practice of excluding Mexican children after the sixth grade.
16. See Montejano, *Anglos and Mexicans*, 266, for a photo comparison of Mexican and Anglo schools from Texas school segregation litigation.
17. Brown v. Board of Education of Topeka, 347 U.S. 483 (1954).
18. Independent School District v. Salvatierra, 33 S.W. 2d 790 (Tex. Civ. App. 1930), cert. denied, 284 U.S. 580 (1931).
19. Lupe S. Salinas, "Legally White, Socially Brown: Alonso S. Perales and His Crusade for Justice for *La Raza*," in *In Defense of My People: Alonso S. Perales and the Development of Mexican-American Intellectuals*, ed. Michael A. Olivas (Houston: Arte Público Press, 2012), 75, 88, describing the litigation of Delgado v. Bastrop Independent School District.
20. Rangel and Alcala, "Project Report," 316.
21. Ibid., detailing the vestiges into the 1970s of Texas de jure segregation of Mexican American children.
22. San Antonio Independent School District v. Rodriguez, 411 U.S. 1 (1973).
23. Kelly Hildebrandt, "War on Poverty: After 40 Years, Have Things Changed for Laredo?," http://madmax.lmtonline.com/textarchives/051401/b1.htm.

24. Perea, "Mi profundo azul," 101.
25. James Crawford, *Hold Your Tongue: Bilingualism and the Politics of "English Only"* (Reading, MA: Addison-Wesley Publishing, 1992), 72.
26. Juan F. Perea, "English-Only Rules and the Right to Speak One's Primary Language in the Workplace," *University of Michigan Journal of Law Reform* 23 (1990): 265, 284.
27. Cantú, *Canícula*, 89.
28. Lupe S. Salinas, "Linguaphobia, Language Rights, and the Right of Privacy," *Stanford Journal of Civil Rights and Civil Liberties* 3 (2007): 53, 65n65.
29. Perea, "Mi profundo azul," 102–3.
30. Douglas S. Massey, "Only by Addressing the Realities of North American Economic Integration Can We Solve the Problem," *Boston Review* 34 (May/June 2009): 16. See generally Kevin R. Johnson, "The Beginning of the End: The Immigration Act of 1965 and the Emergence of the Modern U.S.-Mexico Border State" in *The Immigration and Nationality Act of 1965: Legislating a New America*, ed. Gabriel J. Chin and Rose Cuison Villazor (New York: Cambridge University Press, 2015), 116.
31. Alan Weisman, *La Frontera: The United States Border with Mexico* (San Diego: Harcourt Brace Jovanovich, 1986), 42.
32. Daniel D. Arreola, *Postcards from the Rio Bravo Border: Picturing the Place, Placing the Picture, 1900s–1950s* (Austin: University of Texas Press, 2013), 16; see also https://mx.usembassy.gov/embassy-consulates/nuevo-laredo/nuevo-laredo-history/.
33. Cantú, *Canícula*, 7–8.
34. See generally Bender, *Run for the Border.*
35. Ibid., 48.
36. See generally Elvia R. Arriola, "Voices from the Barbed Wires of Despair: Women in the Maquiladoras, Latina Critical Legal Theory, and Gender at the U.S.-Mexico Border," *DePaul Law Review* 49 (2000): 729.

IMAGES, IDENTITIES, AND REALITIES IN *ROMANCE OF A LITTLE VILLAGE GIRL* (1955) BY CLEOFAS JARAMILLO AND *CANÍCULA: SNAPSHOTS OF A GIRLHOOD EN LA FRONTERA* (1995) BY NORMA E. CANTÚ

VANESSA FONSECA

IN "THE WRITING OF *CANÍCULA*, BREAKING BOUNDARIES, FINDING FORMS" in *Chicana Feminisms* (2003), Chicana critic and writer Norma E. Cantú reflects on her own personal journey while writing *Canícula* (1995). As a Chicana who is trained in many fields of study and who writes in various genres, she often found it difficult to separate her knowledge of numerous literary, historical, and anthropological forms in order to create a novel that adheres to a specific genre. Thus, when *Canícula* was published, she labeled it a "fictional autobioethnography." This label allowed her not only to combine different narrative strategies but to also break conventional lines of thought about how a novel should be categorized or structured. The genre of fictional autobioethnography allows Cantú to produce a novel that is semiautobiographical in form while weaving in elements of fiction and ethnography, which serve to represent both her own identity as a borderlands *chicana/tejana* and also the identity of a larger community that has called this geographic space their home. Cantú states in the introduction to *Canícula*, "I was calling the work fictional autobiography, until a friend suggested that they really are ethnographic and so if it must fit a genre, I guess it is fictional autobioethnography" (xi).[1] Although her novel is representative of a new literary genre, it is not without its precursors. Cantú borrows from Tey Diana Rebolledo and Eliana S. Rivero in stating that her literary foremothers include Cleofas Jaramillo, Jovita González, and Aurora Lucero-White Lea as well as Josefina Niggli and Sara Estela Ramírez ("The Writing of *Canícula*," 104). Rebolledo and Rivero maintain that these foremothers have been the foundation and lifeblood of our culture and creativity as we enter a new age of Chicana writing (39). Genaro Padilla adds to this observation when he affirms that "the formation of autobiographical consciousness—with all of the ideological and rhetorical stresses it now evinces—originated in prior narrative marking of individual and collective experience" (7).[2]

This project examines the connection between the literary production of Cleofas Jaramillo, literary foremother, and Norma E. Cantú, contemporary Chicana writer, in regard to their use of multiple genres as a means to represent formations of identity in New Mexico from the late nineteenth century to the mid-twentieth century and in the Texas borderlands from the 1940s to the 1990s, respectively. As a precursor to Chicana literary authors, Jaramillo was essential in establishing a feminine literary corpus in New Mexico that served as an example of the use of various narrative strategies—including poetry, autobiography, folklore, and photographs—to convey a certain sense of identity for herself and for her fellow *nuevomexicanos* in the face of Americanization efforts following the Mexican-American War (1846–48). In the case of Cantú, we see similar strategies throughout her work that also serve as identity markers within the borderlands of Texas during the post–World War II era. The photographs used in each text will be analyzed to show their potential for representing identity formation as well as social, cultural, and political realities for Chicanas/Hispanas in the Southwest within different geographic spaces and time periods. As a theoretical mark, this paper utilizes the foundational studies of Chicana feminism employed by Tey Diana Rebolledo as it applies to early Chicana writers as well as more contemporary studies by Emma Pérez in which she proposes a decolonial imaginary as a multidimensional strategy to identity formation and the recuperation of history. Furthermore, Susan Sontag's and Roland Barthes's studies on photography will serve as a basis for analyzing the two texts from a visual literacy perspective. We will see throughout this study how both Jaramillo and Cantú use their personal knowledge of folklore, history, and cultural politics, as well as a variety of genres, to reflect an identity unique to their respective geographic spaces and time periods.

DEVELOPING A THEORETICAL MODEL

Chicana critic Tey Diana Rebolledo has been fundamental in developing a critical corpus on early Hispana/Mexicana writers. She has written extensively about the foremothers of Chicana literature, giving close attention to the work of nuevomexicana writers in the early twentieth century. Just as Luis Leal has characterized Chicano literature into different historical periods, in *Infinite Divisions: An Anthology of Chicana Literature*, Rebolledo and Rivero divide the Hispana/Mexicana writers into various categories and assert a historical presence of women writers as precursors to Chicana literature: "Las Pobladoras (The Colonizers)"; "The Mexican National Years to 1848"; "1848 and Beyond: Accommodation, Assimilation, and Survival"; "The 1920s–1950s: Flowering of a Literature of Resistance"; "The Second World War"; "The Chicano/Chicana Renaissance"; and "Contemporary Trends in Chicana Literature."[3] Luis Leal argues that the early writers, including Vicente J. Bernal, María Cristina Mena, Nina Otero-Warren, Fray Angélico Chávez, Cleofas Jaramillo, Fabiola Cabeza de Baca, and Mario Suárez, did not represent a specific generation of writers, a school of thought, or an inclination to particular literary forms.[4] However, it is important not to look at them as a whole and to separate women's writing from men's because, given the historical, political, cultural, and social atmosphere of the early Southwest, it is undeniably certain that women's goals for writing were different from those of their male counterparts. The distinction between male and female literary production lies in the themes and strategies utilized to reflect their unique experiences. By uncovering the contributions of early Mexicana/Hispana writers, Rebolledo and Rivero claim a space for female writing that predates the Chicano movement politics of the 1960s and 1970s, when Chicana feminism emerged as a theoretical tool and thus reignited Chicana literary and cultural production.

Rebolledo and Rivero place the majority of the literary foremothers to which Cantú dedicates her literary formation in the category of "The 1920s–1950s: Flowering of a Literature of Resistance." During this period many writers confronted a variety of identity issues as colonized people; as mothers, sisters, wives, and children; as public figures; as guardians of family values and culture; and as storytellers. They expressed these different identities through yet another persona: the female writer. Through the use of multiple narrative strategies and by mixing literary, historical, and cultural genres, these foremothers were able to express just what it meant to be Hispana/Mexicana with multiple identity markers. Concerning nuevomexicana writing, Rebolledo and Rivero state at length one of the defining strategies as

> the blending or blurring of various forms: the oral with the written, history with creative autobiography, recipes and narrative, family history and romance. The mixing of genre (recipes with fiction, autobiography with poetry) was seen by these writers as acceptable because it was a *recuerdo*, a remembering, and because all the narration was underscored by the *cuento* storytelling tradition. In Hispanic storytelling the mixture of genres with strong attention to personal detail was acceptable, even expected. [Thus] the personal subjectivity incorporates all the discourses of history, sociology, psychology, and geography, but it is the personal storyteller that binds it together. (18)

The use of several narrative strategies and genres is a technique that is later employed by contemporary Chicana writers in their attempts to develop self through writing and cultural expression. Rebolledo and Rivero state that Jaramillo's autobiography, *Romance of a Little Village Girl* (1955), aims at understanding cultural and historical borders that were imposed by the Mexican-American War (1846–48) and Americanization efforts that left the Hispana population culturally and linguistically displaced in a space they once considered their own (31). The idea of borders extends itself literally to Cantú's novel *Canícula* as she continues to struggle with not only cultural and historical borders but also the geographical borders of Laredo, Texas, and Nuevo Laredo, Tamaulipas. As Emma Pérez argues, a Chicana past is often constructed by means of crossing geographic terrains and political borders (xiv). By traversing these borders, both Jaramillo and Cantú reflect the multidimensional experience of living within a culture that consistently looks to negotiate cultural identities.

In both the introduction and prologue to *Canícula*, Cantú mentions Roland Barthes and his book *Camera Lucida: Reflections on Photography* (1981). This immediately impels the reader to seek out Barthes and look for the inspiration Cantú might have drawn from him in the creation of her own work. The tejana writer does not allude to the importance of Barthes in her own story; rather, she invites her readers to be active participants in deciding how these images create meaning. While Cantú places her photos throughout the text, Jaramillo places eight photos, accompanied by captions, at the beginning of her autobiography. Those who have produced critical works on Cantú's novel have utilized both Roland Barthes and Susan Sontag's *On Photography* (1977) as tools for analyzing the use of photography in *Canícula*. These studies are equally useful for exploring the use of photos in Jaramillo's text. Both authors place images in their works as a sort of visual literacy technique and summon the reader to treat the photographs as a complementary text to the narration. In *On Photography*, Sontag examines the various uses for photography, which include, among others, memorializing the achievements of individuals considered as members of families (as well as of other groups); constructing a portrait chronicle of self; giving people imaginary possession of a past that is unreal; and helping them to take possession of a space in which they are insecure by offering indisputable evidence while at the same time enabling them to refuse experiences (8–9). Barthes looks at photography in much the same way by analyzing the level of truth implied by photography, how it reflects identity formation, and the privileging of certain photos over others, as well as our innate attraction to visual imagery to represent certain ideologies. While neither Jaramillo nor Cantú guide the reader to an analysis of the visual strategies, both show an awareness of the role that the photos play in autobiography as a means for communicating personal ideology.

In *The Decolonial Imaginary: Writing Chicanas into History* (1999), Emma Pérez uses a postmodern approach to recuperate Chicana histories. She maintains, "I take a postmodern approach for a number of reasons. Postmodernism is often infuriating for the same reasons that postmodern claims are useful. Nothing is taken for granted. Nothing is accepted at face value. Nothing is real. All is imagined and therefore disputable" (xiv). In an effort to define the *decolonial imaginary*, the multidimensional space between colonial and postcolonial history that allows one to analyze disjointed identities and realities, Pérez utilizes Chela Sandoval's concept of *differential consciousness*, which looks at the idea that identities can mobilize and transform according to sociopolitical and historical factors. Pérez considers Sandoval's concept to lie within the decolonial imaginary. While Jaramillo was not aware of these concepts as a theoretical tool for writing, she nonetheless uses strategies within her text to affirm an identity that is altered by various circumstances, while at the same time refusing to adhere to a specific narrative technique. Cantú, as a Chicana critic turned creative writer, was undoubtedly conscious of a postmodern space where everything is questionable and where realities may not be what they seem. The use of various strategies for narratives that do not follow a chronological order adheres to Pérez's strategy of approaching history and Chicana subjectivity through multiple nonlinear dimensions. Cantú references this point in her introduction to *Canícula*: "It is not a narrative strung out in keeping with Freytag's pyramid: it does not adhere to conventions of plot development. Instead it is a collage of stories gleaned from photographs randomly picked, not from a photo album chronologically arranged, but haphazardly pulled from a box of photos where time is blurred" (xii). While Jaramillo adheres to a chronological order when relating her autobiography, she uses multiple narrative strategies to write her story, including autobiography, ballad forms, photography, history, and folklore. Cantú's novel adopts the various narrative styles as well as a nonlinear development, more closely matching what Pérez has deemed the space of the decolonial imaginary.

Jaramillo and Cantú utilize geographic space as an indicator of social, historical, and political factors that contribute to the formation of their individual identities. While Jaramillo's autobiography is situated in northern New Mexico, Cantú's autobioethnography deals with the borderlands of Texas. Whereas both spaces suffered linguistic, cultural, and political displacement due to the Mexican-American War, the authors portray these conflicts in very different manners, mostly because of the different geographic locations of their lived experiences.

CLEOFAS JARAMILLO AND *ROMANCE OF A LITTLE VILLAGE GIRL*

In *Romance of a Little Village Girl*, Jaramillo begins her autobiography by ascertaining a lineage of Spanish ancestors, utilizing a traditional Spanish ballad form to introduce her narrative (Rebolledo, xxi). In so doing, she attests to their successful settling of the Southwest and founding of missions to recreate Old Spain in northern New Mexico. In a manner reminiscent of the presentation of genealogical lines in the Holy Bible, Jaramillo lists generations of brave, fearless, adventurous Spaniard ancestors who were fundamental in the establishment of Spanish culture from the sixteenth century to the mid-nineteenth century. Her descriptions of Spanish lifeways and customs are abundant throughout her autobiography and form an integral part of her personal identity as an upper-class Hispana/nuevomexicana. Regardless of where Jaramillo finds herself during her life, she is quick to reference Spanish cultural practices: she describes Spanish plays, such as *Los moros y los cristianos*; she celebrates Spanish saints, such as Saint James; and she expresses Spanish superstitions concerning death and mourning, among others.

Jaramillo's appropriation of Spanish identity is exemplified by her use of photography and references to photography throughout her text. Of the eight images that appear at the beginning of her autobiography, she includes herself in five. One photo in particular shows the author, circa 1900 to 1910, outfitted in a Spanish gown, complete with a mantilla. The lace mantillas were imported from China and Spain and were accompanied by precious jewels and heirlooms handed down from previous generations (177). This style of dress serves as a marker of Spanish identity when she forms La Sociedad Folklórica, an organization whose rules include the composition of only thirty members of Spanish descent and the requirement that all members speak Spanish. The organization shares the common goal of preserving their language, customs, and traditions (176). In addition to a photo showing the members of La Sociedad Folklórica during their ten-year celebration, which includes the author and nuevomexicana writer Fabiola Cabeza de Baca, Jaramillo utilizes photography as a means of cultural preservation. She affirms, "To encourage greater interest in the preservation of the old Spanish customs and the study of our traditions, I donated to the society my fifty-page album with my folklore collection" (183). This photo collection, thus, serves as a historical archive aimed at concreting a Spanish identity seen through the eyes of Jaramillo and those who support a similar ideology.

Critics Rebolledo and Rivero, as well as Genaro Padilla and Maureen E. Reed, have all used photos of Jaramillo in their analysis of her literary production. In *Infinite Divisions*, Rebolledo and Rivero use Jaramillo's photo (and those of other writers) as a way to visually capture the writers included in their text, and they do not necessarily connect the image of the writer with a Spanish heritage. The photo does not appear within the body of the text but, rather, places Jaramillo within the context of other women writers. The same photo used by Rebolledo and Rivero appears as the cover for Padilla's book *My History, Not Yours: The Formation of Mexican-American Autobiography* (1993). Padilla also includes another image of Cleofas Jaramillo within the text, one that serves as an example of her traditional style of dress for the Santa Fe Fiestas. This photo is accompanied by Padilla's analysis of the illusionary identity that Jaramillo has created for herself by constructing an autobiographical romance that negates New Mexico's mestizo heritage. He reads her work as a compensation for the socioeconomic struggles she faced after the death of her husband, Venceslao Jaramillo (220). This visual and written text offered by Padilla is in direct contrast to the justification of Spanish identity Jaramillo herself proposes throughout her narrative. In her book *A Woman's Place: Women Writing in New*

Mexico (2005), Reed utilizes four photos of Jaramillo in order to structure an analysis based on class identity, Jaramillo's wedding to prominent nuevomexicano and cousin Venceslao Jaramillo, the murder of Angelina Jaramillo (daughter of Cleofas and Venceslao), and her formation of the Sociedad Folklórica.

The use of family photos in Jaramillo's text signifies a desire to maintain a status quo that adheres to structures of Spanish colonial power. The images indicate an interest in keeping things just the way they are—or, in the case of Jaramillo, just the way they were. Although this status quo may not be reflective of Jaramillo's descending status as an elite nuevomexicana, she combats these notions by immortalizing Spanish dress and customs as a way to link to a past identity that she wishes to preserve in a contemporary Anglo American society. Her current status as a widow who has lost her wealth and her prestige as a landed upper-class woman does not serve as the backdrop for her photos. Rather, the picture serves, as Sontag argues, "as a thin slice of space as well as time. In a world ruled by photographic images, all borders ("framing") seem arbitrary. Anything else can be separated, can be made discontinuous, from everything else: all that is necessary [is] to frame the subject differently" (22). Thus, Jaramillo's framing allows her to create an identity on her own terms. Since she is the primary subject, she has the liberty to leave out any details, even major ones, that do not correspond to her personal ideology. As a writer, she is ultimately in charge of all decisions concerning how her identity is portrayed to the reader, regardless of the level of truth perceived by the reader/viewer.

In her article "La forma testimonial y la novelística de Miguel Barnet," Elzbieta Sklodowska argues that testimonial literature that does not adhere to reality is inherently problematic, as it replaces veracity with personal ideology that may or may not reflect what is historically true. She states:

> Sería ingenuo (en el caso del testimonio) asumir una relación de homología directa entre la historia y el texto. El discurso del testigo no puede ser un reflejo de su experiencia, sino más bien su refracción debida a las vicisitudes de la memoria, su intención, su ideología. La intencionalidad y la ideología del autor-editor se sobreponen al texto original, creando más ambigüedades, silencios y lagunas en el proceso de selección, montaje y arreglo del material recopilado conforme a las normas de la forma literaria. Así pues, aunque la forma testimonial emplea varios recursos para ganar en veracidad y autenticidad—entre ellos el punto de vista de la primera persona-testigo—el juego entre ficción e historia aparece inexorablemente como un problema. (379)

Sklodowska states that silences or lacunae, in *testimonio* can create further ambiguities about the seemingly true text. Padilla and Rebolledo both allude to these created silences, or lacunae, in Jaramillo's autobiography. As a Spanish woman, Jaramillo would be concerned about what does and what does not protect her identity as a member of the elite class; she would not have divulged too much information as it pertains to her familial unit. As readers, we are left to wonder about such events as the illness of her husband and her daughter's murder. By keeping silent, she herself participates in the ongoing process of forgetting or attempting to forget the sadness, loss, and struggle that has interrupted her utopian vision of Spanish-ness in northern New Mexico during the first part of the twentieth century. As a writer, she grazes over these elements to focus instead on the preservation of a diminished past as a strategy to combat Anglo American hegemony.

Her decision to become a writer was influenced, in part, by the overwhelming desire to preserve her personal Spanish identity in the face of the fact that other writers during her time period attempted to take this identity away from the native population. In the introduction to *Romance*, Rebolledo states:

> Jaramillo had the feeling that she and the Hispanos were being co-opted and that people outside the culture were trying to steal her writing just as they were trying to appropriate the culture. Although such fears might seem paranoiac, they were not groundless. In a sense Mary Austin, Mabel Dodge Luhan, and others who helped create the mystique of New Mexican culture during the period were, in effect, appropriating the culture they found so fascinating. (xxiv–xxv)

When considering a publisher for her book *Shadows of the Past*, she decides that the best option would be to self-publish, as it is clear that everyone else is interested only in stealing her ideas: "One professor said he was writing a book. Would I permit him to use two or three of my stories in his books? I then understood. All they wanted was to read my manuscript and get ideas from it" (168). It is interesting to note, however, that Jaramillo's fear of appropriation can be seen as a direct reflection of her own appropriation of other cultures. In essence, in creating her "Spanish" identity, she is also to blame for stealing ideas from surrounding cultures.

There are moments in her text where Jaramillo stakes her claim on a Mexican heritage as a means for appropriating without recognition. Jaramillo's extensive description of Spanish grandeur at the beginning is preluded by Rebolledo's assertion that Jaramillo's maternal grandmother was from Chihuahua, Mexico. This immediately debunks any myths pertaining to a pure Spanish bloodline while at the same time establishes a basis for Jaramillo to incorporate her Mexican heritage as a part of her identity. While she references Mexican history, cultural items, and traditions at various times throughout her text, however, she appropriates them as being Spanish rather than Mexican. She mentions that her maternal grandmother brought a statue of Nuestra Señora de los Dolores from Mexico, but she ties the icon into the larger theme of Holy Week and its importance in carrying on the medieval age of faith, presumably Spanish, into Lenten ceremonies practiced in northern New Mexico (35–36).

When referring to Spanish-style housing, she alludes to a hacienda-style home furnished with Saltillo *sarapes*. A traditional *sarape*, or serape, originates in Saltillo, Mexico, rather than Spain and is used as a blanket or poncho by Mexican men. She does not mention that these items, used as curtains to adorn the Spanish home, came from Mexico. In another scene, she is sewing a *china poblana* outfit, clearly a symbol of Mexican dress, for her daughter, Angelina, yet she does not elaborate on the origins of this style, simply brushing the incident off as part of her everyday duties.

In chapter 16, Jaramillo writes about a trip to Mexico with her mother, her father, and her sister. The abundant adjectives she uses to describe Spanish customs and places are notably absent in her narrative of Mexico. She names places and portrays the landscape in a way that most often returns to discussions of Spanish heritage. When describing Cuernavaca, for example, she writes, "One has to see Cuernavaca to succumb to the charm of its antique picturesqueness. This city dates back to the time of Cortez, 1529. . . . The Morelos, where we lodged, I figured, must have been built by some Spanish grandee" (102). She continues with a description of the Spaniard Hernán Cortés as well as other prominent leaders: "Amid blooming oleander and citrus fruit trees rose a grey monument to the memory of the intrepid Cortez. Inside, the walls were covered with large pictures of Iturbides, Hidalgo and other famous generals in gorgeous uniforms, showing their proud Spanish heritage" (103). As anyone who studies Mexican history would know, Father Miguel Hidalgo would more than likely have been proud of his Mexican (rather than Spanish) heritage, given that he was responsible for the Grito de Dolores, the battle cry that led to Mexico's independence from Spain in 1810. Instead of including this history, however, Jaramillo decides to occlude it as either something she is not familiar with or simply something she refuses to acknowledge as truth. Rather, she focuses her account of her trip to Mexico on Spanish architecture and historical presence while playing up the simplistic elements of the country.

If we look at the descriptions she gives of Mexico versus those of her own hometown of Arroyo Hondo, New Mexico, it is not hard to see which she favors more. As Jaramillo and her family leave Mexico, she describes nothing more than a simple country that is foreign to her: "Five months' rest in this languid, exotic land of leisure that lies drowsing under scorching suns, in this paradise of souls, where the sole ambition of most is to obtain just enough for their daily needs, has restored my mother's strength sufficiently to fight her ills for a number of years" (106). Now, if we look at the description of her hometown, settled by brave and courageous Spanish conquistadors, we see a stark contrast: "Through the center of the basin splashes the noisy, rocky river. Its crystalline waters create green-carpeted meadows and fields. On the west the river surges through the stupendous gate of the Rio Grande and mingles its crystal waters with the musky green ones of the Rio Grande. Three picturesque villages add charm to this small section of the beautiful Taos Valley" (7). The descriptions of both places indicate a preference not only for an environment framed by a Spanish presence but for one whose beauty, in the narrative sense, cannot be surpassed by the simplistic elements of Mexico, a country that is labeled as merely sufficient in ambition and purpose.

Jaramillo mentions in her text that she is aware of Mexican customs but perhaps has forgotten them over time (105). This does not indicate that the nuevomexicana writer had any close ties to her maternal grandmother's place of birth and could be her way of negotiating identity by refusing to acknowledge the influence of Mexican culture in the development of her own Spanish identity. In fact, there are only a couple places in her autobiography where *lo mexicano* is even mentioned. After the death of her and Venceslao's second baby, Jaramillo comments that their nurse, Vita, was good at preparing Mexican dishes (111). This is the first time in her narrative that food is referred to as Mexican, rather than Spanish. In another scene, Cleofas and Venceslao are discussing the sale of sheep. When Cleofas explains to Venceslao that they don't have very many sheep and wants to know why he is selling them, he replies, "Because we Mexicans can only make money with sheep, and land is getting scarce" (125). Venceslao's appropriation of a Mexican identity provides a sharp contrast to Cleofas's portrayal of him as a landed upper-class Spanish *político*.

Reed makes an interesting point when she calls upon the studies of Arthur L. Campa to explain how identity markers in New Mexico differ on the basis of language usage. She states, "He showed how Spanish-speaking New Mexicans used the term [*Spanish*] selectively, and the pattern of their selection reveals their motives" (78). While Spanish speakers would often use "Spanish American" to refer to their identity in English, their language was described, not as Spanish, but as "mexicano." For many nuevomexicanos, there is a clear distinction between a *mexicano* and a *mexicano de México* (78). It is unclear whether the original conversation between Venceslao and Cleofas took place in English or Spanish. If it was, in fact, the latter, it is possible, although unlikely, that Jaramillo may have made an error in translation when communicating this conversation to the reader and represented Venceslao as a mexicano de México as opposed to a mexicano.

In one of the photos that appears at the beginning of the text, we see a young Colonel Venceslao Jaramillo, circa 1897, in a uniform signifying his position as a militia aide to Territorial Governor Miguel A. Otero. If we read this picture as a representation of a social rite and power, as Sontag suggests (8), we immediately see how Cleofas was first attracted to him. As a member of a Spanish land grant family and a cousin to Cleofas, Venceslao became more and more attractive to her for a variety of reasons. From a Spanish bloodline standpoint, her marriage to Venceslao would strengthen the alliance between two of the older Spanish families in northern New Mexico. From a military standpoint, Cleofas was drawn to the uniform that he wore and the power that he possessed as a member of Otero's military staff. Thus, Cleofas presents her husband, not as a Mexican, but, instead, as Spanish.

It is possible that while Jaramillo viewed herself and her community as identifiably Spanish, others, such as her own husband, recognized their *mexicanidad* as an integral part of their identity. This possibility is eclipsed, however, by the first-person narration that Jaramillo provides in her text, leaving no room to elaborate on identities that do not suit her. As in other instances, she is quick to overlook Mexican identity as a contributing factor to social and cultural norms in northern New Mexico during the mid-nineteenth century. She develops a strategy of exclusion based on her own ideologies, which function as a type of truth for herself and those who subscribe to the idea of Spanish lineage and heritage within this geographic space.

In Jaramillo's text, she presents herself as undeniably Spanish, although context clues signify otherwise. A close reading of her narrative suggests a geographical space that is more heterogeneous than Jaramillo would like to believe, comprised of Native American, Anglo American, Hispanic, and mestizo cultural and linguistic influences. While her narrative may not reflect the true nature of the mixed identity of New Mexico during that time period, it does not take away the fact that this was her reality. Reed observes:

> Mestizo qualities did not suit her conceptions of what it meant to be a Hispanic New Mexican. Jaramillo quite determinedly saw and wrote about herself as "Spanish." To those New Mexicans who today identify as mestizo/a, mexicano/a, or chicano/a, and to those who doubt that any New Mexican family could have maintained a "blood line" as "pure" as Jaramillo claims, her Spanish identity, regardless of its origins, may seem a myth perpetuated by racist prejudice. Nevertheless, to Jaramillo, this identity was very real. (74–75)

Jaramillo's use of various narrative strategies and genres to frame her personal identity provides a path for future Chicana writers to utilize similar techniques in the development of self based in different time periods and distinct geographical spaces. Jaramillo's assertion of her identity as Spanish in a changing political, linguistic, and cultural landscape can be seen as a defense mechanism in a New Mexico borderlands defined by colonial relationships. Jaramillo's reality is constructed through narrative and photography as a means not only to communicate nostalgia for a disappearing past but to reassert a Spanish presence in Anglo American society.

NORMA E. CANTÚ AND *CANÍCULA*

Concerning the focus of literary foremother narratives, Rebolledo and Rivero assert, "Interestingly enough, many of the themes and topics covered by these women are frequently seen today in contemporary writing, even though the approach may be different" (39). While Jaramillo writes about northern New Mexico's transition from Spanish/Mexican control to Anglo American following the Mexican-American War, Cantú's autobioethnography deals with a different geographic space in the period following World War II. Her narrative takes place in the linguistic, political, and cultural borderlands of Laredo and Nuevo Laredo. Cantú's narrative emphasizes the land in between the Mexican and U.S. border, which complicates notions of identity based on racial heritage and geographic space.

By labeling Cantú's work as a fictional autobioethnography, the reader cannot take what they see or read at face value. Further, while one would assume that Cantú sat down with a series of photos to create the story on the basis of her hindsight memory of these subjects, this is not the case. In her article "The Writing of *Canícula*," Cantú explains, "I did not have the photos with me as I wrote, I was able to confirm the theory of how memory actually frees the past and photos freeze the moment. When I went back to Laredo to look for the photos and complete the text, I found that the narrative proved the tenuous nature of memory and the apparent rigidity of the photograph" (103). While Cantú could have returned to the narrative to match it to the photo, she chose not to do so. Her process coincides with what Barthes describes as the *punctum*, the ability to think back on a photo and develop a personal relationship with it when it is no longer in front of you. This allows the individual to create a memory that is based, not on a frozen object, but, rather, on an ability to engage in a vivid description of a past not guided by the inflexibility of the referent. Barthes elaborates by declaring, "I may know better a photograph I remember than a photograph I am looking at, as if direct vision oriented its language wrongly, engaging it as an effort of description which will always miss its points of effect, the *punctum*" (53). Cantú utilizes this observation in her own narrative. In "Last Piñata," Nena, the main protagonist and Cantú's fictional persona, describes a moment in which she has lost a photo: "I don't even know where it is, in one of my Mother's other boxes, or in one of Espy's albums, perhaps. It remains crisp and clear in my mind" (55). Although Nena does not have the object at hand to accurately describe her memory, she is suggesting that perhaps her own memory of the photo is more important than the photo itself.

While Jaramillo focuses her narrative on the assertion of Spanish identity and the consequent negation of an Anglo American or mestizo heritage, Cantú begins with a Spanish background and focuses on a present borderlands space defined by Mexico and the United States. Her prologue starts with two lovers in a seventh-floor *piso* in Madrid in 1980, going through a collection of photos that offer a visual representation of identity for the male partner while leaving his female counterpart with no story to tell, because her pictures are not present. The narrator states, "She has no photographs to offer, to share her life through. Her photographs, silent witnesses of her life, her history, lie an ocean away, across the Atlantic, across the United States, across Texas, at the borderland where Mexico meets Texas" (1–2). The narrator sets the stage wherein the protagonist, Nena, will be able to create her story and her identity through a series of photographs that will appear later in the text. Due to the fictional nature of the narrative—and Cantú has affirmed this—the photos do not always match the text.

Life on the borderlands for the tejana/mexicana community is not the same as that which Jaramillo portrays in northern New Mexico. In the section "Las Piscas," the reader is led through a scene reminiscent of a migrant farmworker camp. The entire family is working side by side, picking cotton in August in weather that is so hot that "pus-filled ampulas burst and burn with the sun" (3). The economic situation of Nena's family is apparent as each *saca* of cotton collected earns the household from fifty cents to a dollar. In this scene, the jet in the sky drops pesticides over the cotton fields as its pilot looks down on the primitive labor below. The photo described in this section, although we do not see it, represents a hardworking family who forces smiles through serious faces. The depiction gives way to an emotional response from the reader, as we all empathize with the backbreaking labor that overwhelms the life of the campesino mexicano.

The end of the Mexican-American War in 1848 brought drastic changes to the residents of the Southwestern United States, including unhealthy living conditions for farm laborers such as (but not limited to) long hours in the sun, lack of indoor plumbing, low wages, and health risks caused by pesticides and unsanitary living conditions. Cantú's narrative reflects this common image of the Chicano farmworker in the Texas borderlands, which is then shared with the larger border community. Later in life, Nena finds herself protesting with the farmworkers and marching in anti–Vietnam War efforts, all the while wearing a César Chávez button and reading Karl Marx (31). Her childhood as part of a farmworker family provides the backdrop for Chicano movement politics in the 1960s, which emphasized a Marxist approach to class struggle and a desire to improve the Chicano condition.

Nena's life on the border provides a space to negotiate cultural identities. In the section titled "Mexican Citizen," we see two photos that accompany Nena's immigration papers. Though these official documents would suggest some sort of veracity, the reader is led to believe from the beginning that not everything the narrator presents is inherently true. The images offered appear to be doctored to the extent that sections of the documents are taped over and replaced with other images and signatures. What is interesting insofar as cultural identity is concerned is that while Nena (Azucena) is described as *blanco* in color earlier in life, at sixteen years of age, she is described as *moreno*. This is a simple testament to life on the border and the cultural negotiations Nena makes by being American or Mexican, depending on which side of the border she finds herself and how she is perceived by those around her.

Nena mentions a trip she takes to Mexico with Mamagrande in which her cousins tease her and refer to her as a *pocha*.[5] Though she may perceive herself to be mexicana, those who view her as a traitor to her Mexican culture do not reciprocate the sentiment. This causes Nena to long for her American identity, full of American cultural markers such as *The Ed Sullivan Show* and Glass Kitchen hamburgers. She struggles constantly with linguistic registers that cause her to feel like an outsider in Mexico because she cannot express herself adequately in Spanish nor participate fully in the cultural environment of her cousins. She mentions that her U.S. immigration papers claim she is a Mexican citizen, but it becomes apparent that she does not feel as if Mexico is her home. Sontag's observation of photos is appropriate in this context as we view the documents as an attempt to lay claim to another reality (16). In this case, Nena wants to be more Mexican that she is perceived to be by her Mexican cousins.

Nena's longing for her American identity is later contrasted by the United States' refusal to incorporate Mexican culture and customs into the overall landscape of the country, so that throughout the narrative, Nena struggles not only with being an outsider in Mexico but also with being looked upon as an *extranjera* while in the United States. In the section titled "Papi's Horse," she mentions *sopa de arroz*, *guisados*, *postres*, mole, *cabrito*, and tamales as traditional Mexican foods, served on "linens whiter than white" (17). The emphasis on the color of the linens would lead the reader to believe that while the family is celebrating Mexican identity in a culinary sense, they are living within the confines of a white Anglo American governing body that continually oppresses the tejano/mexicano. In "Políticos," the narrative attests to the injustices suffered in the border communities. Papi asserts:

> Our money lines their pockets, paves private roads on their ranches, while our streets remain unpaved, run like rivers after every rain, while our public library remains as small as someone's private library; while the dropout rate remains between 50 and 80 percent; while judges, mayors, sheriffs, high and low powerful ones abuse, rape, embarrass, harass, taunt, demean women. (30–31)

These inequalities represent the reality of the borderlands, a land that was incorporated into the United States through war and bloodshed at the end of the Mexican-American War. This is the same space in which Anzaldúa, with the publication of *Borderlands/La Frontera* (1987), calls for the United States to admit what it has done in an effort to heal the ever-open wounds of this geographic space. While mexicanos proclaim a historical and cultural presence in the borderlands, they are constantly faced with overwhelming political forces that promote cultural erasure in favor of assimilation. As Cantú's narrative shows, inherent in borderland identity is the unfortunate recognition of an appalling reality characterized by dropouts, violence, and greed.

Both Cantú's and Jaramillo's texts point to the spaces that are claimed by colonial powers. While Jaramillo's autobiography attempts to reconcile the shift from conqueror to conquered, Cantú's narrative shows the everyday consequences of empire, which include political, cultural, and linguistic erasure in the borderlands. In her article "Literary (Re)Mappings: Autobiographical (Dis)Placements by Chicana Writers," Norma Klahn proclaims that Cantú's text points to a space where contemporary writers such as Cantú, Sandra Cisneros, and Mary Helen Ponce contest hegemonic notions of domination and marginalization of minority cultures (123). Her photos, unlike the ones in Jaramillo's autobiography, are meant to show everyday people. While Jaramillo looks to link her photos to an upper-class Spanish lineage, Cantú merely wants to show that the people on the borderlands exist, as it is apparent that Anglo American society rarely acknowledges their presence.

There are but a few instances in which we can pair up photos from each text and analyze the overall significance to the development of identity. Both Cantú and Jaramillo include wedding photos in their narrative. In the case of Jaramillo, we see a young Cleofas and Venceslao, circa 1898, in a portrait taken while on their honeymoon. Jaramillo mentions the photo later in her narrative and states that it was taken at a fine studio during their monthlong travels (81), indicating that the couple had the means to be able to travel at leisure for an extended period of time. In Cantú's text, we see a photo of her parents, also taken at a studio. The backdrop of the photo, however, is quite plain in comparison to the portrait of Jaramillo and her husband. Nena's parents did not have their picture taken while on their honeymoon but, rather, within a few hours of getting married. Nena imagines her parents as two Mexican cultural icons: Jorge Negrete and María Félix. Though Nena mentions the Spanish lace mantilla that her mother wears in the photo, it is clear that the intention is not to link the object with Spanish identity, as Jaramillo has done, but to link her parents to Mexico via Negrete and Félix.

Although we do not see a picture of the china poblana outfit that Jaramillo sews for her daughter, Angelina, we can compare this narrative to the visual image that Cantú provides in *Canícula*. In *Romance*, Jaramillo refuses the notion of being linked to a Mexican identity, even when her husband refers to them as such. She further negates this possibility when she sews a china poblana outfit for her daughter. Rather than commenting upon the significance of the Mexican national dress, she merely states that she made it. In Cantú's narrative, we see a photo of Mami in a china poblana outfit with the words *Viva Mexico* written across the charro hat she is wearing (40). In the previous section, "China Poblana One," Nena is also wearing a china poblana outfit and has her hair braided in green, white, and red, the colors of the "bandera del soldado" (38). The dual images of Nena and Mami in Mexican dress suggest a generational attachment to Mexico. The visual images grow even more meaningful as Nena continues to mention Mexican movie stars, Mexican foods, and Mexican cultural practices throughout this section of the narrative.

The last set of pictures that are important to the narratives of Cantú and Jaramillo are those of Venceslao Jaramillo and what appears to be a picture of Tino. In *Romance*, we know that many Hispano men used military service as a strategy for inclusion during the transition from Hispano political control to Anglo American. In the photo of Venceslao, circa 1897, we see him as a militia aide to Miguel A. Otero, a territorial governor of New Mexico during that period. Through Jaramillo's narrative, we learn that Venceslao was a highly valued political figure from a well-known nuevomexicano family. His life, up until the time of his illness, suggests he was a man of means who was highly respected by all. His illness comes at a time when nuevomexicanos were losing their power within a new political system. In "Tino," Nena points out Tino in a photo as the one on the right shooting a gun (14). Perhaps this is to foreshadow Tino's later life as a soldier in Vietnam and his unfortunate fate while serving a country that sent an alarming number of Chicanos to the front lines. Nena explains that Tino was ill as a three-year-old child but has survived with the help of prayers, medications, and *remedios*. His tie to a Mexican identity helped him to survive the ailments that he suffered early on in life. Yet when he enlists in the American army as a seventeen-year-old, he appropriates a new identity under the United States flag and is sent back home in a coffin. While Venceslao's illness can be read as the inevitable decline of the elite Hispano, Tino's death in Vietnam, as was the case for many Chicanos, was a invitation to die on the front line while serving a country that would never extend respect to those who gave their lives for inclusion and acceptance.

As Rebolledo and Rivero have stated, the literary foremothers provided a space for contemporary Chicana writers to express topics and themes important to Chicana literature and cultural production. In this study, we have looked primarily at the theme of identity as a developing element in Chicana narratives. In the case of Jaramillo, the reader is drawn to her exaggerated descriptions of a Spanish identity that is based on the historical presence of a colonial legacy. Jaramillo uses various narrative techniques—poetry, photography, folklore, and autobiography—to draw on the past as a means for survival in the present. The images she has chosen as a visual literacy strategy affirm her upper-class nuevomexicana identity. Although many critics have called Jaramillo's clinging to tradition a lie (Reed, 73) because it negates the historical presence of both mestizo and indigenous identities, her identity is nonetheless real to her. Throughout her narrative, she negotiates cultural identity as she straddles the border between old and new colonial powers.

Cantú looks to her foremothers as precursors to a Chicana literature and a tradition of autobiographical narrative. She extends this narrative to include fiction and ethnography in her attempt to portray a border identity in South Texas. This identity is constantly struggling to be accepted and defined as both sides of the border push, pull, swallow up, and spit out the communities that inhabit this geographic space. Cantú's narrative and use of photos implements a postmodern approach, following a nonlinear structure in an attempt to portray the harsh realities of border life in the post–World War II era.

NOTES

1. In 2007, while I was enrolled in a course on Chicano/a autobiography at the University of New Mexico, Tey Diana Rebolledo stated it was she and Erlinda Gonzales-Berry who had suggested the incorporation of ethnography into Cantú's description of her novel.
2. In *My History, Not Yours: The Formation of Mexican-American Autobiography* (1993), Padilla examines the contributions of Mariano Vallejo, nineteenth-century California women's personal narratives, Rafael Chacón, and Cleofas Jaramillo as precursors to contemporary Chicano/a or Mexican American autobiography.
3. In "Pre-Chicano Literature: Process and Meaning (1539-1959)" (1993), Luis Leal divides Chicano literary production into distinct historical categories: "Colonial Literature (1542–1810)," "Toward Literary Autonomy (1810–48)," "Territorial Literature (1848–1912)," and "Mexican-American Literature (1912–59)."

4. Leal, 78–79.
5. A *pocha* is a person of Mexican heritage who is living in the United States and who is seen as a traitor, culturally and linguistically, by a native-born Mexican.

WORKS CITED

Barthes, Roland. *Camera Lucida: Reflections on Photography*. Translated by Richard Howard. New York: Hill and Wang. 1981.

Cantú, Norma. *Canícula: Snapshots of a Girlhood en la Frontera*. Albuquerque: University of New Mexico Press, 1995.

———. "The Writing of *Canícula*: Breaking Boundaries, Finding Forms." In *Chicana Feminisms: A Critical Reader*, edited by Gabriela F. Arredondo et al., 97–108. Durham, NC: Duke University Press, 2003.

Jaramillo, Cleofas. *Romance of a Little Village Girl*. Albuquerque: University of New Mexico Press, 2000.

Klahn, Norma. "Literary (Re)Mappings: Autobiographical (Dis)Placements by Chicana Writers." In *Chicana Feminisms: A Critical Reader*, edited by Gabriela F. Arredondo et al., 114–45. Durham, NC: Duke University Press, 2003.

Leal, Luis. "Pre-Chicano Literature: Process and Meaning (1539–1959). In *Handbook of Hispanic Cultures in the United States: Literature and Art*, edited by Francisco Lomelí, 62–85. Houston: Arte Público Press, 1993.

Padilla, Genaro M. *My History, Not Yours: The Formation of Mexican-American Autobiography*. Madison: University of Wisconsin Press, 1993.

Pérez, Emma. *The Decolonial Imaginary: Writing Chicanas into History*. Bloomington: Indiana University Press, 1999.

Rebolledo, Tey Diana. "Introduction." *Romance of a Little Village Girl*. Albuquerque: University of New Mexico Press, 2000.

Rebolledo, Tey Diana, and Eliana S. Rivero. *Infinite Divisions: An Anthology of Chicana Literature*. Tucson: University of Arizona Press, 1993.

Reed, Maureen E. *A Woman's Place: Women Writing in New Mexico*. Albuquerque: University of New Mexico Press, 2005.

Sklodowska, Elzbieta, "La forma testimonial y la novelística de Miguel Barnet." *Revista/Review Interamericana* 12, no. 3 (1982): 379.

Sontag, Susan. *On Photography*. New York: Farrar, Straus, and Giroux, 1977.

A CHICANA DAUGHTER'S BLUES

Canícula: Snapshots of a Girlhood en la Frontera

MARÍA ESTHER QUINTANA MILLAMOTO

TRANSLATED BY ALDO ULISSES RESÉNDIZ RAMÍREZ, MARÍA ESTHER QUINTANA MILLAMOTO, AND ADRIAN ORTEGA

"In the photo, Mami squints in the sun, she is beautiful and angry, impatient. The weight of all of us on her shoulders."

—NORMA ELIA CANTÚ

IN THE PREFACE to Norma Elia Cantú's *Canícula: Snapshots of a Girlhood en la Frontera*, the narrator, who reveals herself as a foreign woman living in Spain, is in a room with her Spanish lover, looking through a sheaf of photos through which "she pieces together her lover's life."[1] Upon describing some pictures, she mentions the dinner he has cooked for her and the red wine whose color reminds her of her mother's blood-red roses, a mother who is thousands of miles away from the foreign woman.[2] In the ensuing scene, the narrator again recreates the past, but this time her mother replaces her lover as the person with whom she goes through a collection of pictures, these stuffed in a shoebox, a metonymic archive for the family's memories. In the first scene, the lover's association with a maternal figure—through the image of the roses and the reference to the dinner he has fixed—indicates a recurring urge in women, that is, the attempt to transcend the dissatisfaction of maternal love through a partner (Flax, 179). According to Jane Flax, women's desire for a romantic lover stems from their unfulfilled need for maternal nurturing, as well as their wish to return to the symbiotic stage of total identification with the mother (175).

However, in said scenes, replacing her mother with her lover is unsuccessful, as evidenced by the foreign woman's need to return to her birthplace, where she and her mother will take it upon themselves to relive memories through a series of photos that will set the story in motion. Cantú herself explains, "The story emerges from photographs, photographs through which, as Roland Barthes claimed, the dead return" (xii), a statement that, along with numerous references to the protagonist's longing for her maternal figures, suggests a melancholic state, the reluctance or inability to let go of a loved one or lost object (Freud 1966–74, 244).

In this essay I argue that in *Canícula*, the mother of her childhood becomes the object of melancholy for the protagonist/narrator, Azucena (or Nena, as she is endearingly called) as a result of Nena's inability to recover from losing the undivided attention and exclusive care of her mother because of the birth of her nine younger siblings. The text becomes a site of mourning within which Cantú attempts to overcome her dissatisfaction with maternal love as well as her grief over the death of Bueli, her maternal grandmother.[3]

By portraying the protagonist's desire to recover her maternal figures through writing, *Canícula* explores mother-daughter relationships in female development, a leitmotif in the so-called ethnic coming-of-age novel by female authors, as I have argued in my book *Madres e hijas melancólicas en seis novelas étnicas de crecimiento de autoras latinas* (*Melancholic Mothers and Daughters in Six Ethnic Coming-of-Age Novels by Latina Writers*). In this book, I identify the protagonists as melancholic daughters yearning for the mothers of their childhood and wishing to satisfy their unfulfilled desire for maternal love. I posit that the adult protagonists strive to recover their maternal figures (who become lost objects in their minds) by reimagining their relationship through writing, painting, and dancing. I called these narrative strategies, and the narratives themselves, "mourning sites" that allow the fictional daughters to overcome their dissatisfaction with maternal love (Quintana Millamoto 2014, 13). In *Madres e hijas melancólicas* I pursue Sigmund Freud's notion that melancholy is a sense of loss that comes from the disappearance of an object, either an ideal or a person, but I differ in his view of melancholy as a pathological condition that requires breaking away from the lost object through the work of mourning (Freud 1966–74, 249). On the contrary, I propose that in the corpus analyzed, the work of mourning has a different role in that it helps the protagonists reconnect with or reaffirm their links with maternal figures and thus reimagine new mother-daughter relationships.

I posit that in *Canícula*, as in the novels studied in my book, the protagonist/narrator channels the pain of losing the mother of her childhood by sublimating it through art. In this essay, I examine the relation between *Canícula* and Latina coming-of-age novels, underscoring the crucial role of the mother-daughter relationship in the formation of women's subjectivity. Drawing upon Lucy Wilson's argument that women tend to define themselves on the basis of their personal relationships as a result of the early bond between daughters and mothers (20), I propose that Cantú's sense of self emerges from her personal connections and that her longing for her past is motivated by all those experiences that she shared with her family members, friends and neighbors, many of whom are no longer alive.

CANÍCULA AND MELANCHOLY

In *Mourning and Melancholia* (originally published in 1917) Sigmund Freud establishes an essential point of reference whenever the topics of mourning and melancholia are discussed. Freud describes melancholia as an unconscious and sorrowful reaction to the loss of a loved one (1966–74, 245). He also maintains that while the subject of mourning is able to recover from a loss by investing psychic energy originally channeled into the lost object to another object, the melancholic subject is unable to psychologically detach from the beloved object (245). Quite to the contrary, the lost object gets incorporated into the ego of the melancholic subject through a narcissistic identification (251).

In *The Ego and the Id* (1927) Freud extrapolates his theory of melancholia to that of the Oedipus complex, positing the need for the boy to break away from the maternal figure (the lost object) while identifying with the father in order to become an individual. Paradoxically, Freud does not suggest that girls should necessarily be separated from the mother at the end of the oedipal phase but argues, rather, that women can continue to be identified with her (1927, 41).

Regarding the tendency for females to continue to identify with the mother figure, Julia Kristeva suggests that women's inability to commit psychic matricide makes them melancholic subjects (30). For her, achieving autonomy requires the psychological murder of the mother, followed by her recovery by means of a relationship (heterosexual, in the case of man, homosexual or heterosexual in women) or of intellectual or aesthetic productions, such as literary writing (27). In reality, what Kristeva proposes is to replace the mother with language or, in other words, to find consolation through language for the loss of the maternal object (Clewell, 51).

Juliana Schiesari opposes the idea of psychological matricide when establishing that the work of mourning is not a simple denial or detachment of the lost object but, rather, that it may help reshape the relationship of the ego with the beloved. Therefore, melancholia can serve to reconfigure the relationship between the mourner and the lost object, that is, with the maternal object (38). Accordingly, I posit that in *Canícula* pictures constitute a metonymic image of the psyche that preserves the memory of the maternal lost objects, and writing constitutes a mourning site that Cantú uses to revisit and reconfigure her bonds with her mother figures, as previously stated. She does so by deviating from Mami's and Bueli's roles of mothers and wives, as Cantú pursues a different path through education and writing.

Moreover, I argue that melancholia takes on another dimension as it channels a critical reconsideration of Cantú's personal and collective past as a Mexican American woman, in order to better understand her cultural history and its impact in her life. In relation to this, David Eng and David Kazanjian claim the epistemological potential of melancholy when they state that "melancholia's continued and open relation to the past finally allows us to gain new perspectives on and new understandings of lost objects" (quoted in Pérez-Torres, 201).

For Chicanos, these "lost objects" have to do with their silenced past and the need to transcend the exclusion of their individual and collective experiences from the Mexican and U.S. national imaginaries, which prompts Mexican Americans to articulate new identities: "This ultimate act of creation of a new self and consciousness transcends the act of (historical) silencing, and is articulated in contrast to that which has been silenced within one's own personal experience" (Velasco, 328).

As for individuals of Mexican descent in the United States, the annexation of Texas to the United States in 1848 created a rift in their history as well as the colonization of their culture: "Even if people there stayed in what is now a shared 'space,' it is through the imposition of the colonizing language and the accompanying literacy that the sense of place held by peoples of Mexican descent and embedded in cultural history, legend and language was (and continues to be) disrupted" (Klahn, 127).

One of the most dramatic ways to disrupt the lives of people of Mexican origin in the United States is to expel them from the country, as Azucena herself recounts, alluding to the deportation of many Texan-born Mexicans (including her grandfather) in 1935. The injustice described in the narrative emphasizes the vulnerability of the legal status of Azucena's Mexican-descended grandparents in the United States and explains the narrator's observations about her grandparents' feelings coming back years later: "And in 1948 crossing meant coming home, but not quite" (5).

While on the one hand *Canícula* sets out to reclaim the obliterated history of the Texan Mexican community, on the other hand it shows the need to reconcile the personal desires of the protagonist with the social and family values that hinder such desires. This issue is a central theme of so-called ethnic coming-of-age women's novels, that is, those stories—both fictional and autobiographical—produced by a writer belonging to the so-called minority groups and centered on a so-called ethnic protagonist (Feng, 15). In the following pages I analyze the connection between *Canícula* and female ethnic coming-of-age novels, particularly in their mutual focus on the pivotal role of women's socialization by their maternal figures. I also study Cantú's novel in relation to autobiography because the author herself associates her novel with this genre. Furthermore, the lack of clear boundaries between the two discourses in *Canícula* points to its hybrid nature: autobiography and fiction, text and image.

COMING-OF-AGE WOMEN'S ETHNIC NOVELS

By representing the ongoing psychological bonds between Azucena—the author's alter ego—and her mother figures, *Canícula* is associated with the female coming-of-age novel, as one of the prominent features of this narrative genre is the preservation of the mother and daughter's psychological ties (Abel, Hirsch, and Langland, 10). The early and ongoing bond between daughters and maternal figures results in a tendency for women to connect with others and define their identity, as well as their autonomy, on the basis of their personal relationships, more so than men (Wilson, 20). This relational orientation, which stems from a continued identification between mothers and daughters, is a fundamental difference between the coming-of-age women's novel and the male bildungsroman, in which the hero tends to break away from the feminine characters (Heller, 24).

While the community is crucial in the formation of women, social demands may be contrary to the personal desires of the protagonists in these novels, so the goal of growing up is to achieve a balance between societal/family rules and personal fulfillment (Quintana Millamoto, 19). In the case of coming-of-age ethnic female novels, the protagonist has to negotiate her individuality not only with the dominant society but also with her ethnic community. On the other hand, she challenges discriminatory stereotypes about her ethnic culture, which misrepresent her heritage and block her own fulfillment (Quintana Millamoto, 16). This process of simultaneous articulation of both personal identity and collective identity is characteristic of coming-of-age ethnic novels, in which the affirmation of the community goes hand in hand with the affirmation of the protagonist, as the reclaiming of cultural pride parallels the search for agency that the society in power denies the subjects considered as minorities (Japtok, 25).

Maria Karafilis asserts that unlike the traditional hero of the bildungsroman, who adopts the values of the dominant society, in many coming-of-age novels by women of color, the value system the protagonist decides to adopt is not that of the dominant culture but rather that defined by her own culture (65). While it is true that contemporary female minority writers portray the close ties between the protagonists and their native or heritage cultures, they also tend to criticize patriarchal patterns that oppress them within their communities. In this regard, Juan Velasco notes that although the community and its history occupy center stage in contemporary Chicano autobiographical writing, the authors simultaneously undermine the repressive cultural values of Mexican Americans:

> As the "I" expands into the total Self, a new text emerges—an autobiography that implies personal and communal, experiential and political knowledge, as well as the historical and the mythological dimensions of a common culture. As such, Chicana/o autobiographical discourse also allows for a new sort of strategic agency. This writing allows Chicanas, for example, to emphasize community, but also to replace inherited repressive values within the community with new options. (334)

Similarly, the authors of coming-of-age ethnic novels, especially about women, rebel against an identity prescribed by the community as they affirm women's right to fulfill individual goals (Japtok, 81). However, they also articulate a notion of ethnic solidarity while preserving their bonds with their ethnic communities: "Ethnic forms [of autobiographical fiction] thus communalize individualistic forms and are answering to different, more communal demands. The 'I' becomes a 'We'—if not, at least the work has to justify why this is not so, and even then the individualization takes place within an ethnic framework" (Japtok, 108).

In *Canícula*, Cantú foregrounds the idea that subjectivity emerges in a relational manner by making space for other characters while she separates the work from the individualistic tendency of traditional autobiography. This becomes apparent in the prologue to the novel, where the narrator, Cantú's alter ego, states that her story is not only hers but it's also the story of her family and her community (2).

Norma Klahn underscores the testimonial nature of what she calls "autobiographical fictions" such as *Canícula*, a narrative form inspired by verifiable events but presented as fiction. These texts foreground the intimate connection between the protagonist's development and her community in a way that the protagonist "cannot be seen outside the group or class situation that has historically marked her as marginal. It is from this culturally or politically rooted position that the narrator becomes the voice, her own, of a self who recollects her memories and those of other members of her community" (Klahn, 120).

Such emphasis on the community in *Canícula* deviates from the aesthetics of autobiographical writing, a "retrospective prose narrative . . . where the focus is his *individual* life, in particular *the story of his personality*" (Lejeune, 4; emphasis mine). In the following section I discuss how Cantú breaks away from expectations of traditional autobiography and the effects that cause such disruption as Azucena aims for a balance between self-determination and ethnic solidarity.

CANÍCULA AND AUTOBIOGRAPHY

In *Touching the World*, Paul Eakin postulates that autobiography's referential expectation is a real taboo theme in the poststructuralist theory that sees as outdated the "simplistic" notion of the "true" nature of this genre (2). Eakin describes Roland Barthes's famous statement "Do I not know that, *in the field of the subject*, there is no referent?" as paradigmatic of poststructuralist reviews of autobiography inasmuch as it illustrates the erosion of the concepts of representation and the subject in postmodernism (3). Despite Barthes's drastic statement, Eakin emphasizes the paradoxical nature of autobiography: on the one hand, part fiction, and on the other hand, referential. Eakin adds that even though *Roland Barthes by Roland Barthes* is the most fictional work by the French critic, "he does not shake free from the pull of reference" (23).

Like Eakin, Cantú underscores the ontological ambivalence of the autobiographical text by revealing, on the one hand, the fictional nature of what may seem as referential in *Canícula* and, on the other hand, the factual context of the author's fictional anecdotes: "In *Canícula*, the story is told through the photographs, and so what may appear to be autobiographical is not always so. On the other hand, many of the events are completely fictional, although they may be true in a historical context" (Cantú, xi). The combination of fiction, extratextual events, words, and photographs inspires her to categorize *Canícula* as a "fictional autobioethnography" (Cantú, xi).

Cantú seems to be aware that, as noted by Eakin, "the constraint of fact is not necessarily a limitation of artistic freedom, and conversely, the invention of fiction in autobiography may be undertaken in the pursuit of *biographical truth*" (Eakin, 31; emphasis mine). Cantú articulates a truth based on the performative act of writing to challenge, from its marginal position, the restrictions and historical misrepresentations that the dominant culture has imposed upon Chicanos (Velasco, 313).

The blurriness/ambiguity of the protagonist/narrator's identity achieved by a metafictional effect (for example, the discrepancy between the protagonist's signature and the name of the author) underlines the artifice and reworking of the narrated events while hampering the illusion of the sovereign subject in traditional autobiography. In fact, inasmuch as Cantú/Nena shares her role of the protagonist with her family, friends, and neighbors, the self that emerges in the story transcends the classical individualist autobiography, as Velasco maintains in reference to the autobiographies by Chicano authors, including Cantú: "The total Self recognizes the multiplicity of voices created in these works as a way of breaking away from the imprisonment of the small 'I'" (328). Therefore, *Canícula* represents an identity and autonomy forged in a specific context of relationships and molded after a complex set of social factors, such as gender, race, ethnicity, and class, among others—in other words, a relational autonomy (Mackenzie and Stoljar, 4). Lucy Wilson identifies *relational autonomy* as a distinctive feature of the ethnic female coming-of-age novels, in which "the protean 'other' [the protagonist] takes on a variety of shapes: mother, friend, lover, community. These narratives trace the expansion of the protagonist's consciousness as she recognizes and acknowledges the complexity of the world, defining herself in relation to it" (16).

Accordingly, Cantú challenges the concept of autonomy in the humanistic model as a "self-sufficient, independent, self-reliant, [and] self-realizing individual who directs his efforts towards maximizing his personal gains" (Mackenzie and Stoljar, 6). She does so by bringing to the fore a relational autonomy that takes into account family, community, and social responsibilities. At the same time, she undermines cultural racist, misogynistic, and classist hegemonic patterns as well as patriarchal Chicano values that restrict Chicanas' self-realization. Consequently, in *Canícula*, Azucena strives to defend her desire for self-realization while simultaneously defending the values and history that tie her to her Mexican American community.

AZUCENA'S TWO MOTHERS

Cantú's/Azucena's longing for maternal love is a widespread sentiment in patriarchal societies, as Adrienne Rich declares: "Few women growing up in patriarchal society can feel mothered enough; the power of our mothers, whatever their love for us and their struggles on our behalf, is too restricted" (Rich 1976, 243).

For Azucena, this lack of fulfillment in her relationship with Mami (as she endearingly calls her mother) in the infant stage is due to her mother's inability to devote her entire attention to her oldest daughter because she keeps having more children who also require her care. The narrator reveals her need for maternal nurturing when as a child she resorted to such ploys as pretending that she had lice so that her mother would caress her hair. Moreover, she shares with the reader her sadness at having lost her privileged place as the sole recipient of her mother's care. Significantly, in "Nena at Three" the narrator's melancholic state is conveyed by her description of herself as deeply saddened, "as if I were thinking of the pain, the loss, the burden that are to come" (54). It is revealing that the narrator immediately adds, "All those brothers and sisters, all the work, and the worry" (54). The authorial voice refers to the loss of exclusive maternal love and to reaching the end of childhood, which means taking on the responsibility for caring for her siblings early on. This section is paradigmatic of how Cantú uses writing as a mourning site to overcome the loss of the joyous time when she was an only child.

Cantú poignantly portrays the topic of dissatisfaction with maternal love in *Canícula* by referencing how Nena has to hand down some of her toys and clothes to her little brothers. In "Wooden Horse," the two-year-old girl is riding a toy horse made by her grandfather. Although the narrator says as the oldest she can have her pick of the toys made by him, she also notes that these are passed on to her younger siblings after a while. At the end of the vignette she recounts that on the day the picture of her riding a horse was taken, she suddenly burst into tears, and her mother came to comfort her. Although the adult narrator provides an explanation for the girl's tears (having picked up on her grandfather's inexplicable sadness), the association between her need to be comforted by Mami and the revelation of turning her most prized possessions over to her siblings is evident.

Her mother´s metonymical portrayal through different objects that at some point belonged to Nena is underscored in the vignette "China Poblana One," in which the narrator refers to the pain she felt when Mami told her she would have to pass her favorite *china poblana* dress (the traditional dress of the state of Puebla, considered the most iconic in Mexico) on to her sister: "Mommy tells Bueli that I'm growing so fast the costume won't fit by next year, and Dahlia will wear it to the parade. I cringe and want to cry, but I won't let the thought spoil the present" (39). The narrator replaces the lost dress/mother with words in an attempt to overcome the melancholia felt by the adult daughter, who has to come to terms with the symbolic separation from the mother of her childhood. Azucena's identification with Mami includes her sense of national allegiance, modeled after her mother's. In "China Poblana Two," the narrator ponders the ambiguous nature of national identity as she notes the contradiction between the dress, which symbolizes Mexican nationality, and the fact that Mami was born in the United States. This national identity that overflows geographical boundaries is previously underlined in "China Poblana One" by the fact that the protagonist wears her Mexican dress during a parade for George Washington, an iconic American hero. In "China Poblana Two," Azucena states that her mother did not go to Mexico until she was ten and could not speak Spanish because of the linguistic oppression of people of Mexican descent during Mami's youth. Despite her mother's upbringing in the United States, Mami's identification as Mexican complicates the idea of nationality linked to geographical origin. This concept is further compounded in the case of Azucena, who develops some ambivalence about her Mexican descent: although she has ties with Mexico through her family's background, she feels alienated when visiting her paternal grandmother's home in Monterrey because her cousins call her a *pocha*, that is, someone heavily influenced by North American white culture. The fact that Azucena does not feel fully accepted as a citizen in Mexico despite having a Mexican passport demonstrates that official/legal nationality does not mean cultural acceptance and explains why, in the case of the protagonist, this feeling of not belonging in Mexico triggers a sense of alienation. Rafael Pérez-Torres argues that a defining characteristic of Chicano discourse is a sense of national and linguistic destitution, described by the critic as a melancholic state: "The loss implicit in Chicano discourse within this frame is intensified by the sense of distance experienced by the orphaned Chicano left bereft of both a national fatherland and a native language. Betrayal and abandonment are compounded in the experiences of Mexican-descended populations north of the border" (199). In *Canícula*, the protagonist resents a dual sense of national abandonment because, although she feels a foreigner in Mexico, she also feels uncomfortable as a U.S. national because of the military and interventionist foreign policy of the United States and the corruption of local politicians.

The pictures of mother and daughter wearing the china poblana dress, which codifies Mexican culture, are presented as unreliable images inasmuch as they conceal the complexity of national identity among those living in the borderlands. Besides the association between the poblana dress and national identity, the similarity of dresses worn by Azucena and Mami points not only to their intimate connection but also to the traditional roles passed down from mother to daughter. This learning occurs on both a symbolic and a literal level: the protagonist learns to become a seamstress like Mami and at age twelve is able to earn enough to pay for her own expenses. Beyond the sense of economic independence that learning her mother's trade provides, Azucena's admiration for Mami as a seamstress and her willingness to learn Mami's trade convey Nena's identification with her mother during her adolescence. Furthermore, this vignette shows that despite Azucena's longing for maternal love, the bond between her and her mother has not been broken.

Her mother also taught her childcare, a task that Nena takes on from an early age, as well as cooking for the family when her mom is giving birth or is otherwise absent. In one paradigmatic example, the paternal grandmother and aunt visit the family while Azucena's parents are absent, and Azucena burns her hand when a hot pan turns over. Her parents severely scold Nena because she could have caused a serious accident, revealing the extent to which they expect their daughter to take care of her siblings. Her parents' high expectations and demands explain, in turn, Azucena's melancholy over the early loss of her childhood. The socialization of the protagonist can be described by what Mary Anne Ferguson describes as initiation "rituals of human relationships" (228). In the specific case of Mexican American women, their duties consist primarily of taking care of family and community, especially of men, and to perform the role of "a dutiful daughter" (Castillo, 131). Although Azucena does not complain about her role as a caretaker, in "Mexican Citizen" she says that during adolescence she worries that her breasts may not develop if she continues to hold her siblings in her arms; her obligations interfere with the ideal body image that she dreams of having as a woman.

Nena's maternal grandmother becomes her surrogate mother, thus compensating—albeit not entirely—for her longing for maternal love. One vignette emphasizes the closeness between Azucena and her grandmother during the girl's formative phase. In "First School" she narrates how she would cross the streets on her way to Señora Piña's house, her first unofficial school: "Bueli would watch—I could see her waving far, far away, as I turned to wave. . . . And at noon [we'd] repeat our ritual" (102). It is significant that Nena copies her grandmother's good-bye gesture. Bueli becomes the symbolic mirror of the protagonist, especially in regard to language, as Azucena's maternal grandmother is her first instructor of Spanish. In his autobiographical work *Roland Barthes by Roland Barthes*, Barthes refers to his mother tongue, French, as the umbilical cord that connects him to his mother (115). In *Canícula*, Spanish is for Azucena a symbolic umbilical cord that connects her with her maternal figures.

Bueli also passes her magical thinking on to her granddaughter, including the power of incantation to save one from danger. For example, in "The Flood," the protagonist crosses a river that has overflowed after a hurricane. To her grandmother's unusual prayer to keep her safe— "Vente Azucena, no te quedes" (Come Azucena, don't drown)—she replies by saying, "Ay voy, ay voy, ay voy" (I'm coming, I'm coming, I'm coming), "wanting to reassure her [grandmother] that [she's] not staying with the river spirits" (9). Magical thinking, such as the belief in spirits, and alternative medicine (especially *curanderismo*) bond Nena and Bueli while instilling a sense of cultural pride in the protagonist.[4] Through Nena, Cantú mourns for her maternal grandmother, as evident in "Bueli," in which the narrator relates to the reader how Bueli appeared to her on the night of the funeral: "She sat rocking back and forth on her sillón in the living room. She told me to take care of the baby. . . . I get up and check. Azalia's fine. But Mami's crying. We both cry, hug" (25).

Despite the deep connection felt by Nena with her two maternal figures, young Azucena is conflicted by, on the one hand, her desire to continue to identify with her maternal figures and, on the other hand, her need to separate from them. Nena reaches an epiphany when her boyfriend from Monterrey says he shall ask for her hand in marriage. While she had dreamed of a "Mexican life," she dreads the idea of playing the role of a housewife: "I freak out. . . I imagine myself married, with babies like Mami, and with a jolt realize I don't want that" (127). Azucena's words reveal her wish to escape the pattern Ferguson describes: "The pattern for the female novel of development has been largely circular, rather than spiral: women in fiction remain at home. Instead of testing their self-image through adventures in the outside world, they are initiated at home through learning the rituals of human relationships, so that they may replicate the lives of their mothers" (22).

Azucena's rebellion against the pattern of domesticity depicted in female coming-of-age novels is displayed when she disobeys her father's orders to get rid of a pair of shoes with "shiny rhinestones" that he regards as "shoes for a puta" (61). Nena gets to keep them with the help of her mother—who has paid for them with her own money—and challenges paternal authority as she wears them for her fifteenth-birthday photo. Her disobedience reveals her desire to escape the domestic model embodied by her mother, but at the same time Nena deeply admires Mami's self-sacrificing love. In "Tina Two," Azucena recounts Mami's near-death experience. Mami recalls spending a brief period of time in a very peaceful place, then choosing to return "because she didn't want her children to be orphans" (82) and because she wants to save Nena from having to take care of her younger siblings. This lesson of maternal sacrifice intensely moves the protagonist, as does the generosity of the mother who does not hesitate to share what little she has, even in times of great economic uncertainty.

Azucena's admiration for Mami and the closeness that she feels toward her is noted even in the closing vignette, "Martin High," in which the protagonist talks about high school, a time that marks adolescent daughters' impulse of emancipation from their mothers (Wieland, 215). Upon describing a picture in which she is posing with her classmates, Nena reminds the reader of her uninterrupted bond with Mami by alluding to her hand-knit sweater, a Christmas gift from her mother. On the other hand, Nena's desire for autonomy is evident when she alludes to the sense of freedom she feels as a result of being with her schoolmates and away from adults (131). Nena's relational autonomy is evident in this vignette as she connects it with her school friends, whose names and destinies she names one by one. Furthermore, Nena's tendency toward self-definition through her connections with others is underscored when the narrator switches from the first person singular "I" to the plural "us." She describes a wide variety of occupations and attitudes in the lives of her former classmates:

> All of us, the studious and the lazy; the gay ones and the straight ones; and the privileged and the disenfranchised . . . become lawyers, drug dealers, architects, doctors, teachers, wheelers and dealers, employers, unemployed, employees, managers, secretaries. . . . We are victims, perpetrators, embezzlers, philanthropists, humanitarians, politicians, healers, hunters, watercolorists, musicians. . . . Some of us remember, some of us forget. (131)

Azucena's perspective offers a much more heterogeneous vision of the Mexican-American border than that offered by the media of the hegemonic culture, which portray the border as a war zone populated by dangerous people and thus as a threat to national security (Velasco, 313). Moreover, "Martin High" conveys Cantú's melancholy for "the joy, the happiness of youth" (131), which she tries to recover through memory and literary language.

In the end, Azucena/Norma Elia Cantú learns the lesson of generosity from her mother and grandmother. Full of purpose, she returns to be the voice of her generation; to show that she has forgotten neither her family nor her community; to tell us that she hasn't forgotten who she is or where she comes from; and to remind us that the text, like the melancholic, preserves our loved ones and our mutual past while it saves our memories from oblivion.

NOTES

I would like to express my deepest gratitude to Adrian Ortega and Dianna Mena for their valuable feedback to improve this essay. *¡Muchas gracias a los dos!*

1. Norma Elia Cantú, *Canícula: Snapshots of a Girlhood en la Frontera* (Albuquerque: University of New Mexico Press, 1995), xii. All subsequent quotes from this novel come from this edition.
2. *Canícula*, 1.
3. In my book *Madres e hijas melancólicas en seis novelas étnicas de crecimiento de autoras latinas* (Pamplona: Instituto Benjamin Franklin de Estudios Norteamericanos and Universidad de Alcalá, 2014), I coined the term *mourning site* to describe different artistic forms (such as dance, painting, and writing) that help women to overcome melancholy for the mother. The novels examined in my book are *Silent Dancing: A Partial Remembrance of a Puerto Rican Childhood* by Judith Ortiz Cofer, *Caramelo; or, Puro Cuento* by Sandra Cisneros, *In the Namé of Salomé* by Julia Alvarez, *The Conquest* by Yxta Maya Murray, *Soledad* by Angie Cruz, and *Peel My Love Like an Onion* by Ana Castillo.
4. However, it is important to note that the belief in magical practices is not always accepted by Azucena; for example, when her father goes to Mexico to consult with a curandera, both Nena and her mother doubt the healer can cure him. It is significant that Nena trusts in the local curanderas recommended by her grandmother but distrusts those who are unknown to her family. This reaffirms the importance of the Texan community as an extended family for Azucena and thus as a network in which the youth can trust.

WORKS CITED

Abel, Elizabeth, Marianne Hirsch, and Elizabeth Langland, eds. *The Voyage In: Fictions of Female Development*. Lebanon, NH: University Press of New England, 1983.

Barthes, Roland. *Roland Barthes by Roland Barthes*. Translated by Richard Howard. New York: Farrar, Strauss, and Giroux, 1977.

Cantú, Norma Elia. *Canícula: Snapshots of a Girlhood en la Frontera*. Albuquerque: University of New Mexico Press, 1995.

Castillo, Ana. *Massacre of the Dreamers: Essays on Xicanisma*. Albuquerque: University of New Mexico Press, 1994.

Clewell, Tammy. "Mourning Beyond Melancholia: Freud's Psychoanalysis of Loss." *Journal of the American Psychoanalytic Association* 52, no. 1 (2004): 43–67.

Eakin, Paul John. *Touching the World: Reference in Autobiography*. New Jersey: Princeton University Press, 1992.

Feng, Pin-chia. *The Female Bildungsroman by Toni Morrison and Maxine Hong Kingston: A Postmodern Reading*. New York: Peter Lang, 1997.

Ferguson, Mary Anne. "The Female Novel of Development and the Myth of Psyche." In *The Voyage In: Fictions of Female Development*, edited by Elizabeth Abel, Marianne Hirsch, and Elizabeth Langland, 228–43. Lebanon, NH: University Press of New England, 1983.

Flax, Jane. "The Conflict Between Nurturance and Autonomy in Mother-Daughter Relationships and Within Feminism." *Feminist Studies* 4, no. 2 (1978): 171–89.

Freud, Sigmund. *Mourning and Melancholia: The Standard Edition of the Complete Works of Sigmund Freud*. Translated by James Strachey. Vol. 14, *On the History of the Psycho-Analytic Movement, Papers on Metapsychology and Other Works (1914–1916)*, 243–58. London: Hogarth Press and the Institute of Psycho-Analysis, 1966–1974.

———. *The Ego and the Id*. Translated by Joan Riviere. London: Hogarth Press and the Institute of Psycho-Analysis, 1927.

Freud, Sigmund, Gerhard Fichtner, and Ludwig Binswanger. *The Sigmund Freud–Ludwig Binswanger Correspondence, 1908–1938*. Translated by Arnold J. Pomerans and Thomas Roberts. New York: Other Press, 2003.

Heller, Dana A. *The Feminization of Quest-Romance: Radical Departures*. Austin: University of Texas Press, 1990.

Japtok, Martin. *Growing Up Ethnic: Nationalism and the Bildungsroman in African American and Jewish American Fiction*. Iowa City: University of Iowa Press, 2005.

Karafilis, Maria. "Crossing the Borders of Genre: Revisions of the *Bildungsroman* in Sandra Cisneros's *The House on Mango Street* and Jamaica Kincaid's *Annie John*." *Journal of the Midwest Modern Language Association* 31, no. 2 (Winter 1998): 63–78.

Klahn, Norma. "Literary (Re)Mappings: Autobiographical (Dis)Placements by Chicana Writers." In *Chicana Feminisms: A Critical Reader*, edited by Gabriela F. Arredondo et al., 114–45. Durham, NC: Duke University Press, 2003.

Kristeva, Julia. *Sol negro: Depresión y melancolía*. Translated by Mariela Sánchez Urdaneta. Caracas: Monte Ávila Editores Latinoamericana, 1997.

Lejeune, Philippe. *On Autobiography*. Edited by Paul John Eakin, translated by Katherine Leary. Minneapolis: University of Minnesota Press, 1989.

Mackenzie, Catriona, and Natalie Stoljar. Introduction to *Relational Autonomy: Feminist Perspectives on Autonomy, Agency, and the Social Self*, edited by Catriona Mackenzie and Natalie Stoljar, 3–34. New York: Oxford University Press, 2000.

Pérez-Torres, Rafael. *Mestizaje: Critical Uses of Race in Chicano Culture*. Minneapolis: University of Minnesota Press, 2006.

Quintana Millamoto, María Esther. *Madres e hijas melancólicas en seis novelas étnicas de crecimiento de autoras latinas*. Pamplona: Instituto Benjamin Franklin de Estudios Norteamericanos and Universidad de Alcalá, 2014.

Rich, Adrienne. *Of Woman Born: Motherhood as Experience and Institution*. New York: Norton, 1976.

Schiesari, Juliana. *The Gendering of Melancholia: Feminism, Psychoanalysis, and the Symbolics of Loss in Renaissance Literature*. Ithaca, NY: Cornell University Press, 1992.

Velasco, Juan. "Automitografías: The Border Paradigm and Chicana/o Autobiography." *Biography* 27, no. 2 (2004): 313–38.

Wieland, Christina. *The Undead Mother: Psychoanalytic Explorations of Masculinity, Femininity, and Matricide*. London: Karnac, 2000.

Wilson, Lucy. *In Due Season: Essays on Novels of Development by Caribbean Women Writers*. Lanham, MD: University Press of America, 2008.

WORD IMAGES

An Interview with Norma Elia Cantú

GABRIELLA GUTIÉRREZ Y MUHS

GABRIELLA GUTIÉRREZ Y MUHS: What changes have occurred in your life lately?

NORMA ELIA CANTÚ: My life is a series of changes . . . that is the only constant. And while for the first twenty-six years of my life I lived in the same town—Laredo, Texas—I have since moved various times: to Kingville, Texas; Lincoln, Nebraska; Madrid, Spain; Santa Barbara, California; Washington, DC; [and] San Antonio, Texas, where I helped build the PhD program in English with an emphasis in Latina/o literature, with moves back to Laredo in between. After retiring from UTSA [the University of Texas at San Antonio], I ended up in Missouri building an undergraduate Latina/Latino studies program.

Among the many changes that moving to a new place brings is the realization that life takes you where you may not have ever imagined you'd be. For me that is Missouri. I've learned that we must keep going along our path, our life, to the next phase, and now mine happens to be in the Midwest.

GUTIÉRREZ Y MUHS: Tell us about your new life teaching at the University of Missouri–Kansas City.

CANTÚ: Yes, it is truly a new life. My position is professor of Latina/o studies and English. We are building a new program, so the first two years have been

---

This interview with Norma Elia Cantú was conducted in 2014.

all about establishing a presence and designing new courses. We got the minor in Latina/o studies approved, and now we are working on the next phase. It will take years to get the program where it should be, because while the demographics and history of the population in the area make you think things should already be way ahead, the truth is that they are not at all where they should be. The work is challenging.

GUTIÉRREZ Y MUHS: I saw in your blog that you're working on a new book about the Camino de Santiago. How many times have you gone on pilgrimage? How did the decision to turn your blog into a manuscript come about?

CANTÚ: I have walked the full Camino Francés once and the last one hundred kilometers once. I hope to walk the long one again when I am seventy, if not earlier. It is a long story, how I came to walk it. In 1979, when I was a grad student and first went to Spain on a Fulbright, I heard about the pilgrimage and wanted to make the walk, but I didn't have the money or the time; I was under pressure to finish my research for my dissertation. A few years later, when I had a second Fulbright, this time to study fiestas, I thought I would make the Camino, but again I just didn't have the time. I tried again in the late 1990s, but Elvia, who was going with me, sprained her ankle, and we ended up spending the time I had allocated for walking the Camino in Santiago [de Compostela], where I wrote stories for "Champú," the novel I am still working on. In 2004, when my friend Rebecca Vela went, I really wanted to go, but work and family commitments prevented that. Finally, in 2010, when I had a sabbatical, I made the transformative walk with Becky, in the winter. We started walking in St. Jean Pied de Port on December 17, 2010, and arrived in Santiago on February 1, 2011. It was on that walk that I realized I could do anything I set my mind to doing—it may be a little late, but it's still an important lesson.

I have to tell you that it was never my intention to write about the Camino. When I was packing I didn't even want to take a camera, but my sisters Elsa and Elvia got me a tiny camera, and I couldn't refuse. When I was on the path, on one bright winter day with snow everywhere, I came upon a bright blue mechanical pencil neatly placed on a white snowdrift. I remember standing in front of it and looking at it and sensing or hearing a voice that said, "If you pick it up you have to write about the Camino." So I picked it up and began keeping a log of where we stayed and what we were eating and such. Eventually it became more of a journal. A year later, I wrote a blog [elcaminoayearlater.wordpress.com], and last year I began turning it into a book. I am not quite finished with it, as I am still undecided about all that needs to go into the book, but I do know I will finish it and publish it. After all, it is a commitment I made when I picked up that bright blue pencil.

GUTIÉRREZ Y MUHS: What are you reading lately, and specifically what Latin@ authors are you reading?

CANTÚ: Well, I just finished Lucha Corpi's collection of autobiographical essays, *Confessions of a Book Burner*. Before that I read Michael Nava's *City of Palaces*, and earlier in the summer I read *At Night We Walk in Circles* by Daniel Alarcón. I also found myself reading Ire'ne Lara Silva's collection of short stories and several poetry books, mostly by CantoMundistas, which I picked up in Austin at this year's CantoMundo. I am always reading unpublished manuscripts too—for presses or for friends. Laura Pérez's collection is by my bed right now.

GUTIÉRREZ Y MUHS: I know you are very involved with CantoMundo. In fact, you were one of the founders. Who are your favorite Latin@ poets?

CANTÚ: That's a hard one . . . I love them all! No, seriously, there are so many fresh and lovely new voices—Laurie Ann Guerrero, J. Michael Martinez, Carmen Giménez Smith, Eduardo Corral, Celeste Guzmán [Mendoza], Natalia Treviño, Pablo [Miguel] Martínez, Deborah Paredez, and many, many more. I also love Benjamin Alire Sáenz's and Ire'ne Lara Silva's work.

GUTIÉRREZ Y MUHS: How has the publication of *Canícula* impacted you professionally?

CANTÚ: Wow! Another hard one to answer. I can't begin to tell you how much that little book has changed my life professionally. I have been working in academia for more than thirty years, but when *Canícula* was published is when I began to get noticed as a scholar and as a writer. It just changed everything. I started to see myself as a writer who teaches instead of a teacher who writes. Also, I can't begin to describe the satisfaction that comes with knowing that others are reading your words and that it makes a difference in their lives—although in my community of Laredo, Texas, not everyone knows about *Canícula*, even though on some level they were the ones I wanted most as an audience.

GUTIÉRREZ Y MUHS: When is your next novel coming out?

CANTÚ: That depends on when I finish it—it is still in draft form! Then it takes a while to get the press to move on it, but if all goes well, I suspect it will be in

2018. The twentieth anniversary edition of *Canícula* came out in 2015, with some added pictures and stories, so I have worked on both books until now. My novel [manuscript] "Cabañuelas," which follows *Canícula*, is with readers from one of the presses I work with. I intended to work on "Hair Matters" first, but you know how it is, ya sabes como son las cosas.

GUTIÉRREZ Y MUHS: Chicana writers have long contributed to the expansion of subjectivity with the representation of Latin@ characters, especially in regards to intersectionality, sexuality, and gender. Can you tell us how the characters in your work contribute to this expanding subjectivity in literature?

CANTÚ: I wish I could say that I purposefully set out to expand subjectivity, but I don't necessarily think about such things when I am writing. It really just happens because my characters are based on real people and what happens to real people, so subjectivities emerge from the lived experiences of the people I write about, mostly men and women along the U.S.-Mexico borderlands. It is indeed a pleasant surprise to have the characters engage in such questions of identity and of the oppressions they face just because they happen to live on the border, or happen to be female, or happen to be lesbians.

GUTIÉRREZ Y MUHS: Could you talk to us about the plot of "Champú, or Hair Matters"?

CANTÚ: There is not a traditional plot line à la Freytag's Pyramid, if that is what you mean by plot. It is a very fluid text with various story lines and connected characters that are living at a specific time and in a specific place: Laredo, Texas, in the early twenty-first century. They contend with the vagaries of everyday life on the border, with both humor and stoicism. I am just amazed at how people survive, how they manage to still have hope and believe in the future, when they exist in such dismal and oppressive circumstances. Violence is at the core of the book, but it is a generic violence, not just the kind perpetuated by the drug cartels or the gay-bashing haters; it is in the poverty, it is in the lack of access to quality education. Somewhere I wrote that poverty is a kind of violence, and I really believe that. So are poor schools and unsanitary conditions, such as contaminated water sources. Poverty is a violence that kills as surely as the guns and knives we usually associate with it. The endemic violence wrought by years and years of living under a political machine and a militarized zone makes the border susceptible to a "ni modo" response, as people are apt to accept what is and shrug.

GUTIÉRREZ Y MUHS: Tell us about your role as a folklorist.

CANTÚ: I love my folklore work. It began really early, I think when I went along with my grandmother Celia Becerra Ramón to cut the herbs for teas, for healing. She taught me about healing herbs but also told me folktales and stories. So when I was in college—I went to night classes and worked during the day at an office—I found out that it was a field of study. My mentor, Allen Briggs, first introduced me to the notion of folklore studies, and I presented under his tutelage at a meeting of the Texas Folklore Society. Then in the nineties I finally joined the American Folklore Society [AFS], and when I was inducted into the Fellows of the Society it was a milestone for me, as it recognized the work I had been doing practically all my academic life—my dissertation was a semiotic analysis of a folk play, *la pastorela*, and I am currently engaged in a research project with some of my undergraduate students to document and survey the traditional practices of the Mexicano/Latino community in Kansas City. Folklore is my passion, you could say. I know that for many Chicana/o scholars it is a bad word, because they don't want us to focus on the traditions lest they reinforce stereotypes, but really, if we don't do the work, then outsiders will do it, and you have a more likely scenario that stereotypes will be perpetuated.

GUTIÉRREZ Y MUHS: When did you start being identified as such? How does your work as a folklorist complement your role as a scholar and writer?

CANTÚ: I began seeing myself as a folklorist when I joined AFS. I jokingly call myself an undocumented folklorist, as I do not have a degree in folklore, nor have I ever taken courses or trained in the discipline. My work as a folklorist definitely complements my work as a scholar and as a creative writer. I suppose it is because the research I do as a folklorist informs so much of my academic and creative work that I can claim the "autobioethnographic" nature of my work. I do not necessarily segregate these aspects of the work I do. When I write a poem it is just as likely to draw from my research with the community as from the more scholarly work. I see my role as following in the footsteps of many other writers, including the *folcloristas* from New Mexico, such as Aurora Lucero-White [Lea], and from Texas, like Jovita González, along with writers whose work is infused with traditional cultures, such as Josefina Niggli and Américo Paredes.

GUTIÉRREZ Y MUHS: I saw that you were listed as a juror for the prestigious Neustadt International Prize for Literature for 2012 and that you nominated

Elena Poniatowska, Mexico's most important *femme de lettres*, for the award. What motivated you to nominate Poniatowska?

CANTÚ: Elena has always been for me an enigma. She's a brilliant writer and has a huge following, yet not many have recognized her brilliance as a writer until recently—she received the Premio Cervantes. I think Mexican writers are often ignored or not recognized for their art. I am currently translating a poet from Monterrey, Minerva Margarita Villarreal Rodríguez, a wonderful poet whom no one in the States knows about yet. She has won several major awards in Mexico.

Elena is the most important femme de lettres, and while I was a little upset that she didn't get the Neustadt, I am happy that an Indian writer received the award [Rohinton Mistry, in 2012]; it is always so difficult to judge. Lately I have served on the Tejas Foco Premio committee, and I have in the past judged poetry contests as well, and while it is wonderful to read all the great works that are submitted, it is agonizing to have to select just ONE for the award. I think I will stop being a judge, because it causes such distress! After all, who am I to judge who is the best? We are all writing the best way we know how, and whether we win prizes or not is not the issue, although the award or prize means more sales, of course. I truly believe that the passion for the work is reward enough. I feel blessed that I can write, that I can share my visions and dreams with others.

PART II

CANÍCULA TEACHING METHODOLOGIES

CANTÚ'S DECOLONIAL IMAGINATION THROUGH THE LOOKING GLASS

ALDO ULISSES RESÉNDIZ RAMÍREZ

"We're reclaiming the agency of reinscribing, taking off their inscriptions and reinscribing ourselves, our own identities, our own cultures."

—GLORIA ANZALDÚA, *INTERVIEWS/ENTREVISTAS*

NORMA E. CANTÚ'S *Canícula: Snapshots of a Girlhood en la Frontera* takes its title from the colloquial Spanish term given to the scorching, sun-laden summer days that overshadow the cotton-picking season in the South Texas farmlands. Mostly written during such dog days in 1993, which marked the cusp of a five-hundred-year era of indigenous resistance to European invasion and unrelenting neocolonization, *Canícula* came into existence during a momentous time that witnessed a renewed call for decolonization and the shedding of internalized, self-destructive colonial practices, a battle cry that came from multiple fronts and across many native tribes and nations the world over. *Canícula* should thus be read in such a light, as a reinscription of Chicana feminist narrative—on such a historical occasion, the renowned queer theorist Gloria E. Anzaldúa, a fellow Tejana and contemporary of Cantú, would indeed summon writers to do as much—in an effort to uproot hegemonic discourses of oblivion and contribute to the ever-expansive Chicana decolonial imagination.

In this journey through her self-described fictional autobioethnography, photography becomes Cantú's primary medium for recollection of herstory. A tool of colonial documentation and modern-day imperial and white supremacist cultural voyeurism that often serves to reduce "local," "native," and "ethnic" communities to nothing more than still subjects for Western/White curiosity and consumption, family pictures and portraits in Cantú's hands turn the settler-colonial gaze on its head. No longer the outsider looking in but now the insider looking out, Cantú in *Canícula* makes no claim to the universal; instead, the writing clings to the image metaphors of the author's childhood set against the backdrop of the Laredo borderlands.

With its use of imagery, *Canícula* allows for what Barton and Hamilton (2000) describe as the process through which "people can be incorporated into the literacy practices of others without reading or writing a single word." Indeed, the book guides the reader through what Toni Morrison once referred to as "visual literacy," opening up the possibility for literacy to be experienced through visual signs, colors, and shapes. This is the way in which many children first learn to understand the world and, in fact, the way that those who are denied the ability to read and write use their senses and their social and cultural systems of representation, whether individually or collectively, to "do" literacy.

Cantú not only gives the reader a set of vignettes or interconnected tales but masterfully spins the thread of her *historias*, that is, stories that tell histories, like in Spanish. Indeed, she does so by reinscribing the story of Azucena, the child protagonist, and bringing her family to the forefront of the annals of Texas history, thereby correcting a facsimile error, the product not of omission but of historical exclusion. *Canícula* works to reinforce positive self-concepts of girlhood and Mexican-ness on both sides of the border while simultaneously contradicting prevailing negative images and stereotypical representations.

It is difficult to agree on one single definition of what is or what constitutes cultural authenticity, particularly as it relates to multicultural literature. However, there is a prevailing belief that the best way to describe it is that authenticity cannot be defined but "you know it when you see it" (Bishop 2003). Chicana writers, in their roles as insiders, have an understanding of issues of power within and outside their communities; yet no one writer can represent an entire group of people or any particular experience (Botelho and Rudman 2009). Moreover, *Canícula* can be positioned in the tradition of *testimonios*. Much in line with Chicana/Latina epistemologies, "there is a tradition in Latin American countries known as testimonio. It is the responsibility of those who survive the struggle for freedom to give testimony. To tell the story in order to keep alive the memory of those who died" (Álvarez 2002).

By virtue of its interdisciplinary approach to visual storytelling, *Canícula* can serve as a tool for engaging in critical pedagogy, one that goes beyond its use in the discipline of Chicana and Latina literature but itself is the product of sociological and anthropological inquiry through which the readers may critically analyze racialized constructions of gender and sexuality and engage in discussions of how Chicanas have been historically, socially, and discursively shaped. Anchoring the text in a working-class ethos intrinsic to Mexicana and Chicana aesthetic, *Canícula* not only asks questions but demands answers, not a fortuitous feat, since "the interrogation of class alongside race and gender is a direct attack on U.S. power relations" (Botelho and Rudman 2009).

The bilingualism in *Canícula*, everywhere from its title to the unapologetic use of nonitalicized Spanish words, some in nonstandard varieties, disrupts English language hegemony and makes for an important resource in the bilingual classroom. Similar to the experiences of Azucena, Anzaldúa (1987) describes her experience growing up in the Texas borderlands and what she calls the "linguistic terrorism" to which she was subjected because of the prejudice she experienced toward her first language, Spanish. She explains, "In childhood we are told that our language is wrong. Repeated attacks on our native tongue diminish our sense of self. The attacks continue throughout our lives." Azúcena's experience is not unlike that of other Spanish speakers who used to be barred from—and, in fact, punished for—speaking Spanish at school and in other public settings.

The narrative in *Canícula* makes use of *translanguaging*, or the language practice that characterizes bilinguals whereby they make use of their complete linguistic repertoire, strategically selecting and deploying linguistic features in more than one language to communicate effectively and "make sense of their bilingual worlds" (García 2009). This dynamic, hybrid, and simultaneous type of meaning construction is not the effort of the sole bilingual speaker; rather, as aptly captured in the book, it involves entire families and communities who are engaged in the process. The linguistic repertoires and language practices of the characters in *Canícula* cut across a cross-section of geographic, social, and stylistic variation, styles, and registers, at each juncture indexing a particular social identity. This is accomplished in the face of a number of challenges, since Spanish bilinguals have to contend with linguistic policing not only by English speakers in white spaces but oftentimes also in Spanish-dominated spaces among members of their own linguistic and ethnic group.

The potential for using *Canícula* to introduce translanguaging as a critical pedagogical tool opens the door for teachers to draw from language varieties, styles, and registers distributed across separate languages in order to engage in a strategic meaning-making process and to facilitate students' learning. Introducing translanguaging in the classroom through bilingual texts and allowing for the free linguistic expression of students solidifies the notion that students are there to add a standard variety of Spanish, an academic register, and literacy practices to the rich linguistic repertoire they already possess, expanding their vocabularies, registers, and styles. Translanguaging then allows learners to develop their own linguistic systems, taps into students' "funds of knowledge," and creates an "asset-based" approach to their learning (García 2009). In this process, regardless of their background, teachers of Spanish bilinguals can learn from and welcome into their classrooms their students' linguistic and cultural knowledge and the expression of their home and community culture. By making students aware of their rich linguistic knowledge, translanguaging can be linguistically, socially, and academically empowering.

The translation of *Canícula* into Spanish, which Cantú herself executed, makes for a different read with the inclusion of pictures that do not appear in the English text. This allows for both versions of the book to be used in fields such as translation studies and comparative literature, since there are only a handful of contemporary works of Chicana literature that have been translated by the author herself.

Beyond linguistics and bilingual education, the chapters in the second part of this anthology also speak to various other uses of *Canícula* in the classroom, particularly in cultural and ethnic studies. Indeed, in *Canicula*, Cantú inscribes the borderlands Tejana experience into the Chicana literary canon simultaneously giving us a critical pedagogical tool with which to be actively engaged in decolonial epistemologies.

WORKS CITED

Anzaldúa, Gloria E. *Borderlands/La Frontera: The New Mestiza*. San Francisco: Aunt Lute Books, 1987.

———. *Interviews/Entrevistas*. Edited by AnaLouise Keating. New York: Routledge, 2000.

Álvarez, Julia. *Before We Were Free*. New York: Alfred Knopf, 2002.

Barton, David, and Mary Hamilton. "Literacy Practices." In *Situated Literacies: Reading and Writing in Context*, edited by David Barton, Mary Hamilton, and Roz Ivanič, 7–15. London: Routledge, 2000.

Bishop, Rudine Sims. "Reframing the Debate about Cultural Authenticity?" In *Stories Matter: The Complexity of Cultural Authenticity in Children's Literature*, edited by Dana L. Fox and Kathy G. Short, 25–37. Urbana, IL: National Council of Teachers of English, 2003.

Botelho, María José, and Masha Kabakow Rudman. *Critical Multicultural Analysis of Children's Literature: Mirrors, Windows, and Doors*. New York: Routledge, 2009.

García, Ofelia. *Bilingual Education in the 21st Century: A Global Perspective*. Malden, MA, and Oxford: Blackwell/Wiley, 2009.

THE HIDDEN CURRICULUM OF *CANÍCULA*

Critical Educational Lessons in Becoming a Mujer

AURORA CHANG

"I must learn to keep secrets otherwise Papagrande will be angry. I listen and obey, learn the lessons of growing up."

—NORMA ELIA CANTÚ (23)

SPEAKING SECRETS

IN THE QUOTE ABOVE, Azucena captures the intense and commonsensical expectations of a Latinita's paradigm regarding the construction of female knowledge—or what it means to become a *mujer en la frontera*. "Keeping secrets," as Deena J. González (1998) notes, "is never easy" (46), yet it seems to become the key to avoiding unwanted emotions, like anger, and simultaneously pleasing the patriarchy—or at least keeping it at bay. Even beyond keeping secrets to placate others in her life, Azucena learns that there are consequences to speaking those secrets, such as being shamed, creating conflict, appearing *atravesada*, and/or positioning oneself as antiauthoritian. Such consequences have a price that Azucena learns to pay; in the process, she navigates the world of *niñez*, the school of critical educational lessons.

Like Azucena of *Canícula*, I grew up in a family of secrets and *apariencias*—everything was about our appearance to the outside world, *el ¿qué dirán?*, what would others say. As a young girl, I learned to keep certain things to myself, mainly the stuff of female desire, but as the years passed I began to feel compelled to express myself. Speaking my secrets (González, 46) was like setting a bomb off in the already fragile walls that seemingly protected our household; that which was once hidden—the unspoken rules, the insidious expectations, and the constant denial of female desire—was now exposed for the world to see. This was considered the behavior of a "bad" female, the equivalent of a *malcriada*. However, before I spoke my secrets, I learned how to keep them. Or, perhaps more accurately, I was taught to keep secrets, quietly absorbing the alchemy of female longing, daughterly appropriateness, and family image—an inculcation that required a nuanced dance.

In many ways, Azucena engages in this dance, intimately intertwined in the work of what Sandra K. Soto (2010) calls mastering the "de-mastery of desire" (2), what I recognize as that expertise fostered by the painful internalization of separating the flesh from the spirit, a visceral comprehension that desire is something to be tamed and disciplined, not explored or celebrated. In this essay, I argue that Azucena illustrates the value and heaviness of the hidden, and that within the seemingly quotidian and minute interactions of everyday life Azucena learns the always consequential and often bittersweet lessons of becoming a mujer. Drawing from Chicana feminist epistemology, I demonstrate how Azucena utilizes her community cultural wealth to develop familial and resistant capital, ultimately utilizing the experiences of her niñez to inform her notions of and foster her fortitude in becoming a mujer. I conclude by discussing potential implications of using this type of work in classroom settings for the purposes of teaching and learning.

CONCEPTUAL FRAMEWORK

In this chapter, I combine the educational concepts of hidden curriculum and community cultural wealth to frame the literary analysis and explain the implications of Azucena's experiences. It is important to frame these vignettes in an educational context for a variety of reasons. First, social science scholars often neglect literary pieces or replace them with nonfiction in curricula to assert some type of mythological objectivity in teaching young people. I believe that Azucena's narratives are accessible, rich, and laden with meaning—literary opportunities to engage youth in the enterprise of learning. Second, and perhaps more importantly, my experience as an educator, as well as the existing research, has taught me that when a teacher centers her instruction on the lived experiences of her students, students are more likely to respond positively, creatively, and deeply. *Canícula* is an ideal vehicle for effectively engaging students in the practice of self-reflection, demonstrating as it does the importance of personal experience and of using one's voice to tell her truth. Indeed, *Canícula* embodies the intent of culturally responsive teaching.

Culturally responsive teaching (Gay 2002, 113) treats students as whole children, using their cultural knowledge, prior experiences, and performance styles in order to make learning effective for them. Gay notes that culturally responsive teaching "argues that explicit knowledge about cultural diversity is imperative to meeting the educational needs of ethnically diverse students" (107). Culturally responsive teaching is also based on the assumptions that racism creates distorted and negative images of the cultures, histories, and possibilities of people of color and that culturally responsive classrooms can become a space where detrimental images are deconstructed and replaced by positive cultural and self-affirmations. In selecting an appropriate conceptual framework for analyzing these vignettes, I knew that it was important to situate it in terms of utility for teacher practice as well as in terms of larger sociocultural issues of the meaning behind becoming a mujer. As a researcher, I can expound on conceptual ideas, but it is equally if not more important for me to provide real-life applications to teaching and learning; using *Canícula* as a central curricular text allows me to do just that.

HIDDEN CURRICULUM

While we tend to view curriculum in narrow terms (the fallacy that it exists mainly within the four walls of a classroom), I also draw from the concept of hidden curriculum, defined as that which is implicitly but effectively taught in schools and is not usually discussed in an explicit manner yet is understood as important (Apple 2000, 29), to illustrate how girlhood as depicted in *Canícula* shapes the understood and sometimes unspoken rules of becoming a mujer. While the concept of hidden curriculum has been used primarily within the context of schooling and specifically within the parameters of educational institutions, I utilize it within the context of community to illustrate the ways in which Azucena gains community cultural wealth (Yosso 2005, 77) embedded in a certain Chicana feminist sensibility. And while hidden curriculum is usually framed in a negative light, the hidden curriculum of *Canícula* is not so straightforward. As Michael W. Apple notes:

> The hidden curriculum in schools serves to reinforce basic rules surrounding the nature of conflict and its uses. It posits a network of assumptions that, when internalized by students, establishes the boundaries of legitimacy. This process is accomplished not so much by explicit instances showing the negative value of conflict, but by nearly the total absence of instances showing the importance of intellectual and normative conflict in subject areas. The fact is that these assumptions are obligatory for the students, since at no time are the assumptions articulated or questioned. By the very fact that they are tacit, their potency is enlarged. (29)

The hidden curriculum in *Canícula* reinforces the basic rules about becoming a mujer in Azucena's specific sociocultural context. It establishes the boundaries of childhood behavior, which Azucena internalizes. Through instances of conflict, Azucena learns what is regarded as questionable and appropriate. The implicit nature of such moments inculcates Azucena with lessons that hold a silent but lasting power. I argue that *Canícula* presents a hidden curriculum comprised of critical educational moments, usually rooted in conflict, some of which may not necessarily be explicit but are enacted nonetheless. Through the descriptive narrative of *Canícula*'s portraits of niñez, the boundaries of girlhood are reinscribed, and girlhood experiences illustrate a series of critical educational lessons about what it means to become a mujer growing up on the frontera and the knowledge and skills required to survive that journey.

COMMUNITY CULTURAL WEALTH

Throughout *Canícula*, Azucena begins to develop and foster community cultural wealth, "an array of knowledge, skills, abilities, and contacts possessed and utilized by Communities of Color to survive and resist macro and micro-forms of oppression" (Yosso 2005, 77). Tara J. Yosso explains that communities of color nurture this cultural wealth through at least six different types of capital: aspirational, navigational, social, linguistic, familial, and resistant. She notes that "aspirations are developed within social and familial contexts, often through linguistic storytelling and advice (consejos) that offer specific navigational goals to challenge (resist) oppressive conditions. Therefore, aspirational capital overlaps with each of the other forms of capital, social, familial, navigational, linguistic and resistant" (77). I focus on two forms of this community cultural wealth, familial capital and resilient capital, illustrating Azucena's overall aspirational dispositions through her longing and desire within her community contexts. As Yosso notes, all forms of capital have an element of aspiration—that strong desire to hope for more.

METHODOLOGY

I treat Cantú's vignettes as data, albeit they represent a "fictional" account of Azucena's niñez. However, as we are well aware, the ways in which we construct memory are often, if not always, subjective; so my treatment of these vignettes is not so different from the treatment of "real-life" accounts of personal experiences. As Cantú notes, "We live life in our memories, with our past and our present juxtaposed and bleeding, seeping back and forth, one to the other in a recursive dance" (xii). Furthermore, the significant findings that these vignettes provide substantiate a serious rendering of their meanings and potential implications. Even the seemingly sporadic nature of the text is purposeful and symbolic of the ebb and flow of the feminine self. Cantú stressed that "chronological order had to go; after all, we don't think in clean, clear chronological order; life doesn't happen in neat little packages. I wanted a narrative that, like my memory, worked in a recursive and overlapping fashion" (102). Cantú challenges conventional forms of storytelling in her refusal to follow any linear progression. In keeping with the counterstory of Azucena, she takes her own path in her own time.

Similarly, I employ a Chicana feminist epistemology (Delgado Bernal 1998, 2), drawing from four sources of cultural intuition, to resist traditional hegemonic ways of knowing and to privilege the narratives of the "other." According to Dolores Delgado Bernal:

> Epistemological concerns in schools are inseparable from cultural hegemonic domination in educational research. The way educational research is conducted contributes significantly to what happens (or does not happen) in schools. In education, what is taught, how it is taught, who is taught, and whose fault it is when what is taught is not learned are often manifestations of what is considered the legitimate body of knowledge. For Chicanas, this is not merely an epistemological issue, but one of power, ethics, politics, and survival. Employing a Chicana

> feminist epistemology in educational research thus becomes a means to resist epistemological racism and to recover untold histories. (2)

In concert with the conceptual framework of hidden curriculum and community cultural wealth, I use Delgado Bernal's Chicana feminist epistemology as my epistemological orientation for analyzing counterstorytelling, the methodology utilized to analyze Cantú's *Canícula*.

Counterstorytelling is "a tool to 'counter' deficit storytelling [and] offers space to conduct and present research grounded in the experiences and knowledge of people of color" (Solórzano and Yosso 2002, 28). It is used to counter "monovocal" stories that become "master narratives" or "majoritarian stories" we all participate in. According to Solórzano and Yosso, these stories can be used as theoretical, methodological, and pedagogical tools to challenge racism, sexism, and classism and work toward social justice. These counterstories offer a challenge to a legacy of racial privilege where dominant stories are presented in such a way that "racial privilege seems 'natural'" (28).

Within this literary analysis, the majoritarian story is one of whiteness and male dominance. Consequently, stories in which male perspectives and female repression are the norm seem natural, while feminist women of color identities are seen as disruptions to this master narrative. Using critical race methodology allowed me to analyze Azucena's counterstory(ies) by focusing on the ever-present salience of Chicana feminism, by challenging the typical male paradigm, and by placing significant value on the complex navigation specific to Azucena's experiences.

Counterstorytelling is defined as a method of telling the stories of marginalized peoples. These counterstories disrupt the otherwise dominant discourse. They are a response to the question of whose stories are privileged and whose are silenced in educational contexts, and they draw from the strength of communities of color. Through the use of what Delgado Bernal describes as cultural intuition (2), I examine how Azucena's counterstories are constructed, bringing to bear research data, existing literature (both traditional and nontraditional texts), and the researcher's professional and personal experiences (including multiple voices of family and friends). Critical race theorists employ storytelling to analyze the myths, presuppositions, and received wisdoms that make up the common culture about race. As such, critical race theorists also integrate their own experiential knowledge, drawn from a larger sense of marginalization in the production and co-authoring of these stories. These stories run counter to otherwise hegemonic narratives that impose stories on those who have been "othered." The value of counterstorytelling lies in the power of "naming one's own reality" (Delgado and Stefancic 1993, 462), rather than having it designated and told from the perspective of another, a likely dominant other. I use the methodological tools of story construction and telling to relay Azucena's narrative. Undoubtedly, my own positionality as a multiracial Chicana feminist educator speaks to my understanding of Azucena's narrative.

My identity as a multiracial woman, coming out as a *racial queer*, defined as "the deviation from monoracial categorization, with or without a conscious intent of challenging normative racial constructions" (Chang-Ross 2010, 107), rather than accommodating myself to appearances, is about speaking my secrets—telling the truth and taking pride in queering what has been my familial norm, no matter how high the stakes. I am the one in my family who is seen as the rock, the pillar, the self-righteous overachiever with strange feminist and activist tendencies. I am possessed with a mission to tell the truth because I strongly believe that my family and I have suffered and continue to suffer from not doing so. One of the first places I felt safe telling the truth was with my teachers in my classroom; there, unlike home, I was rewarded for speaking up. In the classroom, sharing my opinion seemed to correlate to good grades, for the most part. At home, articulating my own opinion seemed inappropriate, rude, and/or insubordinate. In my early elementary years, usually the first thing I would do upon arrival in school was to go to my teacher and say, "I have a stomachache," and I did. I felt something that I can only put into words now: anxiety. This anxiety stemmed from the stress in my home: the combination of my patriotic, paranoid, idealistic, and severe father coupled with my brilliant, afflicted, shamed, and repressed mother and the tension that accumulates with six children sharing two bedrooms and one bath. My home life was traumatic and chaotic. When I went to school, however, I felt as if I had control over my world. It was a safe space where I could forge my own identity. School has always been my sanctuary.

In an academic setting, I was praised and singled out as superior and gifted. I thrived in this competitive environment. Reading, doing homework, writing, exploring, and doing anything that took me to an imaginative place came with ease and joy. At home, academic chores served as an escape hatch from my familial troubles. I could always say that I needed to go to the mobile library, which would visit our neighborhood three times a week as part of an outreach program, and hide out there in the company of infinite books and a soft-spoken librarian. My scholarship was my ticket out of a house full of pain, duality, religion, and strictness. I used it to my every advantage. I yearned for an alternative space. Like Azucena, I longed to find my truth.

FINDINGS

FEMALE LONGING AND DESIRE

A sense of longing permeates throughout *Canícula*. From Azucena's description of straddling Buelito's rocking horse, "built from discarded wood planks, painted the color of the red coyoles—red as memories" (6), we understand her burning desire for the real thing, the real pony. In many ways, this longing sets the underlying tone for all of the moments that comprise critical educational lessons. The vignettes in *Canícula* provide us with glimpses into the depths of community knowledge and community cultural wealth that Azucena draws from, helping us to understand her context and to appreciate nontraditional ways of knowing.

These ways of knowing are introduced through the five senses so indulgently captured in "On The Bridge," in which Azucena describes the portrait of her mama, "beautiful and angry, impatient" after a day of shopping in the *mercado*; she describes the smells that vary from the sweetness of fresh produce to the undeniable stench of the outhouse; and she describes the physical feelings of money moving from hand to vendor and tired legs waiting in line. These are sensory experiences which are allowable and in fact easy to divulge in the presence of others. Yet when we arrive at the end of the vignette, Mami and Azucena buy *Confidencias*, a women's magazine, certainly full of glossy images to consume. Azucena tells us that she will "read a escondidas, during siesta time" (8). "Hiding in the backyard, under the pirul" (9), Azucena fantasizes about the love letters submitted by the magazine's readers by impersonating whom she imagines to be their authors. Interestingly, from an early age, Azucena knows full well that such female desire is to be hidden and shared only among her friends, Sanjuana and Anamaría, in the playground during recess. While the succulence of juicy fruit and the acridity of excrement are experienced in the open air, the warmth of love and lust is to be experienced in the shadows, hidden from view. This act in *escondidas*, while seemingly innocent, relays the message that for girls, desire is something of the occult world. Indeed, the lessons surrounding being a "good girl" are quite prevalent in Azucena's upbringing.

In "Body Hair," Azucena is introduced to the physical aspects of a proper girl. At the painful and awkward entrance into puberty, Azucena describes her "growing pains," which include cramps and other disturbances "for which there was no salve" (60), a reference to a foul-smelling ointment that her mami uses to ease her pain but also a double entendre of the word *salve*. In other words, she will find no salvation from these growing pains, these rites of passage for a growing girl. Once you have passed through that threshold, there is no turning back and nothing can rescue you from its consequences. Perhaps most confusing and hurtful are the mixed messages sent by both males and females about what is appropriate and not when it comes to girlhood, or niñez. When Sarah, the daughter of the Jewish family Mami works for, loudly proclaims within Azucena's earshot that "all I know is unplucked eyebrows and hairy legs and underarms make a girl look like a boy" (60), Azucena breaks into tears. As far as her familial and community knowledge goes, body hair is something prized by and even considered attractive for Mexican women. Her (and her Chicana friends') parents forbid such hair removal. She "feel[s] torn; these same 'pendejas' are sometimes my friends and we work on school projects together" (61)—why then are they punishing her for lessons she has learned at home about the female body? Why is there so much drama among mujeres?

FAMILIAL CAPITAL

That's the thing about being a mujer. Relationships can get complicated but are, "above all, [about] women sharing life, tending to each other. Supporting each other. Teaching each other to mother, to survive, to understand, to live" (36). Through the pain and heartache, they are your *vecinas* and *comadres* who hold onto all of the little victories, especially those of their children, and find just enough hope to "barely stay alive" (36). Azucena possesses the community knowledge of sisterhood and *confianza*, a space in which the mundane is discussed in *platicas* and where the little everyday matters are raised to the level of importance that they deserve—the stuff of weeping, celebrating, and yearning. The term *familial capital* "refers to those cultural knowledges nurtured among familia that carry a sense of community history, memory and cultural intuition [see Delgado Bernal 1998]. This form of cultural wealth engages a commitment to community well being and expands the concept of family to include a more broad understanding of kinship" (79). As Azucena observes, "They share it all, offer sympathy and prayers" (37), bringing a temporal balance to the sufferings of life with a simple acknowledgment of their realities. Azucena reflects on her mami's experiences, "When you give life to eleven children and suffer two miscarriages you don't take worrying or life lightly. Every day brings its weight of worries and of joys, laughter and tears like sunshine and rain" (44).

Like Mamagrande, whose "pains and joys are buried in her heart" (17), Azucena learns that women carry burdens that are sources of both pain and strength. "The keeping up of appearances, of dignity" (17), she notes, is what keeps Mamagrande exhausted. From maintaining the house in a sparkling clean state to the daily ins and outs of cooking meals to fighting off the forever dust that lingers in a rancho, a mujer's attention to the home is paramount. Azucena sees Mamagrande, surrounded by children at her feet, as possessing an understanding of her internal power and the magnetism that fortitude brings. Azucena notices that for Mamagrande, "the work never stops, her handkerchief a la mano in her apron pocket ever ready for the tears of joy and pain" (17). Azucena must wonder, how does Mamagrande survive such intensity? Yosso offers an explanation for the source of her resilience: "From these kinship ties, we learn the importance of maintaining a healthy connection to our community and its resources. Our kin also model lessons of caring, coping and providing (educación), which inform our emotional, moral, educational and occupational consciousness" (79). Azucena is unknowingly receiving her true *educación*, hidden in the masterful art of her grandmother's everyday life.

RESISTANT CAPITAL

Whether you are perfecting a home, like Mamagrande, *chismiando* with the other *primas* and *tías*, or doing the opposite of what is expected of you, *resistant capital* "refers to those knowledges and skills fostered through oppositional behavior that challenges inequality" (Yosso, 80). Often, these oppositional behaviors are not explicitly rebellious. Rather, resistant capital can be verbal and nonverbal activity that feeds the female spirit. The mujeres in Azucena's life "consciously instruct their children to engage in behaviours and maintain attitudes that challenge the status quo. These young women are learning to be oppositional with their bodies, minds and spirits in the face of race, gender and class inequality" (Yosso, 81). In her efforts to talk back to the experiences she finds unjust, Azucena exhibits various agentic and creative types of oppositional behavior. Yosso summarizes Daniel Solórzano and Dolores Delgado Bernal's (2001) notion that

> resistance may include different forms of oppositional behavior, such as self-defeating or conformist strategies that feed back into the system of subordination.

> However, when informed by a Freirean critical consciousness . . . or recognition of the structural nature of oppression and the motivation to work toward social and racial justice, resistance takes on a transformative form. Therefore, transformative resistant capital includes cultural knowledge of the structures of racism and motivation to transform such oppressive structures. (81)

For Azucena, resistant capital takes on various forms. In "Cowboy Boots," Azucena explains how she develops an almost sixth sense, or *facultad*, regarding her knowledge and understanding that Sanjuana, her childhood friend, had been raped by Tom, the man with the cowboy boots. According to Anzaldúa (1987), la facultad is

> the capacity to see in surface phenomena the meaning of deeper realities, to see the deep structure below the surface. It is an instant "sensing," a quick perception arrived at without conscious reasoning. It is an acute awareness mediated by the part of the psyche that does not speak, that communicates in images and symbols which are the faces of feelings, that is, behind which feelings reside/hide. The one possessing this sensitivity is excruciatingly alive to the world. (60)

La facultad is a survival mechanism, an intuitive capacity that arises as a response to others' racism, homophobia, sexual violence, and general intolerance. For those who dwell in a borderland, caught between and among worlds, la facultad is a well of empowerment, a spiritual haven that is ever present.

Although "Sanjuana never said anything," Azucena knew (118). Recalling this memory, she says, "I don't like cowboy boots. I don't wear cowboy boots, and in fact when I see a man, especially an Anglo, wearing cowboy boots, I cringe, react like I do when someone scratches the chalkboard with their nails" (118). Azucena is shocked that she could pick up on anything like this, "since I didn't even know about such things. Mami never talked to me about sex" (119). Once again, the hidden curriculum behind Azucena's mama's act of leaving "a book that explained things on top of the chiffonier" (119) implies that things related to sexuality are not to be discussed, although there is clearly a necessity for some sort of explanation.

This implication is further cemented when Sanjuana is sent away for being impregnated by her rapist: "The next day, after school, I went to her house. Her Mother greeted me saying Sanjuana was gone. She was at her aunt's house in Nuevo Laredo. My friend was going to have a baby and we couldn't even talk"

(119). And yet, as Azucena is sent to pick up groceries by her mama, she still has the resilient capital to go to the store owned by Tom, the rapist. While she doesn't verbally or physically show her anger and disdain toward Tom, she reveals her fortitude through her own passive aggression: "I was so upset I couldn't look at him. Instead, I just looked down as I signed Mamá's name for the pound of baloney and the loaf of bread; all I saw were his cowboy boots" (120). Time and again, Azucena uses her silence, her power of secrets, to garner strength in the midst of tragedy.

"The Flood" narrates perhaps the most symbolic of Azucena's memories, recounting the rising of Zacate Creek and the massive evacuation, "a scary flood, threatening and overwhelming" (9). The women in her life, continually presented with challenging circumstances, are always ready to evacuate and then, when the time is right, return to their homes. Azucena notes that their homes are safe, "for they sit on high stilts" (9), a figurative and literal reference to the heights to which women will go to ensure the family's security and the resilience that allows them to rise above the floodwaters. Azucena begins to identify that strength in herself. She says, "Most kids cry but I am courageous" (10). As happens with life's never-ending cycles, "after the flood Mami and Bueli begin again" (10). They retend the garden, where only watermarks act as reminders of the fear and loss associated with the flood's rage. Mami and Bueli know that there will be other floods, and when they come, they will draw from their resistant capital to figure out what to do.

Azucena engages with and develops the resistant capital to survive as a mujer in several ways. However, it is clear that she is vividly aware of one weapon already in her arsenal. In the vignette "Nacho," Azucena describes how she inflicts revenge on Nacho, her schoolmate, after he tells on her for a silly interaction involving the throwing of a stone. She boldly exclaims:

> How could I tell Mami of the anger, the humiliation, the mixed-up feelings that were held in that stone and in me? She'd never understand. I took my punishment, but already I was plotting revenge. I was going to write him a poem, call him a chimuelo chismoso; that'd serve him right. I savored the joy of having everyone laugh at him, as I read the poem at recess. (32)

Azucena recognizes that one of the most powerful pieces of ammunition she possesses is writing. The ultimate revenge against Nacho is to show him with words. She savors even the thought of using her words, crafting them onto paper and reading them aloud. Perhaps this is where Cantú and Azucena truly intersect—in this space of authorship. It is also the opening where culturally relevant pedagogy has the potential to make an entrance.

DISCUSSION AND IMPLICATIONS IN THE CONTEXT OF CULTURALLY RELEVANT PEDAGOGY

Azucena has learned her lessons well. Through the hidden curriculum of her interactions, her environment, and her understanding of the world, her community cultural wealth is built both with and on the critical educational lessons she learns about becoming a mujer. Through her own cultural intuition, Azucena lives Chicana feminist epistemology by telling her counterstory in nonconventional ways. While she learns that female longing and desire are notions to be carefully navigated, it is precisely through that navigation that Azucena gains the familial and resistant capital she needs to carry her niñez into a world of unknowns. It is indeed a muddy notion, that of becoming a mujer. Azucena allows us to enter her world of niñez to tease out these dilemmas and also to see the critical importance of the skills that are gained as a result of this complexity.

Earlier in the chapter, I discussed my need to connect this text to classroom educators. Here I present various implications from the perspective of teacher education and student learning through the context of culturally relevant pedagogy. Gloria Ladson-Billings (1995) outlines the three broad theoretical underpinnings of culturally relevant pedagogy: "the conceptions of self and others held by culturally relevant teachers, the manner in which social relations are structured by culturally relevant teachers, and the conceptions of knowledge held by culturally relevant teachers" (477). Generally, teachers who possessed the aforementioned traits demonstrated culturally relevant pedagogy by seeing themselves as members of the community; believing in the value of experiential knowledge; understanding their pedagogy as unpredictable; demonstrating a connectedness with students; and framing knowledge in a critical fashion (always fluid, scaffolded, multifaceted) (478–81). Given these tenets, I provide implications as to how *Canícula* might be used pedagogically in a culturally relevant way.

1. Using texts that intentionally place personal experience at the center of student learning, such as *Canícula*, can increase the engagement of learners by

privileging experiential knowledge and showing the teacher's connectedness to the community at large.

2. Discussing female desire in a critical fashion, especially in the context of learning, in a culturally sensitive and empowering way can provide a space for youth to participate in conversations about needs and aspirations.
3. Speaking secrets is a process that individuals arrive at in their own time. Connecting with students about difficult, sometimes taboo subjects requires the intentional development of a safe and open learning environment. Using texts such as *Canícula* can facilitate this opening and lead to valuable, often unplanned, teaching moments.
4. The hidden curriculum of *Canícula* offers an opportunity to consider the ways in which knowledge is constructed both inside and outside of the classroom and specifically within one's own community.
5. Community cultural wealth should be valued and engaged in classroom interactions and knowledge production, as it draws from students' experiences to construct new knowledge.
6. Familial, resistant, and other forms of capital are tools that should be taught, explicitly discussed, and held to high esteem as a way of valuing experiential knowledge and preparing students to become lifelong learners.

CONCLUSION

I began this chapter by acknowledging that speaking secrets is not easy. Using Azucena's narrative in Cantú's *Canícula*, I illustrated the ways in which Azucena, through specific vignettes, demonstrated how these secrets played out in her niñez, underscoring the value and heaviness of the hidden. I pointed out that it is within the everyday interactions of community life that Azucena consumed the explicit, unspoken, and tacit messages of becoming a mujer. Drawing from Chicana feminist epistemology, I applied the notions of hidden curriculum and community wealth to illustrate how Azucena mined her community cultural wealth to develop familial and resistant capital, ultimately utilizing her experiences of her niñez to inform her notions of and foster her fortitude in becoming a mujer.

This analysis represents a specific focus on particular vignettes that spoke to the familial and resistant capital Azucena gained in her coming-of-age narrative. My decision to focus on the idea of becoming a mujer resonated deeply with me as a Chicana feminist educator. Indeed, I have found that our young female students, especially Latinas, are hungry for more texts that reflect their own experiences or, at least, connect with them on a critically personal level. The cultural relevance of Cantu's *Canícula* endures, not in spite of, but because of the salience of the critical educational lessons that transcend time and place.

While I appreciate *Canícula* as a poignant literary text, I especially value its utility and power in the classroom. This past summer, I worked with a group of Latina high school freshmen in a small rural town. I led an intensive writing institute in which these girls wrote relatively lengthy autobiographies, longer than anything any of them had ever written, according to our conversations. In order to scaffold the activity, I used vignettes from *Canícula* as models from which to present the craft of writing and the importance of personal experience as literary/academic work. For many of the girls, Cantú's vignettes were the first they had ever read about a Latina coming of age. I asked them to write a vignette about their own lives, modeling it after one in the book. I was captivated by what they produced. Indeed, the girls spoke of their secrets, and with each secret that was divulged, the courage of such disclosure emboldened the other girls—they followed suit in their writing. Rather than feeling afraid of this exposure, the girls communicated the liberation they felt as a result. Those vignettes gave them permission to create self-authored pieces based on their community cultural wealth. I can think of no better outcome to reading a text than inspiring budding authors to create their own.

WORKS CITED

Anzaldúa, Gloria. *Borderlands/La Frontera: The New Mestiza*. San Francisco: Aunt Lute Books, 1987

Apple, Michael W. *Official Knowledge: Democratic Education in a Conservative Age*. New York: Routledge, 2000.

Cantú, Norma E. *Canícula: Snapshots of a Girlhood en la Frontera*. Albuquerque: University of New Mexico Press, 1995.

Chang-Ross, Aurora. (2010). Reflections of a Racial Queer. *Journal of Multicultural Perspectives* 12, no. 2 (2010): 1–6.

Delgado, Richard, and Jean Stefancic. "Critical Race Theory: An Annotated Bibliography." *Virginia Law Review* 79, no. 2 (1993): 461–516.

Delgado Bernal, Dolores. "Using a Chicana Feminist Epistemology in Educational Research." *Harvard Educational Review* 68, no. 4 (1998): 1–26.

Gay, Geneva. "Preparing for Culturally Responsive Teaching." *Journal of Teacher Education* 53, no. 2 (2002): 106–16.

González, Deena J. "Speaking Secrets: Living Chicana Theory." In *Living Chicana Theory*, edited by Carla Trujillo, 46–77. Berkeley, CA: Third Women Press, 1998.

Ladson-Billings, Gloria. "Toward a Theory of Culturally Relevant Pedagogy." *American Educational Research Journal* 32, no. 3 (1995): 465–91.

Solórzano, Daniel G., and Dolores Delgado Bernal. "Examining Transformational Resistance Through a Critical Race and LatCrit Theory Framework: Chicana and Chicano Students in an Urban Context." *Urban Education* 3 (2001): 308–42.

Solórzano, Daniel G., and Tara J. Yosso. "Critical Race Methodology: Counter-Storytelling as an Analytical Framework for Education Research." *Qualitative Inquiry* 8, no. 1 (2002): 23–44.

Soto, Sandra K. *Reading Chican@ Like a Queer: The De-Mastery of Desire*. Austin: University of Texas Press, 2010.

Yosso, Tara J. "Whose Culture Has Capital? A Critical Race Theory Discussion of Community Cultural Wealth." *Race, Ethnicity, and Education* 8, no. 1 (2005): 69–91.

THE ALTERNATE LIVES OF AZUCENA IN NORMA ELIA CANTÚ'S *CANÍCULA*

CARLOS SIBAJA GARCÍA

NORMA ELIA CANTÚ writes anecdotes of a community living in and around the border town of Laredo, Texas, in her work *Canícula: Snapshots of a Girlhood en la Frontera*. Through the voice of her protagonist, Azucena, *Canícula* documents the lives of her family and friends and recounts the stories by using a narrative that goes from reality to fiction; the "fictional autobioethnography" genre of *Canícula* functions as a warning label informing readers that what Cantú presents can be both nonfiction and fantasy. Cantú begins *Canícula* by stating, "So although it may appear that these stories are my family's, they are not precisely, and yet they are" (xi). This disclaimer allows the author to disassociate her own life from her literature. In the introduction to *Canícula*, Cantú adds, "I was calling the work fictional autobiography, until a friend suggested that they really are ethnographic and so if it must fit a genre, I guess it is fictional autobioethnography" (xi). Cantú relies on fragmented vignettes that reflect the fluidity of living on the border, *en la frontera*, of speaking both English and Spanish, and of understanding both Mexican and American cultures. Cantú herself writes, "As Pat Mora claims, life en la frontera is raw truth, and stories of such life, fictitious as they may be, are even truer than true" (xi). Additionally, Cantú shows us that living in a border town does more than just represent living in a duality; a third way of living, the Tejana/o experience, becomes as important as the Mexican and the American.

Azucena, as the narrator, represents the lives of many Tejanas/os and Mexicanas/os, yet she can speak only for what she understands to be her reality. Azucena understands that her culture is one where silence reigns in order to avoid the truth. It is a paradox where Azucena learns a story without being told directly, where people accept who they are by realizing what they are not, where a border signifies having more than one home. As Azucena herself states, "And in 1948 crossing [the border] meant coming home, but not quite" (5).

Azucena reveals that, at an early age, she learned from her cousin Tina how to keep secrets, and these secrets lead to a fragmented version of reality. In other words, Azucena tells us enough about herself, and at the same time she does not. For instance, Tina's relationship with her boyfriend must be kept quiet. Otherwise, their grandfather will get mad. Azucena shares what Tina explains to her: "I must learn to keep secrets otherwise Papagrande will be angry. I listen and obey, learn the lessons of growing up" (23). Azucena seems to have learned this lesson very well, since she remains secretive throughout the rest of her life. Azucena never shares her true self, presumably because she is afraid of rejection or of not doing the right thing. Azucena's fragmented narration can be attributed in part to her ability to keep secrets.

In several passages in *Canícula*, Azucena wonders what her future would have been like if she had had a different life. First, she questions the possibility of becoming a nun and rejects that lifestyle. Later, Azucena speculates about what it is like to be married to a man and have children, the life of a typical Mexican woman, like many of her relatives and friends. Could Azucena be married but to a non-Latino man? Or is she single because she's never met a man for her? Lastly, she also documents her affinity for some of her close female friends, which hints that she may not necessarily be attracted to men. So the possibility of Azucena being a lesbian also exists.

Katie Acosta's study (2010) concludes that erasure of nonconformity, sexual silencing, and avoidance after disclosure are strategies used by self-identified lesbians, bisexuals, and queer Latinas with their families (64). Acosta argues that these strategies are used to "minimize the risk of familial rejection. They are complicit in erasing, silencing, and avoiding their sexual identities as they attempt to maintain familial bonds" (64). In addition, Acosta notes, "Sexual silence is a way for families to tacitly accept sexual nonconformity without ever directly acknowledging it" (76). It is possible that Azucena is using sexual silence in her memoirs in order to maintain her familial ties and not disturb the notions of heteronormativity that her family might have. In addition, the author, Norma Cantú, could also have intentionally been silent on her character's sexuality in an effort to broaden the book's reception and increase the likelihood of its publication in 1995.

Azucena shares her fascination with nuns in a couple of passages as well as her rejection of that lifestyle. Joining a convent and becoming a nun may be an alternative to marriage for some women. First, Azucena contemplates some of the Catholic Church's traditions after being confused about whether she can eat meat on Fridays; when she is finally told that it is not a sin to eat meat on Fridays, she adds, "At age thirteen I begin to question church rules, so arbitrary, so unfair" (115). This questioning helps the readers understand why Azucena struggles when she takes Communion one day. Taking Communion prompts Azucena to go into a dreamlike state. She imagines herself as a nun, and that unsettles her to the point of declaring, "Please God, let me be me again!" (116). This statement can lead us to ask what "being me" means for Azucena. Later in the passage, Azucena says that she hides this unpleasant image from everybody, including her loved ones, perhaps because of fear. It is clear that Azucena will not end up in a convent.

Azucena adds, "When [that memory of taking Communion] escapes, sometimes in church, or when I'm walking back from school, I wonder what it would be like to be Sister Consuelo, living without children, not married, praying all the time. Boring, that's what I think" (116). Azucena also thinks of some of her friends, the ones who "did want to hide in a convent, marry Jesus. Like my friend, now my comadre, Ana, whose parents sent her to Mexico City with relatives when she announced her intentions [to become a nun] right after graduation" (116). When she says "hide" one can ask, "Hide from what or from whom?"

Azucena seems intrigued by the idea of having the life of an unmarried woman and finding refuge in a convent. Perhaps she does not want to live the life of a traditional married woman, but the alternative at this point is to become a nun, which does not appeal to her; there has to be another way to live.

Another possible life for the protagonist is that of a married woman. Azucena seems to conform to the notions of heteronormativity and playfully admits that she enjoys flirting with some of the boys because she knows that it is only a childish, silly game. However, she becomes scared when a boy named René wants to talk to her parents about their relationship. The thought of an encounter with René and her parents freaks her out. Azucena states, "I imagine myself married, with babies like mami, and with a jolt realize I don't want that" (127), revealing her intention of not living the typical life of a woman who marries and has children.

A similar rejection of marriage is described in Catriόna Rueda Esquibel's (1998) analysis of Sandra Cisneros's *The House on Mango Street*. Esquibel states that Esperanza, the protagonist in *The House on Mango Street*, "does not want to wait for a man to change her life; she wants to write her own changes. Esperanza seeks an alternative to the options provided to her: options prescribed by sexism and institutionalized heterosexuality" (650). These are the precise options constantly questioned by Azucena. It makes sense that a teenager expresses herself in that manner, but at the same time, we cannot know for sure the reasons why the narrator in *Canícula* rejects the life of a married woman. One possibility is that Azucena simply does not want to have a life similar to that of her family members; she has witnessed how difficult it can be to raise children in their economic situation and therefore may not desire that for herself. In addition, Azucena may simply not feel attracted to men. She never talks about her sexual orientation in her narrative, but that does not mean that her sexuality is absent. Azucena tells her story in a fragmented way, and that fragmentation is a reflection of her own life.

None of these revelations states directly that Azucena is a lesbian; however, Azucena recalls her friend Gloria as "the friend of my heart" (127), suggesting that Azucena and Gloria once had a strong bond. In her analysis of Chicana literature, Esquibel defines *lesbian* and explores how some of the characters in texts like *The House on Mango Street* and Denise Chávez's *The Last of the Menu Girls* can be interpreted as lesbian. Similarly, Azucena in *Canícula* can be read as a lesbian character. Esquibel also explains female-to-female relationships and adds, "Within the socially sanctioned system of *comadrazgo*, young Chicanas are encouraged to form lifelong female friendships, and it is the intimacy of these relationships that often provides the context for lesbian desire" (645). Esquibel notes that in these stories the young girls learn of sexuality but "are discouraged—by mothers, families, community, and religion—from recognizing or exploring their sexuality. At the same time, the cultural role of comadres, which raises lifelong friendships to the status of kinship, is both encouraged and recognized" (648). This notion of *comadrazgo* can also be seen in *Canícula*, especially in the relationship between Azucena and Gloria. That relationship is not quite clear, and we cannot be sure if it was romantic or platonic, pure friendship.

Towards the end of *Canicula*, Azucena says: "The callus on my scissor finger hard and rough reminds me of Gloria, and those summer afternoons recruiting shoeshine boys and dreaming of a different life, a life married to René, a beauty shop all my own, a two story house in front of a neighborhood plaza, a life as a Mexican" (p. 129). As a retired woman, one of Azucena's strongest memories is of Gloria. Besides thinking about Gloria, Azucena considers what her life would have been like if she had married René and how different her life would be now. In addition, we don't know what Azucena has done with her life at the point at which she shares these confessions. Azucena's voice at the moment of her narration does not reveal her current identity, social status, or sexual orientation. Azucena is obviously not married to a man, because she ends the passage questioning what it would be like to be married; but she never states if she is alone or with a romantic partner, that partner being a man or a woman. Cantú ends *Canícula* without giving us any additional information on the adult Azucena's lifestyle. Other Chicana writers also follow this pattern, as Esquibel documents: "While both Cisneros and Chávez depict the cultural structures of institutionalized heterosexuality, neither fixes a heterosexual ending for her protagonist; each is alone at the end of the text, with many possibilities open to her" (648). Similarly, Azucena omits important aspects of her life and identity.

We must read some of the passages in *Canícula* carefully in order to consider the possibility that Azucena might not be a heterosexual character. For instance, Azucena confesses her fascination for a women's magazine called *Confidencias* (8–9), a magazine that she has to read behind her parents' back because she is too young for it. Azucena pretends that the letters in those magazines are for her or written by her. This confession leads us to wonder what Azucena means by that statement. In other words, Azucena is as likely to imagine that she is the author of those love letters to women as she is to imagine she wrote the letters to men. We cannot know for sure what Azucena means in this passage, since she does not elaborate on which direction her imagination actually takes. Nor does she provide an example of those letters so that we can understand what Azucena fantasizes about.

Among some of the fears Azucena documents in her childhood, a major one is the fear of growing up, becoming a woman, and discovering her identity. Azucena notes how her eyes are the same when she is a one-year-old baby as when she is twelve years old (both pictures are included in the chapter "Mexican Citizen"). Those eyes make her wonder who she is, and an act of rebellion pushes her to cut her hair very short, just like Mia Farrow does in *Peyton Place* (21). Azucena also speaks of how that young girl in her Mexican document photo is worried about the changes that her body is undergoing. The natural process of developing breasts and body hair gives Azucena a certain level of anxiety. For example, she is aware of body hair and how her breasts may not be growing equally in size. At this age, Azucena and her friend Anamaría are "obsessed by breasts" (22).

Unlike little boys, young girls do have to worry about their physical appearance, because society pays attention to women's bodies, especially to breasts. When we read this passage, it is easy to relate to Azucena's anxiety over growing up, especially in a heteronormative society. As adolescents, both boys and girls can clearly see the physical differences they face when growing up: the pubic hair, the change in their voices, the mood swings, among others. Esquibel writes of *The House on Mango Street*, "Esperanza keeps coming up against adulthood, womanhood—which actually means adult heterosexuality—and her resistance to that change" (652). Esperanza's anxiety is similar to what some girls in *Canícula* face over growing up.

For women in particular, the body can undergo significantly dramatic changes, like the onset of menstruation and the growth of their breasts. We all know that most men find women with bigger breasts more attractive, and this fact is perhaps what worries Azucena. As she grows up, she realizes that her breasts are growing, and she seems to be fascinated by this change.

Although Azucena worries about her body, she also appreciates when girls stand up for their rights. Azucena's friend Dahlia embodies nonconforming gender roles in *Canícula* (64). Azucena recounts how Don Vicente hired the boys to do yard work and Dahlia, jealous, complained about not being able to work because she was a girl. Dahlia argued with Don Vicente, "even fought with the boys, threw rocks at the Lopezes' house till Jose came out and scolded her" (65). Cantú shows how it is possible for little girls to get equal opportunities by voicing their opinions and standing against patriarchy. In the end, Dahlia "got her way," and "soon she too was working on the Baca's yard, getting paid just like the boys" (65).

Azucena learns, though, that men do have the power in her community. Azucena's friend Sanjuana, who is only about fourteen years old, is sent away by her parents when she gets pregnant (118). Sanjuana had to quit school to help her mother with the house chores. Then, after her father lost his job, the family became indebted to the local store, run by Tom, an Anglo. To help pay the debt, Sanjuana began working for Tom, who seduced her, lied to her, and threatened her to keep her quiet. After Tom rapes Sanjuana and gets her pregnant, Tom's wife fires her and calls her names, even though Tom, an older married man, is the one who coerced and abused Sanjuana. In this story, titled "Cowboy Boots," we are reminded that patriarchy blames women and even girls for supposedly seducing men, and these women are left alone and mistreated. Once more, we recognize that Azucena knows what is happening to Sanjuana even though Sanjuana never told her anything. In the end, Azucena finds herself in a difficult situation, because she feels like killing Tom for what he did to her friend. She does not have the courage to face him when she goes into his store, however, and can only look at his feet in his cowboy boots. Those cowboy boots serve as another symbol for machismo. We can recognize that Azucena has negative associations with men and their power over women.

Canícula is not the only work in which Norma E. Cantú deals with the topic of rape. Elizabeth Ordoñez (2006) discusses the poem "Violación" (Rape) by Norma E. Cantú, which reads, "Que te lleve el diablo / por ser tan inhumano" (May the devil take you / for being so inhuman). The poem's persona was raped as a child, and Ordoñez adds that this violent act has left her "unable to love, with a scar of hatred in her heart" (77). Although Azucena does not state she has experienced rape, she does describe a friend's rape and her hatred for the man that did it. This could help explain why she does not venture into relationships with men.

Azucena may never utter the word "lesbian," and, in fact, she never refers to any of her female friends or aunts as such. However, Tía Chita briefly makes the readers wonder if she is a lesbian. Azucena describes her aunts Toña and Chita in the following manner: "Never married. Solteronas" (83) and continues, "Tía Chita read newspapers religiously, could argue politics with the best of them" (83). Azucena never states that these aunts might not necessarily be heterosexual. As readers, we don't know if Tía Chita is a lesbian. Again, the narrator does not tell us about her aunts' sexual orientations, but that does not mean the possibility of them being lesbian does not exist. Besides, *Canícula* is set in a time when even the thought of not being heterosexual must be kept in private. As a matter of fact, these aunts represent the alternate life that Azucena wonders about, since they are not married and neither are they nuns. This passage is important because it shows Azucena's acknowledgment of the older single woman, a state that could be desired by her. These two women do not exhibit the features of the traditional Mexican woman, who remains quiet and submissive.

Conversely, Azucena introduces her Tía Piedad (84) as the official person to go to for matters of femininity. Tía Piedad is in charge of training the cousins in how to be ladies. Azucena explains:

> First there were lessons on everything from posture and yoga to nutrition and etiquette, and even French. Tía Piedad's book on posture and beauty, published with

> the help of her French husband, reputedly a very rich descendent of a family of the nobility who had stayed in Mexico after the political debacle of his countrymen, gave the basics, but there was more, much more. (84–85)

Tía Piedad functions as the ultimate guide to becoming a lady. Unfortunately, Azucena does not find Tía Piedad's teachings appealing or desirable. Like Azucena, her cousin Luz feels that "it wasn't worth so much suffering, so much deprivation just to be a 'lady'" (85). Azucena adds: "I'm sure I would've failed as well, long thin hands and all. I have never been able to sit straight and prefer to drape my long thin body over chairs and sofas, sometimes my legs find themselves under me or over an arm of a armchair—no, the posture, definitely no" (85). Azucena shows how her notions of femininity are not necessarily the same ones as Tia Piedad's. Even though she is talking about the past, Azucena assumes that she would have never been able to succeed in Tía Piedad's training. Azucena seems to disapprove of the traditional Mexican notion of being a lady, especially knowing all the suffering that goes with it.

Lastly, Azucena tells us that perhaps her most "feminine" behavior was her "shoe fetish," during a period when she owned more shoes than clothes, but that still didn't make her think of her Tía Piedad (86). The reason she had so many shoes is, she says, that "I worked in an office and had to wear certain costumes" (86). Shoes become a symbol of her identity as a woman. Azucena does not seem happy when she wears so-called women's shoes and even calls them part of a "costume." The current Azucena, the one who remembers her past life, is happy wearing "a pair of huaraches for summer and a pair of hiking boots for winter" (86). Interestingly enough, Azucena describes the latter as a "much better choice of footwear for [her] politics and lifestyle" (86). While those politics and that lifestyle are never explicitly described in *Canícula*, the suggestion is that they have to do with being a woman who does not conform to the traditional norms of gender that society dictates.

In a different passage, Azucena tells us about Henrietta, who became her best friend in the fourth grade (88). Although they are very young, Azucena shares some of her anecdotes and secrets with Henrietta; for example, although Henrietta supposedly does not speak Spanish, Azucena knows that Henrietta in fact does understand it. Later, the girls end their friendship. Azucena remembers, "We broke our friendship in a ritual screaming match where we almost came to blows, but my other friends intervened" (89). This fight occurs right after Henrietta finds out that the person she believed to be her father was in fact her stepfather. Azucena cannot understand that a stepfather might be a good person, since she says she only knows stories that make stepmothers appear evil. Azucena then accuses Henrietta of lying about her stepfather. This passage also suggests that Azucena had one of her first crushes on Henrietta and perhaps ended her friendship with her because of a fear of revealing her romantic feelings, resulting in an intense verbal fight. Finally, Azucena remembers:

> We agreed to fight after school at the empty lot two blocks away where most school fights settled school feuds. All afternoon I fidgeted and couldn't concentrate on the lessons before me. I considered backing up, just not showing up, but finally I decided I had to show up; after all, even Helen, whom the guys feared and called "toro" had agreed to "hacerme esquina," and help me out if need be; but Henrietta never showed up and the group soon dispersed and went home disappointed. (89)

The fact that Henrietta did not show up suggests that perhaps she was having similar, if not the same, thoughts as Azucena. Both friends are tense and do not know what to do. In the end, Azucena shows up only because she already has a group of friends who would back her up. However, we can tell by the way she describes this incident that Azucena does not want to hurt Henrietta.

On her way back home, by herself, Azucena thinks of Henrietta with nostalgia. Azucena takes a look at the "orange-stained heels of [her] white socks" (90), and the sight of her own dirty socks makes her remember how Henrietta's socks "would never look like that" (90). The very last utterance Azucena makes regarding Henrietta is "I think I loved her" (90), which shows how much their friendship meant. However, Azucena states that Henrietta's secret of having a stepfather "ended [their] friendship" (89).

In Esquibel's interpretation of *The Last of the Menu Girls*, she notes how the character Rocío mentions "the week I fell in love." Rocío does not say whom she falls in love with; however, she does describe a patient, Elizabeth Rainey, whom Rocío finds beautiful and sad. In Esquibel's words: "Rocío avoids actually saying she has fallen in love with Elizabeth. Rather, she articulates those qualities that attract her to Elizabeth Rainey—her beauty, her pain—and then her own inability to reach out, to give comfort or understanding expected of Florence Nightingales of the hospital" (659–60). Both Rocío and Azucena highlight the qualities of the women they feel attracted to on some level. Azucena never explains what type of love she feels for Henrietta. When Azucena thinks of the past, she realizes that what she felt for her friend was indeed love, even though she did not consciously acknowledge it and express it at the time.

Only at the very end of *Canícula* do we see an acknowledgment of sexual diversity. Azucena remembers her peers and friends and lists them: "All of us, the studious and the lazy; the gay ones and the straight ones; and the privileged and the disenfranchised" (235). Finally, Azucena describes her generation in an inclusive manner. In this description, Azucena once again does not share openly with the readers what her sexual orientation is, nor does she state if she married or not. By simply saying "all of us," she carefully chooses to keep her identity private. But the fact that Azucena does not openly state that she is a lesbian does not mean that we, as readers, cannot find hints that indicate that she is not attracted to men.

WORKS CITED

Acosta, Katie. "'How Could You Do This to Me?': How Lesbian, Bisexual, and Queer Latinas Negotiate Sexual Identity with Their Families." *Black Women, Gender + Families* 4, no. 1 (Spring 2010): 63–85.

Cantú, Norma Elia. *Canícula: Snapshots of a Girlhood en la Frontera*. Albuquerque: University of New Mexico Press, 1995.

Esquibel, Catrióna Rueda. "Memories of Girlhood: Chicana Lesbian Fictions." In "Feminisms and Youth Cultures," special issue, *Signs: Journal of Women in Culture and Society* 23, no. 3 (Spring 1998): 645–82.

Ordóñez, Elizabeth. "Sexual Politics and the Theme of Sexuality in Chicana Poetry." In "Colección de ensayos conmemorativos del vigésimo quinto aniversario de Feministas Unidas," special issue, *Letras Femeninas* 32, no. 1 (Spring 2006): 67–92.

A DISCOURSE OF NORMA E. CANTÚ'S *CANÍCULA: SNAPSHOTS OF A GIRLHOOD EN LA FRONTERA* AND THE WORLD OF *NEPANTLA Y NEPANTLERA*

ROSE RODRÍGUEZ-RABIN

I LEFT HOME IN 2000 for graduate school in the Midwest, and I have not lived in Laredo, Texas, since. San Antonio is where I live and where I teach. I travel south only during the holidays and, once in a while, during the summers. In all my *viajes* (travels) south, I visit only my family, rarely straying further than San Bernardo Avenue.[1]

In 2009, I was invited to guest lecture for a Mexican American literature class at Laredo Community College (LCC), one of my alma maters. It had been more than twenty-five years since I'd been on campus, so the changes that had taken place were quite evident and reflective of the times. LCC (situated partly within an old fort), as well as the city of Laredo itself, had changed as a result of a population explosion, NAFTA, and Homeland Security's attacks on immigration.[2] During a quick tour around the campus, I noticed Homeland Security had fenced in the campus's original rock walled fence, creating a fence within a fence. I don't know why this sight struck me so hard. My eyes teared up; I became emotional. Questions raced through my head: "Who is Homeland trying to keep out? Who is it trying to keep in?" In the background, I could see the expanding city of Nuevo Laredo, Tamaulipas, Mexico. The *carrizo* (reed cane) that had once elegantly swayed back and forth were gone, eliminated so the Border Patrol vehicles could move around without obstruction. The change was ugly. I do not remember my hometown as being ugly.

After my breakdown at the fence, I entered the designated building to give my lecture. Smiling, I told the students about my adventures and the work I had been introduced to by scholars who had come from Laredo and the surrounding region. Many of their faces suggested skepticism about my words. Many questioned the works I mentioned, works written by writers and scholars such as Américo Paredes, Jovita González, Gloria Anzaldúa, Sonia Saldívar-Hull, and Norma E. Cantú. I passed around Cantú's book *Canícula: Snapshots of a Girlhood en la Frontera* (1995), with its many pictures and short, quick prose. A student raised her hand and asked, "Why would anyone want to write about Laredo?" I responded that Laredo actually has a wonderful story, but the story needs people, its community members, to tell it.[3] "I don't understand what is so great about Laredo," she continued. I explained Gloria Anzaldúa's concept of *nepantla* and how Laredoans live in a third space, a space between the United States and Mexico, which we ourselves create. After *Canícula* made its way around the classroom and came back around to me, I asked how many recognized a picture, a smile, a dress in the small book. One student commented on the wooden horse in the vignette titled "Rocking Horse" and said his father had one that had been passed down through his family. Another student identified with the dress in the story called "China Poblana Two." "My *abuela* [grandmother] tried getting me to put on a dress like that. I told her no. It's too hot to put on that dress." Little by little, each student related to *Canícula*; each shared his or her own story. Then I asked how many were familiar with the fence within the fence on campus. One student, from Monterrey, Mexico, raised his hand. He said it bothered him, but he did not know why. I told him that it bothered me too, recalling the emotions I felt when I first saw it.

It took an "outsider," the student from Monterrey, to recognize and respond to the fence, while those who lived on the Texas-Mexico border seemed to dismiss it, along with the changes that have been occurring in their Laredo community.

In examining change, I turn to Gloria Anzaldúa's definition of *home* and Américo Paredes's revisionist idea of folklore as they relate to culture in Norma E. Cantú's *Canícula: Snapshots of a Girlhood en la Frontera*. I specifically look at the shifting position of the border culture and border people through the lens of the womenfolk.[4] Américo Paredes's work on folklore and culture on the Texas-Mexico border is important to Chican@ studies. Paredes's juxtaposition of Mexican American folklore and cultural theory with hegemonic ideas of culture and folklore is critical to this examination. To initiate a discussion of *Canícula* without writing about *las mujeres de la frontera* (women of the frontier) will be doing Cantú's work an injustice.[5] Las mujeres de la frontera are a monumental influence on Cantú's work.

To help with the analysis of *Canícula*, Paredes's definition of folklore is vital. In analyzing her own community, Cantú is guided by culture and folklore to illustrate the experience of growing up on the border, thus giving the outside world a glimpse of the Laredo community. Along with the glimpse into the culture and folklore, Cantú also illustrates the sociopolitical dynamics of the once-small border town. To give this short but loaded novel the attention it deserves, I offer a brief history of Laredo, Texas, and the Mexican border, as well as some relevant definitions. It is important for the reader to put on new lenses to recognize the challenges Cantú faced in writing *Canícula* as well as the cultural strategies Cantú used to address culture, politics, and social agency.

The history of Mexican Americans in the United States has been one of violence, dislocation, and forced migration. As a result of the Mexican-American War and the Treaty of Guadalupe Hidalgo, which was signed upon the war's end in 1848, culture lines divided the people of the land on both sides of the Rio Grande. It is after the Treaty of Guadalupe Hidalgo that an established rural community collapsed. In other words, as a result of that treaty, people of the region that surrounds today's border between Mexico and Texas experienced dislocation and forced inclusion into a union that was developed through violence.

What arose from the forced inclusion reflects colonial policies. American policies and western legal documents divided the populations into two groups: those from Mexico and those from the United States. The regions surrounding the Texas-Mexico border had experienced colonial issues before the Treaty of Guadalupe Hidalgo, when those lands endured Spanish colonization. Nonetheless, after the treaty, the land changed masters, and the victor's historiography came to represent the U.S and Texas borders. As a result of these circumstances, from which the State of Texas was constructed, a biased, anglicized version of Texas literature and history was created.

Therefore, American scholars exclude the border history from U.S. history, possibly engendering a fragmented idea of Mexican American existence. As a result of the hegemonic version of border history, descendants of that region's people have raised questions about their history and culture. The controversy over who gets to tell the U.S.-Mexico border story began almost at its inception in 1848. Where were the voices of the people from the Texas Mexican community? Although Euro-Americans told the stories of the lands they had conquered, that conquest did not mean the people native to the region were gone.[6] It did mean, however, that in Texas, Anglo Texan supremacy controlled the way Texas history was written, told, and taught.[7] Anglo Texan scholars' work demonstrated, celebrated, and romanticized the Anglo Texans and reflected their attitudes toward Texas Mexicans.[8]

At the same time Euro-American men controlled the retelling of history through literature, a Chicano writer, poet, and folklorist, Américo Paredes, surfaced with his foundational Chicano text *George Washington Gómez: A Mexicotexan Novel*. However, there were also Mexican American women who wrote about the history and culture along the U.S.-Mexico border: from California, María Amparo Ruiz de Burton; from New Mexico, Cleofas Jaramillo; and from Texas, Jovita González de Mireles. These three women used their education, whether from an academic institution or from life experience, to write about the making of the borderland region.

Norma E. Cantú, another woman from Texas, contributed to the making of this region with *Canícula*. The novel itself is and is not simply a story of Cantú growing up among the conflicts of colonization and identity dispossession in the small border town of Laredo, Texas, which is nestled immediately north of the Rio Grande. Cantú's autobioethnography laces fiction with nonfiction as she leads the reader on a journey punctuated with family photographs, which she has richly annotated with personal anecdotes; historical events; literary notations; and, of course, some fabrication. What truly makes this novel stand out among other fictional texts is her incorporation of and emphasis on tradition, customs, and folklore, which Cantú delivers in a nontraditional, nonlinear format. *Canícula* provides a significant contribution to Chicana cultural studies because Cantú uses customs and tradition to explain and expose conflicts along the Texas-Mexico border.

To navigate through the novel, we need to understand what the author means by the term *autobioethnography*. In her introduction, Cantú explains that *Canícula* is part of a larger project that "consists of correspondence and documents that tell the story of a family" (xi). She quickly emphasizes that, although the pictures might be of her family, the novel is not *exactly* autobiographical (xi). *Canícula* critic Timothy Dow Adams comments on what he calls contradiction not only in Cantú's introduction but throughout the text as well. In his article titled "'Heightened by Life' vs. 'Paralyzed by Fact': Photography and Autobiography in Norma E. Cantú's *Canícula*," Adams asks: "In what sense, then, does the book appear to be more autobiographical than it really is? One answer to that question comes from comparing the actual photographs to the prose that describes them, revealing countless small discrepancies between the words and the corresponding image" (60). One discrepancy he points out refers to an old black-and-white photograph: Sitting between two children is an elderly woman. Standing behind the woman is a fairly older girl. The caption below this picture says, "Bueli," slang for "grandmother." Below "Bueli," Cantú writes: "In the photo, Bueli sits in her high-back rocking chair, her sillón where she'd rocked all of us to sleep, surrounded by Tino, Dahlia, Esperanza, and me" (24). Looking closely at the picture, the reader notices only three girls and the elder woman. There is no Tino.[9] At the end of his article, Adams does recognize that Cantú mediates between her words and her images by manipulating, not the photographic record, but her prose descriptions of the photographs, thereby allowing room for her changing identities (70). His analysis leads the way to our understanding the people of the area, an area oftentimes contentious and restrictive to outsiders. In further commenting on the discrepancies, Adams argues that "*Canícula* is not meant to be read as an exact likeness of its author so much as a transcription of her autobiographical act, the act of emphasizing her borderland existence as a child and as an adult recording her childhood" (70). This point is important in the reading of Cantú's text. While Adams characterizes the novel as full of small contradictions, in actuality, he acknowledges that the contradictions are necessary to demonstrate the duality and complexity of life in Laredo, a city that shares its name with a city situated in another country, with a river as the only division between the two.[10]

Autobiography is another term that warrants definition. *Autobiography* has taken on a different meaning for women of color than the canonic, hegemonic definition. Cantú examines her surroundings, whether through memory or through photographs, to initiate a discussion. This discussion of autobiography will be connected with storytelling. In *Canícula*, Cantú is engaging in storytelling, which in Western thought seems to be a dangerous process because storytelling has its origins in oral narratives and, to the minds of traditional scholars and academicians, oral narratives can always be changed. Embracing change, Cantú challenges the traditional linear narrative. Her text has no actual beginning or ending. Nor does her text have an actual sequence. It is as though she has taken some stories, with all their allegorical expressions, and put them down on paper.

The first time I taught *Canícula* was in a midwestern university, and many of the students rejected the novel, complaining that "it isn't the truth" or "it is confusing and out of order." To teach this text to a predominately hegemonic student body is difficult, to say the least, because students believe, as a result of their academic training, that there is always a beginning, the place where the story starts, and there is always an ending, the place where the story concludes. The reader expects to progress linearly, neatly, from the beginning to the ending. Cantú's novel violates their traditions, their expectations.

In recent discussions on autobiography, it's been noted that marginalized women tend to write against traditional linear narratives.[11] The construct is such that the characters and story are more important than the idea of linearity and order. Thus, is it any surprise that Cantú's novel should reflect this "other" construct? Laredo, situated between two countries, has had to make order out of disorder. Out of the chaos of land dispossession and dislocation has risen a culture derived from two countries. In order to identify with a community, the border people need to disidentify from an imposed identity. An example of this disidentification appears in Cantú's chapter titled "China Poblana Two." The reader is presented with a black-and-white photo of a young woman wearing a "traditional" *china poblana* dress from the state of Puebla, Mexico. Cantú writes that the young woman stands in "the plaza in front of Santo Niño [de Atocha] Church" (40). This woman is wearing what today many people consider the iconic traditional dress of a Mexican woman from the seventeenth century. The dress is most recognizable as the "costume" associated with traditional folkloric Mexican dances. The skirts are long and flowing, with shiny reflective pieces to accentuate movement. The blouses tend to be more traditionally conservative, with a few embroidered flowers around the collar. Usually a rebozo (a shawl-like piece of clothing that traditionally was worn by the peasant women of Mexico) accompanies the dress, but in the picture, the young woman is not wearing one. Instead, she wears a touristy sombrero that says "Viva Mexico" (40).[12] The image alone is laden with contradictions. Historically, the dress is not completely Mexican. The china poblana dress is an evolution of indigenous and early-seventeenth-century Mexican clothing.[13] In addition, the touristy hat is not part of traditional attire. How the reader translates the image of "China Poblana Two" is just as important as how Cantú captions the photograph. Cantú begins what folklorist and scholar José E. Limón calls a "performance centered approach to folklore" (194).[14] This approach to folklore is not a new idea. Paredes, before Limón, analyzed corridos (border ballads) by looking specifically at the metanarrative of the music.[15] When the reader sees the image of the china poblana, the image instantly translates into a young woman from Mexico displaying pride in her nation. Nonetheless, that is not what the caption suggests. Cantú, in a seemingly lyrical way, writes of the young woman, "She who wasn't even born in Mexico, who went there as a ten-year-old knowing only to read and write in English because the nuns at Sacred Heart in San Antonio wouldn't tolerate Spanish" (40). If Cantú were to read this caption for an audience, the listeners would hear the rhythmic tone, that is, the performance behind the words. Cantú herself explains the seeming contradiction between the image and caption. Cantú gives the reader some background about the young woman proudly standing in her china poblana dress. What the reader should see between the image and caption is a story that includes a little folklore, some tradition, and even a political commentary about the treatment of the border people who cross back and forth between countries. It is at this time the reader recognizes Cantú not only as the storyteller but as a folklorist, ethnographer, and even a social and political commentator. All in all, Cantú is a performer. To understand certain works, such as *Canícula*, readers need to focus on the folklorist as the informant, "an artist engaged in a creative act" (Paredes, 83), and then as something like a storyteller.

This example is not a contradiction, as suggested by some critics. Instead it is an undercutting of the structure of a Western traditional narrative. It represents *la mestiza*, which Gloria Anzaldúa (1990) defines as one who "can't hold concepts or ideas within rigid boundaries" (378). In keeping with this idea of la mestiza, it is evident that Cantú's identity does not lie within the definition of autobiography but within the deconstruction of the narrative of tradition and culture. They are always changing. Therefore, in order to make sense of *Canícula*, the reader needs to understand Cantú's influences: the history of Laredo, its people, and its non-linear boundaries. It is this deconstruction of narrative that exposes the cultural spaces between border people, culture, and tradition. The people of Laredo live straddling two countries. Like her community, Cantú "learn[ed] to juggle cultures. She has a plural personality, she operates in a pluralistic mode—nothing is thrust out, the good, the bad and ugly, nothing rejected, nothing abandoned. Not only does she sustain contradictions, she turns the ambivalence into something else" (Anzaldúa 1990, 379).

Here Anzaldúa uses the word *she* to mean women who live and experience border life. The mujeres de la frontera make do with what they have and what they are given. Anzaldúa knows firsthand about life on the border. A scholar of Chicana cultural theory, feminist theory, and queer theory, Anzaldúa based *Borderlands/La Frontera: The New Mestiza* on her life growing up on the Texas-Mexico border. Anzaldúa was born on a South Texas ranch near the Mexican border. When she was young, her family labored as agricultural workers. Growing up along the Texas-Mexico border, with its culture and traditions, Anzaldúa felt she never fit in because of the rigid and stifling rules of her traditional Mexican American home. In *Borderlands*, Anzaldúa depicts her experience of growing up on the Texas-Mexico border and the limiting roles of women. Like Anzaldúa, Cantú, in *Canícula*, incorporated her feelings of social and cultural marginalization into her work.

That "something else" mentioned in Anzaldúa's quote is nepantla. We first see this word used in Anzaldúa's *Borderlands/La Frontera*. It is a Nahuatl word describing a place as an "in-between situation." The Aztecs used this word to describe the place between their world/culture and the Spanish colonization. During the 1980s, Chicanas appropriated the word to describe their marginalized political position.[16] Nepantla describes changing borders and colonial expansion within borders. In Cantú's novel, nepantla describes the culture in between Laredo, Texas, and Nuevo Laredo, Tamaulipas, Mexico.

Further illustrating the tension between the border worlds, Cantú's text includes a vignette titled "Body Hair." She begins explaining the image by pointing out that as "an awkward teen, shy and reticent, [she] face[s] the camera, wearing a sleeveless, morning-glory-blue cotton blouse" (60). She also expresses the "pains of growing up," not only the emotional pains but the physical pains as well. For example, the narrator—presumably Cantú, since the image resembles her—writes about the horrible leg cramps she suffered while growing up. Then Cantú switches from describing the physical pain of stretching muscles to conveying the emotional pain of becoming a teen. Although Cantú shows the reader what may seem like just some teenagers behaving like teenagers, what she is actually demonstrating is the cultural dynamics of a border town. Specifically, the narrator, a teenage girl, mentions a group of Jewish girls who are making fun of her because, as is a social tradition on the border at the time the incident takes place, young women neither pluck their eyebrows nor shave their legs. The Jewish girls are, of course, not originally from Laredo but are transplants from another place. Cantú writes that in a state of frustration, the narrator runs into the bathroom, where she bumps into "some of the chucas" (known as "hometown girls" in the Mexican American communities), who are smoking in there. The families of these *chucas* travel back and forth between Laredo and el Norte, and the girls congregate in the bathroom "wearing makeup and talking dirty" (61). The narrator is torn between the expectations of the Jewish girls, because sometimes they are her partners in school projects, and those of the chucas, because they are hometown girls. The teen tries to reason with herself as to why she should ignore the Jewish girls' taunts and instead follow the chucas' suggestion, which is not to pay attention to the Jewish girls. The narrator reasons that "Mami doesn't shave or pluck her eyebrows either, neither did her comadres [a group of tight-knit women] until much later," and that "most of [the girls] who ride the Saunders bus . . . don't yet shave, much less pluck [their] eyebrows, or wear makeup—[their] parents forbid it" (61).[17] Cantú, in this short but powerful narrative, expresses the conflict every teen at one time or another experiences. The difference from the more common narratives, though, is the social and political commentary this one reflects. On the one hand is the Jewish family that the narrator's mother worked for in a domestic capacity. Such families live in the large and elaborate homes on Laredo's Northside. Also, the families of the Jewish girls are not usually home, leaving the teens alone and unsupervised. On the other hand, the chucas, whose families travel, as agricultural laborers, back and forth to el Norte, are rebelling against the school system (by smoking in the girls' bathroom) and against tradition (by wearing makeup and using foul language). Subsequently, the reader witnesses the narrator and her confusion about what is right and wrong. In the preface to *Borderlands*, Anzaldúa explains this confusion and resentment:

> I grew up between two cultures, the Mexican (with a heavy Indian influence) and the Anglo (as a member of a colonized people in our own territory). I have been straddling that *tejas*-Mexican border, and others, all my life. It's not a comfortable territory to live in, this place of contradictions. Hatred, anger and exploitation are the prominent features of this landscape. (n.p.)

Anzaldúa's experience helps clarify the emotions and dynamics that the narrator, along with most border people, face. Like most of the residents of border towns, in this case the narrator goes into survival mode. Anzaldúa attests that "you face divisions within your own cultures—of class, gender, sexuality, nationality, and ethnicity. You face both entrenched institutions and the oppositional movements of working-class women, people of color, and queers" (Anzaldúa and Keating 2002, 548). In making this comment, Anzaldúa demonstrates that no matter where a person is from, what culture he or she belongs to, or what his or her ethnicity is, a person will come across some sort of opposition. At some point, everyone goes into survival mode, as the narrator does. So what is the narrator to do as she faces opposition from the Jewish girls? What choices does the narrator actually have? Either she can allow herself to succumb to the societal pressures to fit in, or she can go along with the chucas' suggestion. Is the narrator to follow in her elders' footsteps? At the end of the vignette, she explains that she will find a way to get even, academically. The narrator decides she will beat her nemeses by getting the highest grade in her class on her paper.

The narrator in *Canícula* is pulled in multiple directions and "opposing realities" (Anzaldúa and Keating, 548). Cantú was affected by institutional colonization, societal colonization, an example of Anzaldúa's "opposing realities." Cantú's response to colonization is reflected in her resistance to traditional rhetorical strategy. This response is clearly established early on in the introduction to *Canícula*, her "autobioethnography." In order to describe her experience growing up in a land caught between two worlds, where significant political and social events determined the landscape, Cantú decolonized the self and stepped out of the victim role. In writing about culture, ethnography certainly has it conventions. James Clifford in *Writing Culture: The Poetics and Politics of Ethnography* (1986) shares: "I treat ethnography itself as a performance emplotted by powerful stories. Embodied in written reports, these stories simultaneously describe real cultural events and make additional moral, ideological, and even cosmological statements" (89).

Clifford's concept may seem too simple, but this definition of ethnography makes it possible for writers, such as Cantú, to deconstruct and decolonize methodologies that held nonhegemonic cultures within the parameters of Western scientific thought. However, breaking away from writing in a traditional linear format has resulted in criticism for *Canícula*. Cantú's term *autobioethnography* has also been met with criticism. Nevertheless, it is through the criticism that we see *Canícula* blossom. The creative arrangement of *Canícula* situates itself only in a larger frame of reference. That larger frame of reference is the personal struggles that a border person endures growing up along the Texas-Mexico border. Subsequently, as an ethnographer, Cantú takes the experiences and realities of a border person and transforms the experiences into art.

As an ethnographer, Cantú studies, researches, and writes about what she knows and loves: her community. The links between the two countries reach only as far as the people are willing to recognize their differences and similarities. Folklorist Américo Paredes "encountered borders of various kinds—geopolitical, racial, linguistic, cultural, and disciplinary" (Nájera-Ramírez, 69), and Cantú demonstrates the conflicts associated with these kinds of borders in

Canícula. For instance, in "Fridays," Cantú writes that on a Friday the narrator ventures into Nuevo Laredo with her friend and the friend's family. In a traditional Catholic household, when Cantú was growing up, eating meat on Fridays was considered a sin. This is a tradition that the narrator is all too familiar with. On the trip to Nuevo Laredo, the narrator's friend and her family laugh at the narrator when she orders a nonmeat dish simply because it is Friday. The friend tells the narrator that in Nuevo Laredo, it is OK to eat meat. The narrator expresses her disbelief at this news. Back at home, the narrator asks her father whether or not it is OK to eat meat on Fridays in Mexico: "But I ask Papi and he says it's true; it's not a sin" (115). At this point, the narrator questions the rules and regulations of the Catholic Church. The greater reality of the idea of borders does not become any clearer than in this story of eating meat on Fridays. The religious cultures in Laredo and Nuevo Laredo are traditionally similar. The friend and her family tell the narrator that it is not a sin to eat meat on Friday to justify the family's personal values and morals. As Anzaldúa writes, "What you or your cultures believe to be true is provisional and depends on a specific perspective" (Anzaldúa and Keating, 542). In other words, rules and regulations are not set in stone. Even though the narrator's family and the friend's family are of the same ethnicity, the same community, and the same religion, the border values are clearly in a constant state of motion.

The conflicting border values are further highlighted in "Fridays" when the narrator asks the friend's family if she has to cover her hair when she enters the church. Cantú writes, "I ask if covering your hair holds true on both sides [of the border], yes in fact, in Mexico you can't just plop a Kleenex on top and secure it with a hairpin" (115). Then, amusingly, the "usher at the church in Monterrey wouldn't let me in [into the church] until my cousin explained that I was from the United States" (115). While Cantú does not elaborate further on why the usher agreed to let the narrator of the vignette into the church, it can be surmised that the narrator was allowed in because her cousin explained to the usher she was not a local. The vignette "Fridays" is only a page long, but Cantú's short prose creatively expresses the geopolitical differences border people faced daily.

Cultural conflict on the border is a way a life. Life on the border is a blending of cultures that tend to grind against each other. The boundaries established because of culture, skin color, and even gender have given rise to complex but stunning new cultures and theories. Paredes notes that "border dwellers" have had issues with identity since the Texas Revolution (1835–36), when "people of Mexican culture" first encountered Americans (19). The discrepancies and contradictions in *Canícula* create a delineated narrative, which exemplifies the pluralistic life along the Texas-Mexico border. Belonging to and participating in one culture gives some perspective to the "other" culture. Echoing Paredes, Anzaldúa states that "seeing from two or more perspectives simultaneously renders those cultures transparent" (Anzaldúa and Keating, 549). In other words, a person's ability to recognize the worlds in and around him or her helps that person navigate to a new and or different identity, as it did for Cantú.

The search for self is problematic and oftentimes calls into question the author's authenticity. The problem with reading and studying literature like Cantú's *Canícula*, other than the multilayered, multidisciplinary reading it requires, is deeming the literature credible. As mentioned earlier, most students in my midwestern class resisted reading the text. They did not like nor understand its nonlinear format and the code-switching sprinkled throughout the text. Questions such as "Why can't she write in English?" and "It doesn't make sense. Where does it begin?" reverberated throughout the classes. The fact that Cantú writes that some of *Canícula* is autobiographical and some is not only added to the students' confusion and resistance to the text. Mainstream American students expected a traditional format, some sort of structure to guide them through the narrative. What they needed, however, was an understanding of what it means to navigate through a culture as an "other." Chela Sandoval, for example, in *Methodology of the Oppressed* (2000), attests that women who negotiate through masculine culture and base their experiences on marginality work on multiple levels of culture. She calls this "oppositional consciousness" (44). She believes that "subjugated citizens [can] either occupy or throw off subjectivities [in] a process that at once both enacts and yet decolonizes their various relations to their real conditions of existence" (63). What she is proposing is taking the tool of language and restructuring the histories and traditional social and political theories to decolonize a predominantly hegemonic academic institution. Sandoval's "oppositional consciousness" can be what is at the core of *Canícula* when one is reading and studying its perplexity and contradictions.

There is no other better way to decolonize the self than to use one's own culture and familiar surroundings. From Paredes to Anzaldúa to Sandoval, the importance of rediscovering the self is reiterated in their texts and theories. Rediscovering the self establishes not only a sense of belonging but also a sense of community, even in an ever-changing place like Laredo. It is through the rediscovering of the self that mujeres de la frontera decolonize their lives and those of their families and communities. The mixtures of culture along the border help construct an identity. Upon closer inspection, rediscovering the self is a natural response to an association with a larger group. What Anzaldúa and Sandoval do in their work is turn opposition into an instrument of opportunity. Likewise, in *Canícula*, Cantú uses the image to decolonize and define the self. It is through the photos and the folklore within the photographs that she maintains and rediscovers a collective self.

Throughout *Canícula*, the reader learns how Cantú navigates through history, culture, and life on the Texas-Mexico border. It is through this process that the reader encounters the many factors that help shed light on the lives of people surrounding the border areas. Nonetheless, elements such as ethnicity, religion, and nationality play a large role in determining the self. Folklore and culture also tend to help form ideas of people as individuals and as a community. Moreover, what happens to a group of people who have been displaced and colonized? What happens to their traditions and culture? Paredes asserts that "being Mexican meant remaining inviolable in the face of overwhelming attacks on one's personality. Under those circumstances, for a Mexican to accept North American values was to desert under fire. Such a situation—creative of folk groups defined as minorities—is not historically unique" (10). This assessment is understandable considering what Paredes describes as a constant motion of people. In addition, this constant movement on the Texas-Mexico border has led to an "intensified nationalism" on the part of the border people, a resistance to complete Americanization (10).

Canícula demonstrates this complexity and undercurrent of resistance associated with border life. *Canícula* also uses folklore to express culture. Richard Bauman, folklorist and Américo Paredes scholar, reaffirms Paredes's revisionist version of border history by writing that "the generating force out of which such folklore emerges is conflict, struggle, and resistance, and the folklore operates as an instrument of this conflict, not in the service of systems maintenance" (quoted in Paredes, xiv). This conflict acts as a link between struggle and resistance and reflects a theory of "oppositional consciousness" (Sandoval, 44). In "Caminando con La Llorona: Traditional and Contemporary Narratives," Domino Renee Perez (2002) indicates that "folklore . . . acts as a kind of cultural currency through which ideas are exchanged and reinforced within a specific group" (101). In Cantú's vignette "Healing," for example, the reader is introduced to a well-known Mexican American custom, *curanderismo*.[18] The narrator writes about going with her parents to Monterrey by train; they travel to a small hamlet up in the mountains to visit a healer. The father suffers from bouts of arthritis and looks to be healed. The narrator has her doubts about whether the healer will be effective, as does her mother. However, according to a number of letters and postcards pinned on the walls, this healer has helped many. What is important about this piece is that Western society does not accept customs such as healing and labels them antiquated and the product of superstition. But the fact that the healer has numerous written testimonies to prove that her healing methods are "miracles" attests to Mexican Americans' devout belief in such customs. Paredes's revisionist version of border history and culture is extremely useful to an analysis of *Canícula* because it sheds light on the difficult problem of communicating the link between struggle and conflict in customs such as curanderismo (Paredes, xiv).

Throughout *Canícula*, Cantú digs through a box of cherished family photos and describe these mementos in terms of tradition and folklore to bring the reader into her Laredo home in the 1960s. The photographs not only offer a visualization of Cantú's own story but also clarify the rich customs and traditions that have survived colonization and dispossession on the Texas-Mexico border. *Canícula*'s importance is not based solely on the text itself but on what the images it contains reveal. As Betty Bergland (1994) writes in "Rereading Photographs and Narratives in Ethnic Autobiography," images "serve a critical function for readers in the construction of ethnic identity, personal and collective, and thus the construction of ethnic memory and meaning" (46). Images themselves tell a story. The eyes receive the message the images relay, thus drawing the reader into the image. In *Canícula*, while the anecdotes sometimes do not coincide with the image, as Adams notes, what is important is the message the image relays. The images in *Canícula* convey an ethnic identity, a culture that is colonized and fighting to decolonize. An example of this ethnic identity is evident in the image of "China Poblana Two," which was discussed earlier in this essay.

Canícula reveals a web of activity on the border that had not been articulated until this novel was published. Cantú exposes the reader to the political atmosphere of the time, which she unfolds through testimonials, prose, and culture. In *Canícula*, Cantú shares stories—whether autobiographical or fictional—about customs to explain the cultural and gender politics of the Texas-Mexico border. Conquest and colonialism are inescapably tied to clashes of culture and customs, as Paredes notes. The clashes on the Texas-Mexico border relate to the changing political status of Mexican Americans in the United States near the end of the nineteenth century and up to the beginning of the twentieth century. Understanding the history of marginalized groups, such as Mexican Americans, is critical for changing long-held attitudes and, consequently, for reshaping the future. In *Canícula*, Cantú takes the reader to Laredo, a place where people hold on tightly to their traditions but at the same time try very hard to be Americans, as evidenced by their yearly celebration of George Washington's Birthday.[19]

When a person considers his or her own identity, many external factors come into the picture. This idea brings me back to the fence within the fence and the young man from Monterrey, Mexico, who noticed it. After thinking about the fence within the fence and the emotions that seeing it elicited in me, as well as the questions it raised—"Who is Homeland Security trying to keep in?" and "Who is Homeland Security trying to keep out?"—I remembered a family picnic along the Rio Grande when I was about ten years old. My father and uncles fished while my brother Boy, our cousins, and I played in the water. The sun was out, the clouds were white and puffy, and I lay on the pebbles, which were covered by four inches of cool, refreshing water. The water was clean. There were no Border Patrol vehicles speeding along the riverbanks; there were no helicopters flying over with their blades chopping the air. Everything was perfect. It was a simpler time, a time when on Sundays we crossed into Nuevo Laredo to go to the market so my grandfather could get his shoes shined while Boy and I ate popsicles made of succulent pure fruit.

When I look at the fence within the fence, it bothers me because Homeland Security has destroyed the carrizo that the Matachines used to make their dance regalia, a long-held tradition that now is obscured.[20] The fence bothers me because along with Homeland Security come the noisy helicopters that obstruct the sounds of the birds and water swishing against the rocks. It used to be easy to go to the *otro lado* to buy fruits and popsicles.[21] Today, we do not go to the otro lado for anything anymore, and every night, the helicopters fly overhead with their blue spotlights and noisy blades. The factors that help make my identity are not the helicopters, the drones, or the Border Patrol agents walking around in their green uniforms. My identity comes from the traditions and customs handed down to me by my community and family. I learned the folklore from scholars and professors like Cantú and the faculty at LCC and Texas A&M International University. Those are the factors that have influenced who I have become. Now, when I look at the fence within the fence, I resent the black metal that is supposed to keep me from going out, and I resent that it is trying to keep "us" in. As long as there are scholars like Paredes, Sandoval, and Cantú to keep future generations interested in culture and traditions through their works, no fence can stop us from learning about ourselves and how to decolonize. *Canícula*, through its short prose, nontraditional and nonlinear format, and black-and-white photos, reminds the border town readers who they were, because in order to move forward, readers need to look back to see where they came from.

NOTES

1. San Bernardo Avenue is the main street of Laredo, Texas. According to the GPS it is also Highway 35 South, which goes directly into the country of Mexico.
2. For information about historic Fort McIntosh, where LCC is located, see Jerry D. Thompson's *Sabers on the Rio Grande.*
3. I was not trying to sound elitist or essentialist, but in order to engage the students in the discussion, I thought it important to address "our" stories.
4. I will use the term *border people* to describe the people from Laredo, Texas, and the surrounding area. See Américo Paredes, *Folklore and Culture on the Texas-Mexican Border*, page 26, for a better description of how the Rio Grande split a community.
5. In this essay, I will use *mujeres de la frontera* to describe border women.
6. I use *Euro-American* to describe the major hegemonic group.
7. For example, during the 1930s and 1940s, J. Frank Dobie and Walter Prescott Webb, Anglo Texans, became renowned for their work on the history and folklore of Texas.
8. I use *Anglo Texans* to refer to the Euro-Americans who resided in Texas. I use the term *Texas Mexicans* to describe the people who were born, raised, and died on the Texas-Mexico border. Jovita González, Tejana folklorist, uses the term frequently in her article titled "America Invades the Border Towns," published in 1930.
9. Cantú seems to include Tino on purpose. The reader will find out in the course of the book that Tino is the brother of the girls in the picture, who later on is killed in Vietnam.
10. One of the first pages of the text is a hand-drawn picture of the Texas-Mexico border. The author provides this so the reader can have a geographic idea of the place that she is writing about and to demonstrate the closeness between the two cities: Laredo, Texas, and Nuevo Laredo, Mexico.
11. Refer to Betty Bergland's essay "Rereading Photographs and Narratives in Ethnic Autobiography" (1994).
12. See Gauvin A. Bailey's "A Mughal Princess in Baroque New Spain" (1997) for a complete explanation of the origins of the dress.

13. Ibid.
14. According to Limón (1983), "performance centered approach to folklore" is preferred in today's folklore study over "older textual orientations." Limón explains that "performance approach analytically renders the culture specific expressive ways of speaking in a particular speech community" (191–208).
15. Some of Paredes's earlier work centered on corridos, better known as border ballads. His work on corridos is known for its in-depth analysis and political and social commentary. See Paredes's text *Folklore and Culture on the Texas-Mexican Border.*
16. In Anzaldúa's writings, nepantla represents an extension on her theories of the borderlands. Nepantla is a space where transformation can occur. It indicates a space created by a loss of control. Sometimes, it can mean confusion and anxiety. See *Borderlands/La Frontera.*
17. *Mami* is the Spanish version of the English word "mommy." *Comadres* means "girlfriends." Cantú does not italicize the Spanish words in *Canícula*, perhaps because the author wants to give the reader the full effect of being bilingual.
18. *Curanderismo* means "healing" in Spanish. It is a long tradition of healing with herbs and other plants.
19. For a complete history of the George Washington's Birthday celebration in Laredo, Texas, see Elliott Young's "Red Men, Princess Pocahontas, and George Washington: Harmonizing Race Relations in Laredo at the Turn of the Century" (1998).
20. See Norma Cantú's article "Performing Indigeneity in a South Texas Community: Los Matachines de la Santa Cruz" (2012).
21. Border residents usually use *otro lado*, a slang term, to refer to the other side of the Rio Grande.

WORKS CITED

Adams, Timothy D. "'Heightened by Life' vs. 'Paralyzed by Fact': Photography and Autobiography in Norma E. Cantú's *Canícula*." *Biography: An Interdisciplinary Quarterly* 24, no. 1 (2001): 57–71.

Aldama, Arturo J., Chela Sandoval, and Peter J. Garcia, eds. *Performing the U.S. Latina and Latino Borderlands*. Bloomington: Indiana University Press, 2012.

Anzaldúa, Gloria. *Borderlands/La Frontera: The New Mestiza*. San Francisco: Spinsters/Aunt Lute, 1987.

———, ed. *Making Face, Making Soul/Haciendo Caras: Creative and Critical Perspectives by Feminists of Color*. San Francisco: Aunt Lute, 1990.

Anzaldúa, Gloria, and AnaLouise Keating, eds. *This Bridge We Call Home: Radical Visions for Transformation*. New York: Routledge, 2002.

Bailey, Gauvin A. "A Mughal Princess in Baroque New Spain: Catarina De San Juan (1606–1688), the 'China Poblana.'" *Anales del Instituto de Investigaciones Estéticas* 19, no. 71 (1997): 37–73.

Bergland, Betty. "Rereading Photographs and Narratives in Ethnic Autobiography: Memory and Subjectivity in Mary Antin's *The Promised Land*." In *Memory, Narrative, and Identity: New Essays in Ethnic American Literatures*, edited by Amritjit Singh, Joseph T. Skerrett, and Robert E. Hogan, 45. Boston: Northeastern University Press, 1994.

Cantú, Norma E. *Canícula: Snapshots of a Girlhood en la Frontera*. Albuquerque: University of New Mexico Press, 1995.

———. "Performing Indigeneity in a South Texas Community: Los Matachines de la Santa Cruz." In *Performing the U.S. Latina and Latino Borderlands*, edited by Arturo J. Aldama, Chela Sandoval, and Peter J. Garcia, 127–45. Bloomington: Indiana University Press, 2012.

Clifford, James. *Writing Culture: The Poetics and Politics of Ethnography*. Berkeley: University of California Press, 1986.

González, Jovita. "America Invades the Border Towns." *Southwest Review* 15, no. 4 (1930): 469.

Limón, José E. "Legendry, Metafolklore, and Performance: A Mexican-American Example." *Western Folklore* 42, no. 3 (1983): 191–208.

Najera-Ramírez, Olga. "*Encaminándonos*: Américo Paredes as a Guiding Force in Transcending Borders." *Journal of American Folklore* 125, no. 495 (2012): 69–90.

Paredes, Américo. *Folklore and Culture on the Texas-Mexican Border*. Austin: Center for Mexican American Studies, University of Texas at Austin, 1993.

Perez, Domino Renee. "Caminando con La Llorona: Traditional and Contemporary Narratives." In *Chicana Traditions: Continuity and Change*, edited by Norma E. Cantú and Olga Nájera-Ramirez, 100–13. Urbana: University of Illinois Press, 2002.

Sandoval, Chela. *Methodology of the Oppressed*. Minneapolis: University of Minnesota Press, 2000.

Thompson, Jerry D. *Sabers on the Rio Grande*. Austin, TX: Presidial Press, 1974.

Young, Elliot. "Red Men, Princess Pocahontas, and George Washington: Harmonizing Race Relations in Laredo at the Turn of the Century." *Western Historical Quarterly* 29, no. 1 (Spring 1998): 48–85.

CANÍCULA

Snapshots of Interrelationality, Consciousness, and Multiple Selves

JUAN VELASCO

CANÍCULA: SNAPSHOTS OF A GIRLHOOD EN LA FRONTERA (1995) is, at first glance, a collection of Norma E. Cantú's childhood memories in Texas. But these snapshots, autobiographical in nature, also comprise a book that tells a Mexican American story through family vignettes and family pictures. As described by Chicana literary critic Tey Diana Rebolledo (1999), *Canícula* is "a community and family ethnography of life in border Texas in the 1950s. The narrative voice often slips from a childhood present to a known adult future, and details perceptions and reminiscences of Chicano/Mexicano life in South Texas" (46). Gerald P. Lopez, in "Big Time Players," discusses how Latinos are rarely being recognized as a valid part of American society. He states that "we're all to conclude, I suppose, that there are almost no stories to tell, almost no stories to be told about us, and almost no roles we competently fill" (237). Much has been written about the hybrid nature of Cantú's book, but this work, published in the 1990s, is one of the most successful attempts not only at telling the story of a Mexican American childhood but at telling it by connecting autobiographical, visual, and ethnographic accounts of a life spent in the borderlands. Norma E. Cantú's *Canícula* is a collection of eighty-four

This article borrows information from some of my previously published articles on the issue of Chicana/o autobiography and my book *Cultural Resistance and Collective Identity in Contemporary Chicana/o Autobiography.*

vignettes, plus a prologue, an introduction, and twenty-three photographs that make up the subtitle *Snapshots of a Girlhood en la Frontera*. In "Translating Media: Why We Should Rethink Textuality," N. Katherine Hayles states that "once we let go of the assumption that the literary work must be an expression of an immaterial sense—a line of thought dominant in literary criticism at least since the eighteenth century—we see the new forms of textuality that, galloping ahead of textual theory, are already cycling through diverse media in exuberant and playful performances that defy the old verities even as they give rise to the new" (280).

By combining visual and narrative techniques, Cantú makes important disruptions within the existing autobiographical genre but also creates "new forms of textuality" and connects those to a vision of the roles Chicanas/os fulfill in the twentieth and twenty-first century. I have chosen to examine Cantú's *Canícula* because of her innovative form of self-representation, because of the stories she brings forward, and because her work provides some of the most interesting contributions that have been made to the representation of the space of identity *en la frontera*.

CHICANA FICTIONAL AUTOBIOETHNOGRAPHY AND THE NEW FORMS OF TEXTUALITY

Indeed, her fictional autobioethnography presents a unique form of textuality that transcends simplistic representations of the Southwest as a frontier space. Although *Canícula* does not use a traditional form of ekphrasis, I am interested in the ways Cantú includes different forms of representation to create a language and a more complex view of the borderlands than we have traditionally been given. We will distinguish later how the concepts of frontier and borderlands operate differently in her work. First, it is important to clarify that ekphrasis is a form of fiction created through the commentary on a work of art, but, as expressed by Stephanie Coyne DeGhett, this technique has been used "to release storytelling rather than simply to describe art" (98). In her unpublished paper "How I Wrote *Canícula*: Musings on Writing, Reading, and Life," Cantú has credited the influences of Maxine Hong Kingston and Rita Mae Brown but also states that "I came upon the idea of the photos all on my own. I often think up exercises for my writing classes, and in the early '80s I began using the photo for a guided imagery exercise. The students loved it and so did I" (5). That she has used a form of ekphrasis based on pictures and that she started "thinking about a narrative set on the border that used this strategy" (5) show a connection that reveals the structural integrity of her work. Effectively, Cantú's *Canícula* could be seen as using a variation of ekphrasis with the ultimate goal of creating a fictional autobioethnography—thus the creation of a community and family album combining vignettes and photographs. Furthermore, her book brings together personal stories and pictures to create an album of verbal and visual "snapshots."

I am underlining the snapshots, the combination of the mediums of representation, because I see in these new forms of textuality a pattern that is unique to works of Chicana fictional autobioethnography. Sheila and Sandra Ortiz Taylor's *Imaginary Parents: A Family Autobiography* and the storytelling triggered by photographs in Lourdes Portillo's documentary film *The Devil Never Sleeps* are two examples of Chicana autobioethnography using photographs, glimpses into the mystery, and gaps of meaning to create a more complex representation of the traditional family album. In "Exorcizing/Exercising Treachery: Robust Subjectivity in Lourdes Portillo's *The Devil Never Sleeps*," Mónica F. Torres states that "if audience confidence is often assured with photographic evidence, Portillo's use of photographs proves unsettling" (77). As is the case with Cantú, "Portillo includes photographs on which she marks some part of the image that she wants viewers to notice" (81). It is worthwhile to consider these new forms of textuality as a conscious way of using the unsettling aspects of the conflating of images and words, of exploiting the tensions this practice engenders; thus it becomes a technique to release what Cantú named "fictional autobioethnographies."

Indeed, the unsettling feeling that *Canícula* creates in the reader (through the use of text, photographs, and the gaps between them) has driven at least one critic to state that, even though "these mismatches could be thought of as accidental or beside the point, I believe they are deliberate attempts at keeping the reader off balance in terms of the book's genre" (Adams, 62). Certainly, Cantú is advancing these forms of textuality not just to keep us guessing the book's genre but with the goal of representing the subjectivity of the borderlands through a more complex lens than we are accustomed to and also to engage the reader in a particular way by advancing a new understanding of the autobiographical genre. In fact, by the time we finish reading Cantú's work, as in the case of Portillo, we realize "the person thought to precede and produce the text, the person thought to hold the key to any final signified, has been thoroughly problematized"

(Torres, 76). For in Cantu's work, the storytelling being released through her use of ekphrasis moves the reader away from a simplistic version of authorship and to a place that first involves the small "I," then connects the subject represented to family and community, and finally pulls out to capture the whole picture. Similar strategies operate in Carmen Lomas Garza's descriptions of family life and community. In the introduction to *Family Pictures/Cuadros de familia*, Lomas Garza (1990) acknowledges the impact her painting had on helping her to attain her voice. Lomas Garza writes, "I always dreamed of becoming an artist. My family has inspired and encouraged me for all these years" (3). But in her books, by choosing to recount everyday events such as picking oranges, eating watermelon, making tamales, or even hanging out in the kitchen for a good meal, she underscores the importance of the incidental in a representation that values, above all, capturing the whole story: "So when I'm getting ready to do a certain painting, I rely on what I already have in my mind, and then I do move some things around. I do have poetic license to make the picture be able to tell the whole story with all its details" (Lomas Garza 1995). Garza's combination of storytelling and paintings, her use of both English and Spanish, and her deployment of the interaction of written and visual language to create a portrayal of childhood underline the need to represent the whole story.

Her use of these strategies underlines the tensions implicit in this kind of project. Indeed, these Chicana fictional autobiographies are difficult to classify. But by taking "poetic license" to provide the whole story, these artists are employing new forms of textuality to advance complex forms of fictional autobioethnography. I argue that, through a variation on ekphrasis, these artists use "the liveliness of fiction that speaks from both the text of its narrative and from the embedded alternative text of the painting" (DeGhett, 98).

Cantú's commitment to snapshots signals the importance of this unique vision of space, one that involves storytelling and visual language as both a way of adding nuance to the problematized subject being represented and a way of adding multiple layers of "reality" to the autobioethnography. Problematizing authorship allows, for example, Cantú's snapshot of her mother to be the vehicle for the kind of storytelling that includes such aspects of culture as "the descriptions of clothing and the materials from which it is made [which] are constant symbols throughout the narrative" (Rebolledo, 46). But Cantú writes about those everyday relationships as part of a larger whole and embeds a sense of belonging into every aspect of life. Her pictures and vignettes, the combination of Spanish and English, are linked to Cantú's new understanding of space.

This form of representation brings together the elements of cultural experience while envisioning a new sense of home and self.

THE CULTURAL SPACES OF *LA FRONTERA* AND THE MANY SELVES OF A REAL PLACE

Cantú's personal snapshots depict the specificity and memories of growing up as inseparable from the daily events of her hometown in Texas. Her autobio-ethnography indicates the importance of those links by connecting and moving freely between her personal imaginings of home and the goal of creating an album of community and family snapshots.

Some critics have focused on the discrepancies between the written word (the vignettes) and the photographs. Cantú advises the reader, in the prologue, about those instabilities, and her referencing of Roland Barthes let us know that her use of authorship is not a naïve one, but I argue that her strategy is not aimed at erasing the agency of the autobiographical act. In fact, as Melissa D. Birkhofer writes in a 2012 essay on *Canícula*, "Cantú stated that she wanted the readers of *Canícula* to be aware of the U.S.-Mexico border as a real place, a geo-political space where people are dying, not just an abstract, theoretical concept" (48). For Cantú, using photographs in combination with the autobiographical vignettes is a reaffirmation of home and culture and, literally, a way of taking snapshots of her girlhood and of la frontera as "a real place." While some critics have overlapped her questioning of authorship with an erasure of agency, I want to emphasize that the terms of her writing, the unsettling use of different forms of textuality, the presence and absence of multiple subjects, are all part of a structural blueprint that allows for a new form of representation. I suggest that the strategy of conflating the tools of representation (where pictures trigger text and vice versa) creates a form of textuality that allows for a new subject. Adding layers of complexity to the representation of the border is also a way of suggesting to the reader that through her work we will have a glimpse, not just of the frontier experience, but of that of la frontera. It is important to establish the difference between the notions of frontier and la frontera. *Frontier* is the space that separates the zone of civilization from that which is beyond, while the Spanish term *la frontera* conveys the idea of the borderlands as a zone of crossings and interaction. Moreover, we cannot talk about borders or frontiers without inserting their purpose into the semantic field of definition.

The function of every border has always been to stop the interaction, that is, to stop the crossing. While a frontier has traditionally been regarded as a line of separation, the product of an unnatural divide and oppressive dualistic thinking, la frontera in Cantú's work is a space of connectivity, a place where dualistic thinking ceases to operate and instead gives way to interrelationality. Writing that emerges from this kind of comprehension complements her complex understanding of authorship and is best explained by Susan Sontag in "Writing Itself: On Roland Barthes." In that essay, Sontag explains Barthes's interest in self-portraits as a construction of "writing as an ideally complex form of consciousness: a way of being both passive and active, social and asocial, present and absent in one's own life" (72).

The "real place" called home, within the context of Barthes's understanding of writing, points to the recreation, through Cantú's textuality (and her representation of la frontera), of this "complex form of consciousness." Her use of photography and words, her desire to provide a more complex representation of la frontera than we usually see, creates the snapshots of a "real place." *Canícula* then gives us glimpses of the whole picture from within the very specific discourse of truth en la frontera. But in Cantú, the recreation of the "real place" also extends to rendering snapshots "in terms of what is not there [which] is a powerful way to create a mystery in its deepest sense as well as mystery in its what-really-happened sense" (DeGhett, 105). By including in the significance of those events the gaps of representation, her vision of identity is also connected to the recovery of those pieces destroyed by cultural coloniality and those communal voices in need of remembering through autobioethnography. As in the genre Audre Lorde created and called "biomythography," *Canícula* uses photographs and the text to recreate "snapshots" of what is and is not there, of that which exists only in memory and that which was destroyed by history, lost to the colonizing experience. With this technique, she is simultaneously representing la frontera as a space with gaps and disruptions but also as a space of identity that often moves from intersectionality to interrelationality, from the voice of the small "I" to the many selves of a "real place." Gabriella Gutiérrez y Muhs comments on "the broad spectrum of subjectivities she utilizes to tell her autobioethnography: comadres, madrinas, tías, grandmothers, solteronas, and child mothers, all of whom are representative of the layered realities within the Chicana social structure and all of which are verbally photographed in *Canícula*" (11).

This aspect of representation does not imply a refusal of the more autobiographical aspects of her work. Cantú's emphasis on representing the "real place" of la frontera is consistent with a representation of her self in snapshots, in interaction with community, and in a space of interrelationality that is presented as fluid and expanding. Through her family snapshots, Cantú validates the experiences of her unique childhood and always carefully places them in the context of a representation of space inclusive of self, family, and the multiple communities beyond family. Cantú emphasizes in her prologue the merging of la frontera, her story, and the stories of the people living in that space: "The stories of her girlhood in that land in-between, la frontera, are shared; her story and the stories of the people who lived that life with her is one" (2). Certainly, her portrayal of the incidental aspects of experience and the interrelationality of that experience are also conscious decisions to create a space that expands the subject being represented while reinforcing the "real place" of belonging.

In "Fan Letters to the Cultural Industries: Border Literature About Mass Media," Claire Fox states, "*Canícula* is concerned with highlighting those practices and social institutions that forge Azucena's identity and development, ranging from oral histories and kinship relations, to language use, religion, gender relations, education, holidays, literature and popular culture, medical practices, food, clothing, and political struggle" (27). In *Canícula* the representation of certain events reminds us of the deep connections between the political, the cultural, and the personal. Whether in a reflection on body hair or the images of Bueli, the layered, multifragmented representations shake up and redefine assumptions about home and self. The depictions of food, for example, a privileged theme in many of Cantú's snapshots, bring attention to those aspects of experience that dissolve simplistic notions of identity, nourishment, and the representation of Chicano/a life. The arrangement of vignettes and photographs also show a vision from which *Canícula* reveals a sense of the extraordinary within daily life events. Those moments are created through the abundant use of sensory details grounded in the small aspects of experience. The reality of Chicano/a life and self, shaped by a sense of the extraordinary in the midst of community and the incidental, is invisible in the images of mainstream media. Furthermore, her representation of everyday activities reverses the prefabricated identities that populate the mass media and thrives instead on the details of a Chicano/a community, thus reinforcing home and belonging. She pushes for snapshots of experience that emphasize the unique vision of the world emanating from la frontera.

This reconfiguration of home and self, grounded in autobioethnography, cannot be taken for granted. As a counter to the stereotypes of Mexican

Americans created during the 1940s and 1950s, the invisibility of the 1960s and 1970s, the representations driven by marketing and mass consumerism during the 1980s and 1990s, and the images of the undocumented in the twenty-first century, Cantú's autobioethnography shows a home, a past, a childhood en la frontera, escaping the trends of a media invested in images of mass consumption or "illegal" aliens.

Stereotypical representations connected to the immigrant issue and the Mexico-U.S. border are addressed through Cantú's more complex images, like those in the vignette "Crossings." In this piece she describes the back-and-forth movement of those living en la frontera and the effect on those removed from the United States through forceful means, like Nena's grandmother and her Texas-born grandfather; but also the effects on those crossing back to the United States, which Bueli, Mami, and Papi experienced thirteen years later. For Cantú in *Canícula*, that specific crossing "meant coming home, but not quite" (5). This is important since "for Cantú crossing the bridge (or, alternatively, crossing the river) is a permanent referent not only of her family's binational life but also the structural integrity of her tale" (Castillo and Tabuenca Córdoba 2002, 98). In Cantú's fictional autobioethnography, not only is the conflictive nature of the crossings part of the Chicana/o experience, her goal is to represent its ambiguity by making the back-and-forth movement of the crossings a part of the internal structure of her autobioethnography. Cantú's work strives to represent the deep levels of reality in those crossings through the crossings present in the different forms of representation: photography, autobiography, and ethnography. Through the intersection of these different forms of representation, Cantú shows those crossings as a source of conflictive ambiguity—a complex form of consciousness.

AUTOBIOETHNOGRAPHY AS A COMPLEX FORM OF CONSCIOUSNESS

In Cantú, the "real place" called home can only involve new forms of textuality inclusive of subjectivities beyond those offered by traditional autobiography. As such, this autobioethnography is an invitation to literally glimpse individuals within the larger context of crossings and in the context of a representation able to contain the complexities of a new consciousness. Certainly, a book that chooses as a title *Canícula*, a metaphor for both temporal liminality and liminal space, is determined to make its crossings a central point of its representation. The subtitle, *Snapshots of a Girlhood en la Frontera*, written in both English and Spanish, rendered in both roman font and italics on the book's cover, underlines also her investigation of liminality by pointing at the crossings and by looking at the spaces in between, those aspects of experience that are both here and there. For in *Canícula*, the space in between seasons (as time) works as a reminder that the border is a geographical place subject to perpetual change and that in the experience of the border there is a mystery that implies both its presence and absence.

Some critics interpret Cantú's use of Barthes as a reflection on art and memory and a commentary on the limitations of both within the framework of a poststructuralist reading. But I argue that, by using Barthes, "canicular" time, and the forms of textuality discussed earlier, Cantú engages with the more complex realities of the border experience and its representation. For her writing is invested in a fictional autobioethnography that advances a complex form of consciousness—that which is unconstrained or unfixed by traditional notions of subjectivity, time, or space. At the core of this effort are the structural crossings of her writing, which resembles the liminal space of la frontera. As such, she is using the autobioethnography to engage with those liminal spaces, but not just to disrupt traditional autobiographical representation: she does it to point at the border experiences as glimpses into the gaps—a representation beyond dualistic thinking, beyond subject and object, a place to enter interrelationality and multiple selves. Furthermore, the idea of the snapshot suggests the glimpse into the mystery, the moment that holds a whole life in a flash, a moment of consciousness. When Timothy D. Adams states that "Norma Elia Cantú mediates between her words and her images by manipulating not the photographic record, but her prose descriptions of the photograph, thereby allowing room for her changing identities" (70), what he is also acknowledging is that even the subject being represented is a moving identity and that Cantú's writing is an exploration of absence as well as a place of connectivity. Those glimpses the reader experiences into Bueli's border include the fluidity of a truth that is marked by impermanence, that includes what is present and what is not, what was and what will be. In the vignette "Bueli," the narrator incorporates her brother as part of the snapshot, but in fact Tino, who died in Vietnam, is not present in the picture nor in the life of the author when she writes. The tension of presence and absence point to a gap in the way she remembers the picture, but the inclusion of Tino in the vignette alludes to the narrator's voice as a thread to the interrelationality of all beings—his death does not remove Tino from Cantú's childhood or from her life in general. Another example of this strategy is the vignette "Martin High," where Azucena's description of her outfit does not correlate with the one in the photograph. The text mentions a pot of tamales, some corn husks, and people eating, but none of these are present in the photo. The picture instead is a representation of her high school graduating class of 455 people, and of those only twenty-four names are cited. Using both the details and the gaps, one can only guess at a bigger picture of facts and memories as one tries to recreate the particular experiences of the 455 people who appear in the photograph.

Because of her inclusion of multiple subjects, forms of textuality, and experiences, this is a multidimensional writing that is also able to embrace the notion of multiple selves; for even Nena, Azucena, and Cantú are not fixed points of view but rather constitute a project of identity in constant movement, relational in nature, and undergoing a process of presence and absence that enables agency while transcending all boundaries and borders. The critic AnaLouise Keating describes those moments of representation as a political gaze "which moves from interconnectivity to inter-relationality, [and] offers a radically inclusionary approach" (30). Critics usually analyze the spaces between photographs and vignettes as unsettling gaps, but the form of holographic representation used by Cantú suggests Keating's notion of interrelationality. In fact, if we carefully analyze the prologue to *Canícula*, we notice how it starts with the narrator learning about Barthes's death in 1980; then a few weeks later, the narrator, in Paris, buys the *Nouvel Observateur* and reads the special issue on Roland Barthes. His book *Camera Lucida: Reflections on Photography* is born. Also in 1980, she is in Madrid, looking at the photos of her lover before 1936, the time of the Spanish Civil War. According to the narrator, "he has offered his life" to her in photos, but she has no photographs to offer. In 1985, back to her "safe space" between countries, her mother brings out the family album, and the whole family contributes stories. In that moment Cantú returns to her childhood home in Laredo through multiple family narrators and family photographs. The pictures take her to the Laredo of the 1940s; it is through the glimpses into the 1940s that she is triggered to write her fictional autobioethnography in Albuquerque (now without the pictures present), and thus Nena (the narrator and witness of *Canícula*) is born. After the book is completed in the 1990s, she decides to return, in the prologue, to where everything started—to Barthes's death. Some might interpret those events as disconnected, random, or unsettling; I see them as the traces of a deep form of interrelationality interweaving the many lives, times, and spaces she is trying to represent. This prologue is also symptomatic of the kind of crossings (in time and space; in authorship and readership) her writing is addressing. The interconnectivity of elements in time and space and her multiple dimensions of reality and self (life and death, memory and its holographic projections into the past and the future) are not simply "inconsistencies" caused by the instability of meaning. This writing is unfolding a self-portrait that reveals a form of consciousness invested in both presence and absence. It is a movement (a multidimensional crossing) between studium as "commitment" and punctum as a "cut" (time) that arrives at what Barthes describes as obtuse meaning, or those moments of recognition not "located in language used" (60). Just as the image of the *canícula* captures this temporal and spatial entity, a particular experience in between the seasons and in between cultures, languages, and nations, Cantú's autobioethnography thrives not by identifying one story to tell or a nation to belong to but by pointing at the crossings and the extraordinary moments of interrelationality. Thus, the reader also experiences the epiphany of a glimpse into a moment of representation that evokes, according to Barthes, not the *being-there* "but an awareness of its *having-been-there*" (44)—that is, in its presence and absence, in the flash of a moment that brings the interrelationality of experience together. In other words, Cantú's snapshots, juxtaposed against one another, reveal the potentiality for a new language, one that refuses subject and object, avoids the simplistic dimensions of dualistic thinking, and points at those moments experienced from within as a complex net woven of interrelationality and consciousness.

Whether in time, in space, or in the forms of textuality creating a new blueprint of representation, *Canícula* points to the fluidity of relational space, to a new consciousness as a response to an unnatural border, to an imposed dualistic separation that her writing is breaking open. For Cantú wishes us to see those spaces not just as undermining meaning but as a real place, a space of interconnectivity and empowerment. In the cracks of interrelationality this consciousness is a response to the imposed borders, to the boundaries that contain her experience beyond languages, memories, and texts. Furthermore, her snapshots not only consider those complex realities but present the possibility of a breakthrough by looking at interrelationality from within.

In *The Spell of the Sensuous: Perception and Language in a More-than-Human World* (1996), David Abram remarks on philosophy's impossible dream of explaining the deeper structures of reality. Later, however, he comments on how

Maurice Merleau-Ponty opens, in the realm of phenomenology, the possibility of "a philosophy which would strive, not to explain the world as if from outside, but to give voice to the world from our experienced situation *within* it, recalling us to our participation in the here-and-now, rejuvenating our sense of wonder at the fathomless things, events and powers that surround us on every hand" (47). Precisely by transcending traditional forms of autobiographical and ethnographical representation based on separation or dualistic thinking, on the separation of subject and object, Cantú creates a unique album of family pictures and a glimpse into a consciousness wherein lies the possibility for the reader to experience the breakthrough from within.

THE CONSCIOUSNESS OF INTERRELATIONALITY

As we saw in the previous section, Cantu's new form of textuality, and her crossings beyond the linear narratives of traditional autobiography into the intersectional and interrelationality, unfolds a form of consciousness that also allows agency. Through the incorporation of multiple layers of experience, the extraordinary space of representation created in *Canícula* anticipates a consciousness that underlines a relational experience rather than separation or loss. Furthermore, Cantú's affirmation about certain kind of crossings "not being quite home" is also a wake-up call to us to be aware that there are no here and there. Ultimately, in this consciousness, there should be nothing to cross. *Canícula*'s consciousness leads the reader to a decision to live without borders: "you must live *sin fronteras*" (Anzaldúa, 216). As such, the configuration of being borderless goes beyond the language of nation to the creation of a model of subjectivity based on interrelationality—a space of representation in which "those boundaries are disrupted, in which national and cultural affiliations are superseded, in which binaries of centre and periphery, national self and other are dissolved" (Ashcroft, 171).

The sense of interrelationality among family, language, time, space, and community is crucial to nearly every scene of daily life en la frontera. In "Living Theory: Representing Lives in Norma E. Cantú's *Canícula*," Kathryn Quinn-Sánchez points to Cantú's consciousness, recreated textually "as character, memory, photograph, collage, family member, friend, colleague, and as potential" (124). Furthermore, Cantú's *Canícula* shows the interconnectedness of all aspects of experience and, through the arrangement of textuality, offers a glimpse of past, present, and future connected by extraordinary moments. Referring to the vignette titled "Body Hair," Jeraldine Kraver states that "in this simple, two-page recollection, Cantú captures far more than Nena's grappling with identity and adolescence. 'Body Hair' is the struggle of a people and a region caught literally and figuratively between two cultures and two worlds" (81). Through the open-ended quality of this form of representation Cantú is able not only to represent personal experiences but to bring together snapshots of a consciousness that speaks for a "home" that interconnects the spaces of family, school, and community. As stated by Kraver, "Cantú's work reminds us that her story, Nena's story, and the story of all the men, women, and children who people her photographs is shared. Their story is inseparable from the world of *la Frontera*. Even though the reality of the photographs included alongside the text may be lost and the memories maybe rewritten or revised, it matters little" (81).

Cantú transcends the representations of the space of "illegality" by showing the homemaking space of *Canícula* and strives to represent the whole picture of Chicana/o life by showing the interrelationality and by emphasizing the incidental moments of experience reflected from within. This whole picture takes us, not to a nation of people crowded around the television as it shows images of "illegal" aliens, living vicariously through fictitious border-like stereotypical characters, but to those moments of experience when the community members are alive and present to one another, changing through their connections and interactions.

Canícula's fictional autobioethnography advances a new conception of interrelationality as a space where the multiple experiences and the multiple communities the Chicana/o inhabits come together. Cantú is also able to take a snapshot of those spaces and show them as both being a challenge and offering the possibility for a transformation. This space of "home" is linked to a complex form of consciousness that enables multiple subjectivities to act without necessarily eliminating tensions and contradictions. Theoretically grounded in Barthes's understanding of self-portrait, her work reveals the significance of those fragmented dimensions of experience that dissolve the boundaries of time and space, presence and absence, and it emphasizes the snapshots that show life as a web of options and interrelated selves. Those dimensions of experience reveal her understanding of the past as pregnant with the present and the future. Cantú's glimpses of interrelationality disclose the consciousness of a culturally rich community in the process of creating its own future.

WORKS CITED

Abram, David. *The Spell of the Sensuous: Perception and Language in a More-than-Human World.* New York: Random House, 1996.

Adams, Timothy D. "'Heightened by Life' vs. 'Paralyzed by Fact': Photography and Autobiography in Norma E. Cantú's *Canícula.*" *Biography: An Interdisciplinary Quarterly* 24, no. 1 (2001): 57–71.

Anzaldúa, Gloria. *Borderlands/La Frontera: The New Mestiza.* San Francisco: Spinsters/Aunt Lute, 1987.

Ashcroft, Bill. "Literature, Nation, Transnation." In *Ethnic Literatures and Transnationalism: Critical Imaginaries for a Global Age*, edited by Aparajita Nanda, 163–72. New York and London: Routledge, 2015.

Barthes, Roland. *Image, Music, Text.* Translated by Stephen Heath. London: Fontana Press, 1977.

Birkhofer, Melissa D. "Norma Elia Cantú's *Canícula: Snapshots of a Girlhood en la Frontera.*" *Rocky Mountain Review* (2012): 48–57.

Cantú, Norma E. *Canícula: Snapshots of a Girlhood en la Frontera.* Albuquerque: University of New Mexico Press, 1995.

———. "How I Wrote *Canícula*: Musings on Writing, Reading, and Life." Unpublished essay.

Castillo, Debra A., and María Socorro Tabuenca Córdoba, eds. *Border Women: Writing from la Frontera.* Minneapolis: University of Minnesota Press, 2002.

DeGhett, Stephanie Coyne. "Painting in Fiction: Ten Lessons from the Masters of Ekphrasis." *Writer's Chronicle* 46, no. 6 (Summer 2014): 96–107.

The Devil Never Sleeps/El diablo nunca duerme. Written, directed, and produced by Lourdes Portillo. Xochitl Films, 1994.

Fox, Claire. "Fan Letters to the Cultural Industries: Border Literature About Mass Media." *Studies in 20th Century Literature* 25, no. 1 (Winter 2001): 16–31.

Gutiérrez y Muhs, Gabriella. "Subjectifying Entities/Emerging Subjectivities in Chicana Literature Through the Literary Production of Demetria Martínez and Norma Elia Cantú: Madres, comadres, madrinas, niñas madres, tías, abuelas y solteronas." PhD diss., Stanford University, 2000.

Hayles, N. Katherine. "Translating Media: Why We Should Rethink Textuality." *Yale Journal of Criticism* 16, no. 2 (2003): 263–90.

Keating, AnaLouise. *Transformation Now! Toward a Post-Oppositional Politics of Change.* Champaign: University of Illinois Press, 2013.

Kraver, Jeraldine. "Norma Elia Cantú's Fictional Autobio-ethnography: Not-Quite-True Stories About Real Life on la Frontera." *Auto/biography Studies* 20, no. 1 (January 2005): 76–89.

Lomas Garza, Carmen. *Family Pictures/Cuadros de familia.* San Francisco: Children's Book Press, 1990.

———. Interview by Andrew Connors, May 1995. Smithsonian American Art Museum. http://www.scholastic.com/content/collateral_resources/pdf/t/target/DreamArtistStatements_6-8_9-12.pdf.

Lopez, Gerald P. "Big Time Players." In *The Latino/a Condition: A Critical Reader*, edited by Richard Delgado and Jean Stefancic, 237–39. New York: New York University Press, 1998.

Ortiz Taylor, Sheila, and Sandra Ortiz Taylor. *Imaginary Parents: A Family Autobiography.* Albuquerque: University of New Mexico Press, 1996.

Quinn-Sánchez, Kathryn. "Living Theory: Representing Lives in Norma E. Cantú's *Canícula.*" *Hispanic Journal* 32, no. 1 (2011): 119–35.

Rebolledo, Tey Diana. "The Tools in the Toolbox: Representing Work in Chicana Writing." *Genre: Forms of Discourse and Culture* 32, nos. 1–2 (Spring/Summer 1999): 41–52.

Sontag, Susan. "Writing Itself: On Roland Barthes." In *Where the Stress Falls*, 63–88. New York: Farrar, Straus, and Giroux, 2001.

Torres, Mónica F. "Exorcizing/Exercising Treachery: Robust Subjectivity in Lourdes Portillo's *The Devil Never Sleeps.*" *Velvet Light Trap* 57 (Spring 2006): 76–85.

CONTRIBUTORS

Steven W. Bender, a law professor and associate dean for research and faculty development at Seattle University School of Law and former president of the Society of American Law Teachers, is the author of several books encompassing legal, social, cultural, and historical issues: *Greasers and Gringos: Latinos, Law, and the American Imagination* (NYU Press, 2003); *One Night in America: Robert Kennedy, César Chávez, and the Dream of Dignity* (Paradigm Publishers, 2007), recipient of the 2008 Oregon Book Award for general nonfiction; as lead author, *Everyday Law for Latino/as* (Paradigm Publishers, 2008); *Comprende? The Significance of Spanish in English-Only Times* (Floricanto Press, 2008); *Tierra y Libertad: Land, Liberty, and Latino Housing* (NYU Press, 2010); and *Run for the Border: Vice and Virtue in U.S.-Mexico Border Crossings* (NYU Press, 2012). *Mea Culpa: Lessons on Law and Regret from U.S. History* is his latest book, published in 2015 by New York University Press. Many of his published articles address the need and potential sources for compassionate immigration reform, including "Compassionate Immigration Reform" (*Fordham Urban Law Journal*, 2010).

Aurora Chang is an assistant professor in teaching and learning at Loyola University Chicago, where she teaches course work on urban schooling. Chang's research focuses on the intersection of education, identity, and agency within traditionally marginalized communities. Chang's personal and professional values are based on the following principles: (1) the need to understand the impact of identity and agency on students' and teachers' educational experiences and practices and (2) the desire to empower diverse marginalized communities. Currently, she focuses on the ways in which undocumented students' paths of educational survival, resistance, and persistence affect the "American" sociopolitical landscape.

Vanessa Fonseca is an assistant professor of English at Arizona State University Polytechnic, where she teaches courses on Chicano, indigenous, and American ethnic literature and film from the contact period to the present. Her research interests include contemporary manifestations of colonial relationships in Chicana/o literature. She received her MA in Hispanic Southwest studies from the University of New Mexico and her PhD in Spanish cultural studies from Arizona State University.

Gabriella Gutiérrez y Muhs is a full professor in modern languages and women and gender studies at Seattle University. She held the Wismer Professor Endowed Chair for Gender and Diversity from 2007 to 2009 and was the Latin American Studies program director from 2009 to 2012. Gutiérrez y Muhs has also been the director of the Diversity, Citizenship, and Social Justice Core Track for several years. She has published literary and cultural criticism in various journals in the United States and abroad. She works on transnational feminisms and has presented her research on Latina identity and subjectivity all over the world. Gutiérrez y Muhs is a renowned and anthologized Chicana writer and poet as well as a Latina/Chicana cultural worker. Gabriella Gutiérrez y Muhs is the author of several books and is lead editor of the revolutionary *Presumed Incompetent: The Intersections of Race and Class for Women in Academia*. She has authored multiple articles, poetry collections, and encyclopedia entries and in 2015 was awarded the Provost's Inaugural Award for Scholarship, Research, and Creativity at Seattle University. Also in 2015, she was selected universitywide as the director of the Center for the Study of Justice in Society. Her poetry collections *¿How Many Indians Can We Be?* and *The Runaway Poems* are forthcoming from Mango Press and Finishing Line Press, respectively. Gutiérrez y Muhs's research interests lie principally in the areas of Chican@/Latin@ and Latin American literatures, cultural studies, and feminist theory, but her intellectual and teaching interests include literary and cultural theory, Latin American studies, the study of immigration, and the shifting of international positions toward ethnicity and identity. She has an MA and PhD from Stanford University.

María Herrera-Sobek is an associate vice chancellor for diversity, equity, and academic policy and a professor of Chicana/o studies at the University of

California, Santa Barbara; she held the Luis Leal Endowed Chair from 1997 to 2009. She received her PhD in Hispanic languages and literature from the University of California, Los Angeles. Her past appointments include professor at the University of California, Irvine (1975–96); visiting professor, Harvard University (1992 and 1996); and visiting professor at Stanford University (1991–92). She has edited or coedited fourteen books; has published more than 150 scholarly articles and book chapters; and has coedited several international journals. Herrera-Sobek's publications include *The Bracero Experience: Elitelore Versus Folklore*; *The Mexican Corrido: A Feminist Analysis*; *Northward Bound: The Mexican Immigrant Experience in Ballad and Song*; and *Chicano Folklore: A Handbook*. Recently she has published *Sandra Cisneros: A Reader*, was associate editor of *The Norton Anthology of Latino Literature*, was co-editor (with Astrid Haas) of "*Transfrontera*: Transnational Perspectives on the U.S.-Mexico Borderlands," a special issue of the *American Studies Journal*; and was editor of *Celebrating Latino Folklore: An Encyclopedia of Cultural Traditions*, volumes 1, 2, and 3.

Ellen McCracken is a professor in the Department of Spanish and Portuguese and the Program in Comparative Literature at the University of California, Santa Barbara, where she specializes in U.S. Latino and Latin American literature, narrative and semiotic theory, cultural criticism, and digital literature. Her main publications include *Decoding Women's Magazines: From* Mademoiselle *to* Ms. (1993); *New Latina Narrative: The Feminine Space of Postmodern Ethnicity* (1999); *The Life and Writing of Fray Angélico Chávez: A New Mexico Renaissance Man* (2009), winner of a Southwest Book Award; and *Paratexts and Performance in the Novels of Junot Díaz and Sandra Cisneros* (2016). Her edited volume *The* Serial *Podcast and Storytelling in the Digital Age* is forthcoming from Routledge. She is currently writing a book on the new textuality of literature read on portable digital devices.

María Esther Quintana Millamoto is an associate professor of Hispanic studies at Texas A&M University. A native of Chihuahua, Mexico, she came to the United States to pursue a Master's and PhD at the University of California, Berkeley. Her book *Los pícaros, bufones y cronistas de Maluco: La novela de los descubridores* was published by Linardi y Risso in Montevideo, Uruguay, in 2008. Quintana's second book, entitled *Madres e hijas melancólicas en las novelas de crecimiento de autoras latinas*, was published in 2014 by Instituto Benjamin

Franklin and Universidad de Alcalá in Spain. She has also published critical essays in refereed journals in Mexico, Cuba, Spain, and the United States. Her teaching fields are Hispanic literatures, U.S. Latino literature, women's studies, Latin American culture, and the Spanish language.

Aldo Ulisses Reséndiz Ramírez is a Mexican immigrant and queer Xicanx of indigenous hñähñu-xo'oi descent who recently completed his MA in applied linguistics at Teachers College, Columbia University. Reséndiz Ramírez is a writer, cultural worker, community organizer, and language justice promoter in community organizing spaces, working on critical language pedagogy and popular education approaches to teaching emergent bilinguals.

Rose Rodríguez-Rabin is a lecturer in the Writing Program at the University of Texas at San Antonio, teaching courses in freshman composition and often incorporating Native American, Chicano/a, multiethnic, and feminist literature and folklore into her teachings. She self-identifies as a Comanche/Apache/Chicana. She was formerly the president of the American Indian Council of Laredo (1995–2000) and a lecturer at Texas A&M International University (1995–2000). She is working on her PhD in culture, language, and literacy at the University of Texas at San Antonio.

Jesús Rosales is an associate professor of Spanish at Arizona State University. He is the author of *Thinking en español: Interviews with Critics of Chicana/o Literature* and *La narrativa de Alejandro Morales: Encuentro, historia y compromiso social.* He serves as the editor of the annual publication *Puentes: Revista méxico-chicana de literatura, cultura y arte.*

Carlos Sibaja García is a language instructor at the Seattle Central Institute of English. He is passionate about language and literature and has lived and worked in both Seattle and his native Guadalajara, Mexico. Sibaja García completed his Master's in TESOL (Teaching English to Speakers of Other Languages) at Seattle University, with an emphasis on challenging current ESL pedagogy and its effectiveness. His thesis has been used to challenge future ESL teachers regarding accent and comprehension. Sibaja García's essay "Arizona's HB 2281's Attack on Education and Equality: Let's End the Ban on Ethnic Studies" was published in *Global Issues, Local Arguments.* In addition, his poetry has been featured in *Solaluna Revista*, an electronic magazine from Arizona.

María Socorro Tabuenca Córdoba has a PhD in Hispanic languages and literatures from the State University of New York at Stony Brook. She is a professor in the Department of Languages and Linguistics at the University of Texas at El Paso, where she is also the chair of the department; she is the former academic director for the Center for Inter-American and Border Studies at UTEP. From 1992 to 2008, Tabuenca was a researcher at El Colegio de la Frontera Norte, for which she served as the regional director in Ciudad Juárez and the dean for the North West Region. She held the Whichard Distinguished Chair from East Carolina University during the spring of 2008. Tabuenca Córdoba is the author of *Mujeres y fronteras: Una perspectiva de género* (1998); co-author (with Ricardo Aguilar) of *Lo que el viento a Juárez: Testimonios de una ciudad que se obstina* (2000); and co-author (with Debra Castillo) of *Border Women: Writing from la Frontera* (2002). She is the co-editor (with Julia Monárrez) of *Bordeando la violencia contra las mujeres en Ciudad Juárez* (2008). She has another coedited book forthcoming (with Juan Carlos Ramírez Pimienta), *Camelia la texana y otras mujeres de la narcocultura*. Her articles have been published in both national and international journals and have focused mainly on Mexican border women writers, border theory, U.S.-Mexico border representations in film, and representations of the Ciudad Juárez femicides.

Juan Velasco is an associate professor in the Department of English at Santa Clara University, where he teaches courses in nonfiction creative writing, autobiography, and Latina/o literature. In his first academic book, *Moving Borders: Tradition, Modernity, and the Search for "Mexicanness" in Contemporary Chicano Literature* (2003), Velasco examined cultural and literary traditions from both south and north of the Mexican-U.S. border. He has published extensively in Latino/a literature and autobiography. In 2015, his academic publications were included in *Latino/a Literature in the Classroom: 21st Century Approaches to Teaching*, edited by Frederick Luis Aldama; in *Expanding the Circle: Creating an Inclusive Environment in Higher Education for LGBTQ Students and Studies*, edited by John Hawley; and in *Ethnic Literatures and Transnationalism*, edited by Aparajita Nanda. His latest book, *Collective Identity and Cultural Resistance in Contemporary Chicana/o Autobiography*, was published by Palgrave Macmillan in 2016.

INDEX